Tudor Executions

Tudor Executions

From Nobility To The Block

Helene Harrison

PEN & SWORD
HISTORY

First published in Great Britain in 2024 by
Pen & Sword History
An imprint of Pen & Sword Books Limited
Yorkshire – Philadelphia

Copyright © Helene Harrison 2024

ISBN 978 1 39904 332 8

The right of Helene Harrison to be identified as
Author of this Work has been asserted by her in accordance
with the Copyright, Designs and Patents Act 1988.

A CIP catalogue record for this book is
available from the British Library

Typeset by Mac Style
Printed in the UK by CPI Group (UK) Ltd, Croydon, CR0 4YY.

Pen & Sword Books Limited incorporates the imprints of After
the Battle, Atlas, Archaeology, Aviation, Discovery, Family History,
Fiction, History, Maritime, Military, Military Classics, Politics,
Select, Transport, True Crime, Air World, Frontline Publishing, Leo
Cooper, Remember When, Seaforth Publishing, The Praetorian Press,
Wharncliffe Local History, Wharncliffe Transport, Wharncliffe True
Crime and White Owl.

For a complete list of Pen & Sword titles please contact

PEN & SWORD BOOKS LIMITED
47 Church Street, Barnsley, South Yorkshire, S70 2AS, England
E-mail: enquiries@pen-and-sword.co.uk
Website: www.pen-and-sword.co.uk
or
PEN AND SWORD BOOKS
1950 Lawrence Rd, Havertown, PA 19083, USA
E-mail: uspen-and-sword@casematepublishers.com
Website: www.penandswordbooks.com

To Laura.
A fantastic friend and wonderful editor,
it's always great to share a nerdy chat.

Contents

Acknowledgements

A huge thank you once again to the team at Pen and Sword who have helped and guided me through this whole process. I still find it hard to believe this is my second book! Thanks to Sarah-Beth Watkins, Lucy May, Sarah Hodder, and Laura Hirst, as well as Rosie Crofts and the amazing social media team.

Massive thanks go to my friends and family. Mum, Dad, and Matilda for letting me drive you a little bit nuts. Special thanks yet again to Mark for supporting me so completely and dealing with my anxiety when it takes over, pushing me to keep going and nudging me to do things that scare me. I'll never be able to repay you for what you've done for me and continue to do. Also special thanks to editor extraordinaire and my amazing friend, Laura, for checking a lot of my grammar and making sure that what I'd written made sense. That can't have been an easy job! Yet again I owe you cake. Thanks also to Ben and Hattie for the never-ending support and propping me up when things get tricky. You are all amazing, and my friends really are like my family so thank you so much to you all for being there and supporting me to the ends of the earth.

Thank you to my dissertation supervisor when I was studying at Northumbria University, Gaby. I wouldn't be here and able to publish my work without you. I felt so bereft having finished university that I started my blog and it really snowballed from there. Hopefully in the future I'll be able to expand on that exciting research for my Master's dissertation and make it into a book. That's the next dream.

Thanks to Leigh and Aaron at Wheelhouse Coffee Bar for keeping me in hot chocolate and sweet treats during the writing and editing process. Those sugar hits at times have really got me through!

Shout out to the #HistoryGirls community on Instagram; you all inspire me and push me to expand my horizons, and I've had messages from so many of you wishing me luck and spurring me on in those difficult moments. And thank you to all of you bloggers and social media users out there who have reviewed and promoted my first book, *Elizabethan Rebellions: Conspiracy, Intrigue, and Treason*, and listened to interviews and have been so encouraging, even though I'm very jealous of some of your photography. Some gorgeous shots of my book have been shared, and I've saved them all! I do not doubt that you'll be just as encouraging when this book comes out as well.

Thank you to the Wellcome Collection, the National Gallery of Art in Washington D.C., the Yale Center for British Art, and the Rijksmuseum in Amsterdam. Also thank you to some of the amazing historians whose work has been invaluable to me: Nathen Amin, David Loades, Alison Weir, Owen Emmerson, Kate McCaffrey, and Leanda de Lisle. Too many to name really, but everyone who writes and publishes on the Tudors deserves a mention. You all contribute to fledgling history writers like me believing that we can do it. We can, and the field will keep growing.

Illustration Credits

1. An Allegory of the Tudor Succession, 1590. Unknown Artist, 16th Century, after Lucas de Heere 1534–1584. Yale Center for British Art, Paul Mellon Collection.
2. White Tower at the Tower of London. Photograph: Author's Own.
3. Perkin Warbeck reading his confession in the stocks. Wellcome Collection, Public Domain.
4. Memorial to Edward Plantagenet, 17th Earl of Warwick, and Edward Stafford, 3rd Duke of Buckingham, on Tower Hill, London. Photograph: Author's Own.
5. Henry VIII on silvered brass. Unknown artist after Hans Schwarz. National Gallery of Art in Washington D.C.
6. Anne Boleyn, Queen of England, by Jacobus Houbraken, 1738. After Hans Holbein the Younger. Wellcome Collection, Public Domain.
7. Anne Boleyn's uncrowned falcon emblem carved on wall in the Beauchamp Tower in the Tower of London. Photograph: Author's Own.
8. Tower of London Execution Memorial on Tower Green within the Tower of London. Photograph: Author's Own.
9. Katherine Howard, Queen of England, by Jacobus Houbraken, 1747–1752. Yale Center for British Art, Yale University Art Gallery Collection.
10. Interior of the Chapel of St Peter ad Vincula at the Tower of London. Photograph: Author's Own.
11. Site of the scaffold on Tower Hill, London. Photograph: Author's Own.
12. Henry Howard, Earl of Surrey, by Jacobus Houbraken, 1750. Yale Center for British Art, Yale University Art Gallery Collection.
13. Edward Seymour, 1st Duke of Somerset, by Jacobus Houbraken, 1738. Yale Center for British Art, Yale University Art Gallery Collection.
14. Axe and block on display at the Tower of London. Photograph: Author's Own.
15. Etching of the Execution of Lady Jane Grey by Paolo Mercuri. After Paul Delaroche, 1833–1884. Rijksmuseum, Amsterdam.

16. The name 'Jane' and the Grey coat of arms carved on a wall in the Beauchamp Tower in the Tower of London. Photograph: Author's Own.
17. Mary I, Queen of England, by Frans Huys. Rijksmuseum, Amsterdam.
18. Elizabeth I, Queen of England. Unknown Artist. Rijksmuseum, Amsterdam, on loan from the Cultural Heritage Agency of the Netherlands, Amersfoort.
19. Thomas Howard, 4th Duke of Norfolk, by Jacobus Houbraken, 1735. Yale Center for British Art, Yale University Art Gallery Collection.
20. Memorial to Henry Howard, Earl of Surrey, and his son, Thomas Howard, 4th Duke of Norfolk, as well as Edward Seymour, 1st Duke of Somerset, on Tower Hill, London. Photograph: Author's Own.
21. Robert Devereux, 2nd Earl of Essex 1596/1601. Unknown Artist. National Gallery of Art in Washington D.C.; gift of Mrs. Henry R. Rea.

Preface

This is my second book with Pen and Sword Books, and I am so thrilled I got to go through the whole experience again. Writing a book is a bit like a whirlwind as I had no idea where to start but when I got going I just kept writing!

My interest in Tudor history started with an A-Level module on Tudor Rebellions and developed through my undergraduate and postgraduate degrees, with both dissertations on Henry VIII's second wife, Anne Boleyn. It was a bit of an indulgence for me in writing this book to be able to write a chapter on Anne Boleyn's fall and execution, though it was difficult not to get carried away and write a lot more on her than anyone else in this book! In writing my first book, *Elizabethan Rebellions: Conspiracy, Intrigue and Treason* and when studying Anne Boleyn's life and legacy through university and then my own research over the years since, there have been plenty of executions that have also enthralled me. I seem to be drawn to controversy and when I realised that there were no dukes in England from 1572 until 1623, I wanted to know why. What had happened to make the monarchy kill off many of their nobility? That was the basis for this research and eventual book.

There is so much of interest in studying executions and it is more than just death; it is the reasons behind the executions that are so fascinating and how so many nobles came to be accused of treason. How many of them were actually guilty as accused? Or were they in fact conspired against and were innocent of the charges? This book examines these questions but leaves you to make up your own mind. There is also a psychological element; what must it have been like to be tried by people you have been around your whole life (many were tried by a court made up of their peers) and have to listen to them pronounce you guilty and sentence you to death. But also knowing that this would not happen unless your monarch wanted it to. That must have been terrifying. And then the fear as you had to walk to your death, knowing what would happen, but not knowing whether it would be a smooth and fairly painless death or a botched attempt. Sometimes it took several cuts, as happened with Margaret Pole, Countess of Salisbury. On top of that you had to pay your own executioner and forgive him, as was traditional.

A lot of these things we cannot understand in the twentieth century. Executions were something of a spectator sport in the sixteenth century and people did not seem to be as squeamish as some of us are today (I count myself in that number; I cannot watch horror films!). It was a different time, and we cannot judge what people did and thought five hundred years ago by today's standards. We have to try to look at events as they were and without colouring them with our own beliefs and prejudices, which is what I have tried to do here.

The aim when writing this book was for each chapter to be able to be read as a standalone article. So, you do not have to read the entire book, but can dip in and out of it depending on what you want to read at any particular moment, therefore some information is repeated from chapter to chapter. I love doing that with books, dipping in and out, so that was what I wanted to do here. The only exceptions to this rule are Chapters 7 and 8 on the Seymour brothers, which really need to be read in conjunction with each other as the two were so interrelated it is often difficult to separate them, though the falls of each of the brothers deserved their own chapters.

I really hope you enjoy this book and my research into the fall of the Tudor nobility and the often gruesome and gory details that go with them.

Helene Harrison, May 2023

Tudor Royal Family

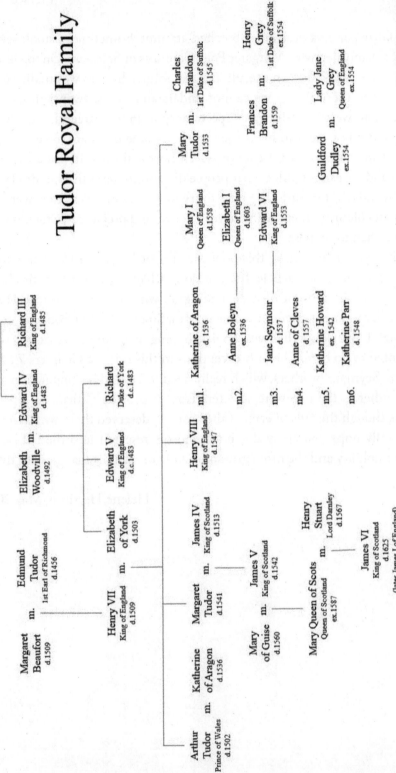

Compiled by Helene Harrison

Stafford-Pole Family

Isabel Neville d.1476 m. George Plantagenet 1st Duke of Clarence ex.1478

George Plantagenet — Edward IV King of England d.1483 — Richard III King of England d.1485

Edward Plantagenet 17th Earl of Warwick ex.1499

Margaret Plantagenet Countess of Salisbury ex.1541 m. Richard Pole d.1504

Children of Margaret and Richard Pole:
Henry Pole Baron Montague ex.1539
Arthur Pole d.1528
Geoffrey Pole d.1558
Reginald Pole Cardinal d.1558
Ursula Pole d.1570

Ursula Pole m. Henry Stafford Baron Stafford d.1563

Edward IV King of England d.1483 m. Elizabeth Woodville d.1492

Katherine Woodville d.1497 m. Henry Stafford 2nd Duke of Buckingham d.1483

Elizabeth of York d.1503 m. Henry VII King of England d.1509

Henry VIII King of England d.1547

Edward Stafford 3rd Duke of Buckingham d.1521 m. Eleanor Percy d.1530

Children: Elizabeth Stafford d.1558 / Henry Stafford Baron Stafford d.1563

Elizabeth Stafford d.1558 m. Thomas Howard 3rd Duke of Norfolk d.1554

Children: Mary Howard d.1557 / Henry Howard Earl of Surrey ex.1547

Mary Howard d.1557 m. Henry Fitzroy 1st Duke of Richmond d.1536

Henry Howard Earl of Surrey ex.1547 m. Frances de Vere d.1577

Thomas Howard 4th Duke of Norfolk ex.1572

Compiled by Helene Harrison

Howard-Boleyn Family

John Howard
1st Duke of Norfolk
d.1485

m.

Katherine Moleyns
d.1465

Thomas Howard
2nd Duke of Norfolk
d.1524

m.

Elizabeth Tilney
d.1497

Thomas Howard
3rd Duke of Norfolk
d.1554

m.

Elizabeth Stafford
d.1558

Edmund Howard
d.1539

m.

Joyce Culpeper
d.c.1528

Elizabeth Howard
d.1538

m.

Thomas Boleyn
1st Earl of Wiltshire
d.1539

Henry Howard
Earl of Surrey
ex.1547

m.

Frances de Vere
d.1577

Mary Howard
d.1557

m.

Henry Fitzroy
1st Duke of Richmond
d.1536

Katherine Howard
ex.1542

m.

Henry VIII
King of England
d.1547

m.

Anne Boleyn
ex.1536

George Boleyn
Viscount Rochford
ex.1536

m.

Jane Parker
ex.1542

Mary Boleyn
d.1543

m.

William Carey
d.1528

Thomas Howard
4th Duke of Norfolk
ex.1572

Elizabeth I
Queen of England
d.1603

Henry Carey
Baron Hunsdon
d.1596

Catherine Carey
d.1569

Seymour Family

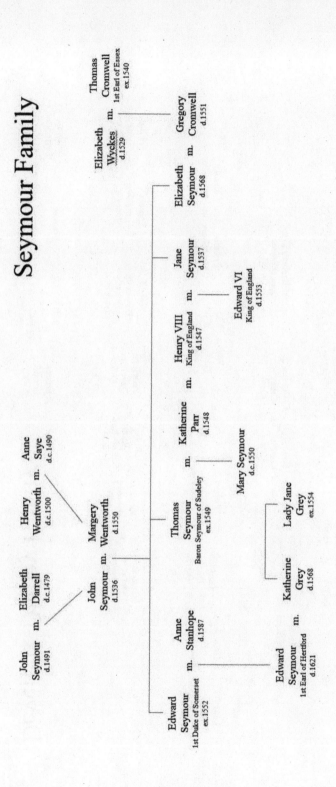

John Seymour d.1491 m. Elizabeth Darrell d.c.1479

Henry Wentworth d.c.1500 m. Anne Saye d.c.1490

John Seymour d.1536 m. Margery Wentworth d.1550

Elizabeth Wyckes d.1529 m. Thomas Cromwell 1st Earl of Essex ex.1540

Gregory Cromwell d.1551 m. Elizabeth Seymour d.1568

Jane Seymour d.1537 m. Henry VIII King of England d.1547

Edward VI King of England d.1553

Thomas Seymour Baron Seymour of Sudeley ex.1549 m. Katherine Parr d.1548

Mary Seymour d.c.1550

Edward Seymour 1st Duke of Somerset ex.1552 m. Anne Stanhope d.1587

Edward Seymour 1st Earl of Hertford d.1621 m. Katherine Grey d.1568

Lady Jane Grey ex.1554

Compiled by Helene Harrison

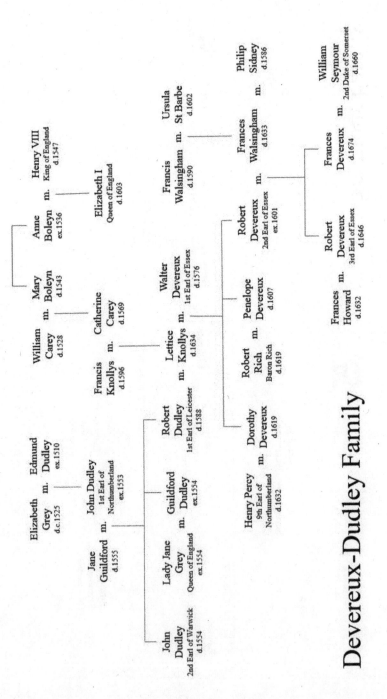

Devereux-Dudley Family

Compiled by Helene Harrison

Introduction

The nobility of England faced a crisis during the reigns of the Tudor monarchs in the sixteenth century. The turmoil of the Wars of the Roses in the mid-fifteenth century led to many of the nobility being killed in battles or executed, as claimants to the throne fought over it. This meant that when Henry VII came to the throne after defeating Richard III at the Battle of Bosworth Field in 1485, the remaining nobility were vulnerable to being exploited. The likes of the Duke of Norfolk had been killed with Richard III and the Earls of Surrey and Northumberland were imprisoned after the battle. By the end of the Tudor age, with the death of Elizabeth I in 1603, there were no dukes remaining in England at all, and many of the nobility had been executed and their titles and lands had reverted to the crown.

This book will examine some of the best-known and most controversial cases of Tudor treason; in eleven chapters, nine men and five women will be discussed. All had a noble background and could expect a comfortable life. All would also end up under the executioner's blade. Three queens, four dukes, three earls, a countess, and three lesser nobles would find themselves accused of treason, imprisoned in the Tower of London, and taken to their deaths. Many were granted the mercy of a private execution on Tower Green within the Tower of London itself, rather than the public Tower Hill nearby. Some may well have been guilty as charged, but others were either set up or used as scapegoats. What we have to remember is that the trial documents and indictments were written to make the accused look as guilty as possible.

The executions span the reigns of all of the Tudor monarchs; from Henry VII through Henry VIII, Edward VI, Mary I, and Elizabeth I. The Tudors were the first dynasty to execute queens and, to a large extent, women. Their gender had protected women from death by execution before, with the likes of Eleanor of Aquitaine, wife to Henry II in the twelfth century, and Isabella of France, wife to Edward II in the fourteenth century, having their lands forfeit and even being put under a form of house arrest and imprisonment but avoiding death. Traditionally, 'the male realm is defined as public, and the female realm as private'.[1] What this means is that the men went out and earned money and made names for themselves, wielding the power, while the women were to stay at home, bear and raise children, and keep house: the traditional roles assigned to the genders one could argue. The sixteenth century saw women stepping fully into the public sphere and wielding power; particularly with the emergence of England's first two regnant queens. The Tudors, however, seemed also to be a new, dangerous dynasty.

By 1572 there were no more dukes in England, and this would remain the case until 1623 under the Stuart king, James I, when he created a new dukedom of Buckingham for his favourite, George Villiers. The Tudors seemed determined to rid the country of all those who threatened their grip on power and the safety of the throne. Many of these happened to be the most powerful and wealthy in the country. Several of them also had royal blood going back to the Yorkist king, Edward IV, and further back to the Plantagenet king, Edward III. Those with this bloodline arguably had a better claim to the throne than the Tudors, who were descended from Edward III through an illegitimate line. This seems to have made the Tudor monarchs, and particularly Henry VIII, feel vulnerable and paranoid. The desire to keep the throne and stop England returning to Catholicism also resulted in Elizabeth I authorising the execution of a fellow regnant monarch to protect her position, although Mary Queen of Scots does not feature in this book as she was a Scottish royal rather than a Tudor noble.

It was also very often a family affair for the Tudors which, in a way, makes it more shocking and surprising. However, as most noble families were interrelated, perhaps it should not be so remarkable. A royal brother and sister were executed over forty years apart (Edward, Earl of Warwick, in 1499, and Margaret Pole, Countess of Salisbury, in 1541). The Howard / Boleyn family suffered disproportionately with Thomas Howard, 3rd Duke of Norfolk, losing a son, grandson, two nieces, a nephew, and a niece-in-law to the executioner. These were Anne Boleyn and her brother George Boleyn, Viscount Rochford (executed 1536), Katherine Howard and Jane Boleyn, Viscountess Rochford (executed 1542), Henry Howard, Earl of Surrey (executed 1547), and Thomas Howard, 4th Duke of Norfolk (executed 1572). The 3rd Duke of Norfolk also nearly lost his own life, being spared only by the death of Henry VIII in 1547 but he would remain imprisoned throughout Edward VI's reign, regaining his liberty only on the accession of Mary I in 1553.

Under Henry VII, Edward Plantagenet, 17th Earl of Warwick, was executed after the rebellion of Perkin Warbeck in 1499. His royal blood made him a danger to the new dynasty, and his sister would later be executed for her royal blood. Henry VIII racked up the largest tally of executions under the Tudors: Edward Stafford, 3rd Duke of Buckingham (executed 1521), Queen Anne Boleyn and her brother George Boleyn, Viscount Rochford (executed 1536), Margaret Pole, Countess of Salisbury (executed 1541), Queen Katherine Howard and Jane Boleyn, Viscountess Rochford (executed 1542), and Henry Howard, Earl of Surrey (executed 1547). This marked the first time that a queen of England was executed, as well as prompting religious turmoil and the Break with Rome. Henry VIII's paranoia about the succession and his own power would greatly influence his children. Edward VI had his two maternal uncles, Thomas Seymour, 1st Baron Seymour of Sudeley, and Edward Seymour, 1st Duke of Somerset, both executed. Mary I executed her main rival and the Nine Days Queen, Lady Jane Grey, along with Jane's top supporter, John Dudley, 1st Duke of Northumberland. Thomas Howard, 4th Duke of Norfolk, and Robert Devereux, 2nd Earl of Essex, were executed by Elizabeth I for their involvement in rebellions against her.

* * *

Before we can start to examine whether the nobility of England under the Tudors were in fact guilty of treason as charged, we need to understand what treason is. Treason is often assumed to be an act against the life of a monarch, but there are actually different types of treason. Petty treason was the act of killing or usurping the authority of a social superior other than the king. For example, a wife killing her husband was petty treason, because the husband was considered to be superior. It was high treason when it was disloyalty to the crown or acting against the monarch. More generally, the Oxford English Dictionary describes 'treason' as follows:

'The action of betraying; betrayal of the trust undertaken by or reposed in any one; breach of faith, treacherous action, treachery.'[2]

The word 'treason' comes from the French word 'trahir', meaning to deliver up or betray, initially from the Latin *traditor*. The 1351 Treason Act declared treason to be imagining the death of the king, queen, or their eldest son, or if a man violated the queen, eldest daughter of the king, or the wife of the king's eldest son. It would also be treason if one levied war against the king in his realm, or assisted the king's enemies, or killed the chancellor, treasurer, or one of the king's justices.[3] The violation of the queen, eldest daughter, or wife of the eldest son was treason because it could imperil the succession, as would be seen in the cases of Anne Boleyn in 1536 and Katherine Howard in 1541/2.

This act was still in place under the Tudors and was modified by the Treason Act of 1534 which was introduced alongside the Acts of Succession and Supremacy. The act also made it treason for a person to deny the king his title as Supreme Head of the Church of England or call him a heretic or usurper.[4] This would result in many more executions as a result of the Break with Rome, including Cardinal John Fisher, and Sir Thomas More. There were further Treason Acts in 1547 under Edward VI and 1554 under Mary I. The 1554 act abolished all forms of treason created since 1351, except the 1351 Treason Act itself. The 1554 Treason Act was eventually repealed in two parts, in 1863 and 1967.

What was new under the Tudors was the ability to condemn someone for treason by an Act of Attainder. This was introduced under Henry VII but would become widely used under Henry VIII who introduced new forms of treason and an expansion of the definition. An Act of Attainder was a way of condemning someone through parliamentary statute without the need for a trial. This meant that there was less chance of a public outcry and revolt. New forms of treason were even created or altered retrospectively.[5] For example, Jane Boleyn, Viscountess Rochford, who was condemned to death for allegedly assisting Henry VIII's fifth wife, Katherine Howard, to commit adultery, was said to have gone mad during her imprisonment. Henry VIII had the law changed so that he could execute mad people, where usually they would be committed to an asylum.

There were also new writings about treason and execution, many of these in the form of poetry or ballads. Tudor writer, John Harington, wrote a short poem called 'Of Treason':

'Treason doth never prosper, what's the reason?
For if it prosper, none dare call it treason.'[6]

This could have been true of Lady Jane Grey, the Nine Days Queen, who actually ruled technically for fourteen days, and is discussed in Chapter 9. Had Mary I been captured, as the Duke of Northumberland had intended, Jane Grey would have kept her head and her throne, and would not have been found guilty of treason because she would have won. Instead, Mary would have been found guilty of treason and executed, and history would have been very different.

Probably the most popular execution covered in this book (and the one that frustrates people the most because it gets so much coverage!) is that of Anne Boleyn in May 1536. The poet, Sir Thomas Wyatt, it was rumoured, had been romantically interested in Anne. He was imprisoned in the Tower of London during the bloody days of May 1536 but was eventually released without charge, possibly due to the intervention of Thomas Cromwell. He wrote a poem while imprisoned called *Circa Regna Tonat*, which translates from the Latin as 'about the throne the thunder rolls' or 'thunder rolls around the throne'. This is just one verse, but perhaps the most haunting:

> 'These bloody days have broken my heart.
> My lust, my youth did them depart,
> And blind desire of estate.
> Who hastes to climb seeks to revert.
> Of truth, circa Regna tonat.'[7]

Wyatt marks this point as the loss of his youth because he saw a sight that should not have happened and marked a turning point in the Tudor period. It is generally accepted today that on 19 May 1536, an innocent woman was executed and vilified. There would be many more executions in the years that followed; but in May 1536 Wyatt had lost several friends, as well as the woman he was said to love. There have been suggestions that Wyatt actually saw Anne die, being able to see the scaffold from the Bell Tower where he was imprisoned. He rued the fact that a desire for more power and wealth had brought him to imprisonment and his friends to death, accused of treason. Wyatt would survive but many others would die at the hands of the Tudor monarchs, accused of treason, because they had reached for wealth, titles, and power. Perhaps this is the curse of the Tudor nobility; always wanting more, whether it was wealth, power, titles, or their pride.

* * *

Noble prisoners condemned to death were executed, in large part, with an axe, though the traditional sentence passed at condemnation was to be hung, drawn, and quartered. However, the monarch would usually commute this to beheading as an act of mercy for traitors of noble birth. It was thought that the force of a swing of an axe intended to sever a head from a neck was then absorbed by the solid wooden block that the condemned person put their head on. Beheading was believed to be swift and humane; an 'honourable and merciful way to die'.[8] The scaffold would be covered in straw to soak up the blood, and the block itself was carved so that there was a dip for the victim to place their head in to expose the neck for the axe. The condemned were supposed to pay the executioner on the scaffold and receive their forgiveness, as well as address the crowd who had gathered to watch them die.

These scaffold speeches were often focused on praising the monarch and acknowledging any sins, so that it could be said that they died well. Victims would not generally speak against their death or their condemnation for fear that the monarch would then react against their surviving family. If the executioner was competent then the execution would be achieved with a single blow. However, if the executioner was inexperienced, or the axe was not sharp enough, then it would take several blows to sever head from body and make the experience longer and more drawn out for the victim, and the watching crowd.

Once the condemned person was dead, the executioner would traditionally hold up the head to the watching crowd and declare 'behold the head of a traitor' or something similar. Legend suggests that this was so that the head could see the crowd and its own decapitated body. It is said that the brain continues to function for several seconds after decapitation while the oxygen supply depletes and then stops altogether.[9] It was not, as some believe, for the crowd to see the proof that the deed had been carried out, though no doubt this was a factor.

Today it is difficult to imagine, in Britain at least, how someone might feel before being judicially murdered. The United States still has the death penalty, although those deaths seem to be carried out largely in private with only a select group of onlookers. In sixteenth-century England, these executions were bloody and in front of quite a large crowd; and were often treated like a spectator sport and an exciting day out. The nobles who were executed were at the very top of Tudor society, on friendly or at least speaking terms with the monarch, and condemned to death on the orders of said monarch.

They were personal deaths. Treason was a personal crime for the monarch and demanded the highest possible punishment.

Death meant that the crime could not be repeated by the same person and their mantle passed on to another. So it was, through all of the executions for treason that will be discussed in this book. One noble died of treason, but there was always another who would continue plotting. Treason remains on the statute book, enshrined in law today, though not an oft used law. When we think of treason and tyrannical monarchs, Henry VIII is usually pretty high on the list. He redefined treason to be what he wanted it to be and, as a result, opened the doors to multitudes of treason trials and the depletion of the English nobility.

In the introduction to the book which accompanied the exhibition at the National Archives in 2022 entitled *A History of Treason*, the following is said, probably most notably applied to Henry VIII:

'It is a crime defined initially by the Crown, and later by the state, which imposes concepts of allegiance, of control, of restriction. But while treason is defined, it places a limit on those that rule, and holds them accountable when rulers verge towards tyranny ... in the pre-modern period, those who expanded the definitions of treason beyond reasonable boundaries were marked as tyrants, and their expansions were repealed at the earliest opportunity. Despite its terrible portent, the codified law of treason was seen as a bulwark against its tyrannical misuse. All trials are theatrical, but perhaps none more so than that for treason'.[10]

Chapter 1

Edward Plantagenet,
17th Earl of Warwick – 1499

The story of Edward Plantagenet, 17th Earl of Warwick, is an incredibly sad one. He was undeniably nobility, the nephew of two kings and the son of a royal duke. His paternal grandparents were Richard Plantagenet, 3rd Duke of York, and Cecily Neville. He was the only surviving son of his parents, though he did also have a sister, Margaret, who would marry Richard Pole and be created Countess of Salisbury in her own right. The title descended from their grandmother, Cecily Neville's, side of the family. Margaret would herself be executed in 1541 by Henry VIII (see Chapter 4). The pedigree of both brother and sister made them a threat to the Tudor ascendency after the death of Richard III at the Battle of Bosworth Field in 1485, though naturally the brother was a more obvious and serious threat, as a male, hence Margaret survived a lot longer.

Warwick's father was George Plantagenet, 1st Duke of Clarence, the brother of Edward IV and Richard III, hence he was also of royal blood. However, he was barred from the succession to the throne of England after the execution of his father in 1478. The children of someone accused of treason lost all rights to lands and titles, which were forfeit to the crown. Famously, Clarence was said to have been 'drowned in a barell of malvesye', or malmsey wine in the Tower of London.[1] Legend says he was allowed to choose his own method of execution and he chose malmsey wine as it was his brother, Edward IV's, favourite. Warwick's debarring from the throne, along with the declaration that the children of Edward IV and Elizabeth Woodville were illegitimate, allowed Richard III to take the throne in 1483. Through his father, Warwick was descended from Edward III through his fourth surviving son, Edmund of Langley. His grandmother, Cecily Neville, was also descended from Joan Beaufort, the daughter of John of Gaunt, who was Edward III's third surviving son. Warwick's mother was Isabel Neville, the daughter of Richard Neville, 16th Earl of Warwick, also known as the 'Kingmaker' for his role in helping his cousin, Edward, ascend the throne as Edward IV. He was thus descended twice over legitimately from Edward III, giving him a very strong claim to the English throne, undeniably stronger than that of the Tudors, who were descended from an illegitimate line of Edward III. He was, in addition, descended from the Neville Earls of Warwick and Salisbury, some of the most powerful families in England at the time. They were great supporters of Richard Plantagenet, 3rd Duke of York, and then his son who would become Edward IV, at least initially. This explains why Henry VII was so concerned about keeping Warwick close and contained.

The Wars of the Roses were a complex time with family in-fighting, and the Nevilles were no exception. Richard Neville, 16th Earl of Warwick turned against his ally Edward IV in 1470 and restored the Lancastrian Henry VI to the throne in his place. He felt he would have more power with the puppet king, Henry VI, rather than Edward IV, who had found his feet as king and embarrassed Warwick with his secret marriage to Elizabeth Woodville. However, Warwick was killed the following year at the Battle of Barnet and Edward IV regained the throne. Clarence had re-joined his brother before the battle, having at first supported Warwick, so ended on the winning side. But the accord between the York brothers did not last, and this led to Clarence's execution.

The marriage of George, 1st Duke of Clarence, and Isabel Neville, angered Edward IV. Until such time as he had a son, Clarence was his successor and the bringing together of Clarence with a daughter of the Earl of Warwick made them more of a threat, particularly any sons they may produce, such as Edward, Earl of Warwick.[2] The Warwick title passed to Edward Plantagenet, 17th Earl of Warwick, as the closest male relative when he was born in 1475 as Warwick the 'Kingmaker' had died in 1471. One of Edward's godparents was his uncle and namesake, Edward IV. Margaret was the elder sibling, born in 1473. The pair also had a younger brother, Richard, who died in infancy with his mother, Isabel, having died soon after his birth in 1476. Warwick was just a year old when his mother died, so likely had no memories of her at all. Even Margaret's memories may have been fuzzy at aged just three. Whichever way you look at it, Warwick and Margaret were born as royal as can be without being the legitimate offspring of a king. Clarence had allegedly hoped to be king but could not bring it to fruition.

Having been imprisoned by Henry VII from a young age, Warwick never married or had any children, so his direct line died out with him. He spent so many years in the Tower that he did not have a chance to marry or reproduce, probably exactly as Henry VII had intended. However, Warwick did have nieces and nephews, as his sister, Margaret, married and had issue. Her descendants are still alive today.

* * *

Edward Plantagenet was born on 25 February 1475 as the son of a royal duke. After the death of his mother in 1476 and the execution of his father two years later, the young Earl of Warwick was made a royal ward. In 1481, he was then made a ward of Thomas Grey, 1st Marquess of Dorset. This was in exchange for a payment of £2,000 (around £1.3 million today). Part of this agreement was that Dorset had the marital rights of the earl, although one would think that he would not act in this without the consent of the king, given that Warwick had royal blood and could be considered to be in line for the throne, despite Clarence's attainder. Dorset was the eldest son of Edward IV's wife, Elizabeth Woodville, from her first marriage to Sir John Grey of Groby, and therefore a cousin by marriage to Warwick. Because of his royal blood, Warwick was considered a very valuable ward to have. Wardship was often bought and sold like this; partly as a way of keeping those with valuable inheritances in the power of those closest to the throne. They could then be married off to benefit those closest to the throne and, by marriage, tie the most powerful families in the country to the crown.

When his father was executed in 1478, on the orders of Warwick's own uncle, King Edward IV, Warwick was just 3 years old. Clarence's execution meant that his titles and lands, including the Warwick earldom, were taken into crown custody. Officially this was for Warwick's minority only, until he came of age and could take control of things himself.[3] Often an attainder meant that the titles and lands were lost to the heirs, but Warwick would be valuable to have onside for the Yorkists, not knowing that they would be ousted by Henry Tudor in less than a decade. This could explain why Warwick did not immediately lose his inheritance. The earldom was also descended from Warwick's mother, Isabel Neville, rather than his father, which could also help to explain why he retained the title.[4] Between February 1478 and November 1482 much of Warwick's inheritance was granted to supporters of the Yorkist king, Edward IV, on the provision that it would be returned to Warwick once he reached the end of his minority at age 21, which would be in 1486.[5] Edward was subsequently referred to as the Earl of Warwick, but the attainder was never officially reversed and even when Warwick came of age, he was never granted the lands and titles that had been Clarence's. Possibly this was because he came of age after the death of Richard III and the accession of Henry VII.

Warwick's Yorkist family were no longer in power, and he was now considered a serious threat to the new ruling dynasty, the Tudors. He was one of the few surviving Yorkist royal males, since the Princes in the Tower were presumed dead, murdered by Richard III. The Princes in the Tower, Edward V and Richard, Duke of York, were the sons of Edward IV and Elizabeth Woodville. Edward V was declared king on his father's death in 1483 but vanished in the Tower of London soon after along with his brother. Another alternative claimant was John de la Pole, Earl of Lincoln, who would be killed fighting for the Yorkist cause at the Battle of Stoke in 1487. Henry VII recognised straight away that Warwick had a stronger claim to the throne than he did, so would not have wanted to honour promises Edward IV made to return his lands, as this would have made him one of the most powerful landowners in the country, and quite possibly have given him the resources to raise an army which could have forced a regime change. Though whether Warwick would have raised a rebellion is unknown. Later in his life he was said to be simple, though as he had been locked away for an extended period without a real education or any interaction perhaps this can be attributed to neglect rather than stupidity or some kind of disability.

After the death of Edward IV and Dorset's flight to join Henry Tudor in exile in France, Warwick was detained by Richard III, largely at Sheriff Hutton Castle in Yorkshire, with John de la Pole, 1st Earl of Lincoln, Warwick's cousin. Lincoln was the son of Richard III's sister, Elizabeth Plantagenet, Duchess of Suffolk. Warwick was present at the coronation of his uncle, Richard III, in 1483, and was knighted, aged 8, at the investiture of Richard's son, Edward of Middleham, as Prince of Wales the following year.[6] Richard III saw no reason not to at least have Warwick involved in some way in court life as he had a son and heir, and Warwick could prove a useful ally to him in the future as well as being his nephew. After this point, Warwick seems to have remained out of sight, probably at Sheriff Hutton, until Richard III's death in August 1485, in all likelihood being educated with his cousin. There does seem to have been some suggestion that Richard may have named the Earl of Warwick as his heir after the sudden and unexpected death of his only son and heir, Edward of Middleham, in April 1484. However, another possibility as his heir was John de la Pole, 1st Earl of Lincoln, who was Richard's nephew and the son of his sister, Elizabeth, who had married John de la Pole, 2nd Duke of Suffolk. Lincoln was thus related to Richard in the same way as Warwick, though through a female line untainted by treason, in contrast to Warwick through a male line, and the son of a traitor.

Warwick's precise position in the line of succession at this point was uncertain. He was the only son of the middle brother of York, so would ordinarily have been in line for the crown ahead of Richard III. However, his father had been attainted for treason and the act of attainder removed any claim to titles from his offspring, including the accession to the throne. Edward IV and Richard III seem to have made some kind of exception to allow him to retain the Earl of Warwick title but would have been reluctant to have him in the succession. However, Edward IV had no reason to even consider Warwick for the succession as he had two sons of his own. He could never have guessed that both would disappear, presumed murdered by their own uncle, who Edward IV seemed to trust implicitly. Richard III claimed the English throne by declaring the marriage of Edward IV and Elizabeth Woodville as invalid, thus making their children illegitimate. His basis for doing so was that Edward IV had supposedly been betrothed to another woman, Eleanor Butler, before he married Elizabeth Woodville. Clarence had been attainted, so his children were barred from the succession. This meant that Richard III considered himself the only viable Yorkist successor in 1483. Before claiming the throne, he placed Edward's two sons, Edward and Richard, in the Tower and they would become known to history as 'The Princes in the Tower'. But not everyone believed that Edward's sons were illegitimate, and this explains the rebellion against Richard III in October 1483 to restore Edward V to the English throne, led by Henry Stafford, 2nd Duke of Buckingham.

Warwick was kept under close supervision during Richard III's reign, but not imprisoned in the Tower as his cousins, Edward V, and Richard, Duke of York, were. Perhaps his father's attainder actually protected Warwick from the same fate as he was barred from the throne anyway by law. Richard still felt threatened by the princes as he knew that the stain of illegitimacy against them was not strong, and many still believed Edward V was the rightful king. Could Warwick potentially have shared the fate of the Princes in the

Tower had he not been barred from the throne due to his father's attainder? Quite possibly. But Richard could not reverse the attainder against Clarence without 'sacrificing the legitimacy of his own claim to the throne'.[7] No one truly knows what happened to the Princes in the Tower in 1483 when they disappeared. The most likely and generally accepted view is that they were murdered, but how and by whom is unlikely to ever really be explained. There have been rumours that King Charles III is in favour of the bones in the urn at Westminster Abbey being examined, which could possibly provide a cause of death and at least confirm whether they are those of the princes. These bones were discovered during excavations at the Tower of London in 1674, buried under a staircase leading into the White Tower. The bones were said to be those of two boys which were assumed to be the princes, buried there after their murder in 1483. The remains were buried in Westminster Abbey in an urn and do not appear to have been examined since. Any testing is unlikely to provide answers aside from the identity of the bones.

As we will see, there have been attempts to claim that one or both of the boys escaped the Tower and survived, and that Warwick himself escaped the Tower overseas to cause trouble and claim the crown. These conspiracies would put him in a dangerous position, even though he was safely imprisoned in the Tower of London throughout Henry VII's reign. There was no chance Warwick was running around on the continent raising rebellion.

With Richard III's death at the Battle of Bosworth Field in 1485 and the accession of Henry VII to the English throne, Warwick was moved to the Tower of London where he would spend the remainder of his life. He was considered too much of a threat to the new Tudor dynasty to have anywhere other than under the nose of the government, even though his cousin, Elizabeth of York, the eldest daughter of Edward IV, became queen of England when she married Henry VII. It is unknown whether Elizabeth saw Warwick again after he was imprisoned in the Tower in 1485, but perhaps she visited him. However, she would be unable to save her cousin from the executioner's axe.

* * *

Warwick was only aged 10 when Henry VII imprisoned him in the Tower of London in 1485, almost immediately after his accession to the throne. Warwick was a pawn with little to no control over his own life or destiny. He was in the same place that his royal cousins disappeared just a few summers earlier and some feared that he would meet the same fate. With the Princes in the Tower believed to be dead at the hands of, or at least on the orders of, Richard III, Warwick was the closest Yorkist heir to the English throne. It would be this proximity to the throne which would prove Warwick's undoing, more than any actual actions that he would take. It has been suggested that it was in fact Henry VII, or his mother, Margaret Beaufort, who had the Princes in the Tower murdered and that they were actually still alive when Richard III was killed at Bosworth. Though, if Henry VII had them murdered, it would have benefited him to display their bodies, perhaps pretending that the bodies had been discovered in the Tower of London during some building or remodelling work. This would have later lessened the impact of pretenders to his throne.

However, that leaves the question of why not do away with Warwick at the same time? As the princes were already believed to be dead, it would have been easy enough to kill them and blame it on the dead Richard III. Warwick, however, was known to still be alive and had been seen since Richard's death as Henry VII ordered that he be brought south to London. It is probably a mystery we will never know the answer to. It would be a similar situation in 1538 for Warwick's sister, Margaret Pole, and her closeness to the throne. She was arrested along with her entire family and would be executed three years later. They were the last of the 'White Roses'; those who could threaten the Tudor's claim to the throne, and who many believed were the rightful rulers of England. The white rose was notably the symbol for the House of York of which Henry VII's wife and Henry VIII's mother, Elizabeth of York, was born into. Margaret and Warwick were Elizabeth's cousins and Margaret's execution will be examined in Chapter 4.

Warwick became unintentionally tied up in the Lambert Simnel and Perkin Warbeck rebellions against Tudor rule in the 1480s and 1490s. The first rebellion was the pretender, Lambert Simnel, who claimed he was the real Earl of Warwick. Simnel emerged in Ireland less than two years after Henry VII won his throne on the battlefield at Bosworth. The surviving Yorkists believed that if no Yorkist claimant to the throne existed, one had to be created.[8] Of course, Warwick did have a claim to the throne but was out of reach to the conspirators, imprisoned as he was in the Tower of London. The council met amidst the growing crisis and concluded the best thing to do was to briefly remove the Earl of Warwick from his chambers in the

Tower of London and show him to the people of London, to directly refute the claim that he was raising rebels in Ireland, so the 'foolish notion that the boy was in Ireland would be driven from men's minds'.[9] Henry VII could prove Warwick was in his custody, which Richard III could not seem to do with the young princes in 1483.

Henry VII paraded the young Earl of Warwick through the streets of London to prove the real Warwick was alive in London, and that those who supported the pretender 'Warwick' in Ireland were wrong (either mistakenly or otherwise). It did not really work as Simnel was crowned in Dublin, Ireland, as Edward VI and made his way over to England with an army including German and Swiss mercenaries under the command of Martin Schwartz, and supported by Margaret of York, Duchess of Burgundy. Margaret was Warwick's aunt, the sister of Edward IV, Richard III, and George, Duke of Clarence. She did not like and was not ready to believe that her family had been overthrown by the Tudors and was determined to restore the House of York to the English throne, whatever it took. Simnel and his fellow rebels were defeated at the Battle of Stoke on 16 June 1487 and Simnel himself was put to work in the royal kitchens as a scullion. He eventually rose to the role of falconer and is thought to have died during the reign of Henry VIII, possibly in the 1520s, though this cannot be confirmed. If Simnel did die in the 1520s then he would have lived to a good age for the Tudor period, into his late-40s or 50s.

Henry VII recognised that Simnel was being used by John de la Pole, 1st Earl of Lincoln, and Francis Lovell, and that he was not responsible for the rebellion against the king. Lincoln was killed at the Battle of Stoke. Lovell seems to have vanished from the historical record, either dead in the battle or fled abroad in the aftermath. Lincoln's involvement in the rebellion is interesting as he initially seemed to accept Henry VII's victory over Richard III and his rule of England and waited eighteen months before fleeing to England to join Simnel. Lincoln possibly wanted to take the crown for himself, exploiting Simnel's pretence as Warwick for his own ends. Lincoln knew that Warwick was in the Tower with little to no chance of his father's attainder being overturned, so determined to use the situation to benefit himself. Richard III and Henry VII had taken the throne against the odds, so why could Lincoln not do the same? Men raised money to aid Lincoln 'then beyng a great Rebell, Enemy, and Traitour'.[10] Like so many other rebels and Tudor nobles, Lincoln ended up with an ignominious death.

The more dangerous rebellion against Henry VII, and for Warwick himself, was that of Perkin Warbeck during the 1490s. It lasted longer and seemed to garner much more foreign support than the Lambert Simnel rebellion; from Margaret of York, Duchess of Burgundy, and James IV of Scotland to the Holy Roman Emperor, Maximilian I, among others. Warbeck was accepted by these supporters as the younger of the Princes in the Tower, Richard of Shrewsbury, Duke of York. Because the bodies of the princes were never produced to prove their deaths, Henry VII could not do what he had done when Lambert Simnel was impersonating the Earl of Warwick and parade Edward V and Richard, Duke of York, through the streets of the capital to disprove rumours from abroad. The Princes in the Tower had vanished in suspicious circumstances, presumed dead, and there were plenty of rumours flying around about their fates. But Henry VII could not prove one way or the other that they were dead. Of course, there is a suggestion that Henry VII or his mother, Margaret Beaufort, may have killed the princes, or ordered their killing, but the king would not want to admit that. He would rather blame it on Richard III committing 'murders in shedding of infant's blood'.[11] With Richard III dead he was not able to defend himself, and if the princes were not alive in 1485 it was natural to assume that Richard was responsible for their deaths.

Polydore Vergil recounted that Henry VII sent spies to try and find out who the pretender really was, and they discovered him as Perkin Warbeck (sometimes spelled 'Werbecque'), 'born of low degree', though from Warbeck's later confession this was not entirely true.[12] His family seem to have been merchants, fairly well off though not noble by any stretch. Either way, it was 'proven' that Warbeck was not of royal blood, an imposter, and in fact had no legitimate claim to the English throne. This meant that either he had duped some of the most powerful rulers in Europe, or that they had wilfully believed the deception for their own ends. As Nathan Amin brutally puts it, the Yorkists believed that 'the Tudor usurper had to fall'.[13] The likes of Margaret of York, and John de la Pole, 1st Earl of Lincoln, believed that the Yorkists were the rightful heirs to the throne and that Henry VII was himself a pretender and usurper with no right. This is how they justified their actions in both 1487 with the pretender Lambert Simnel and throughout the 1490s with Perkin Warbeck. They must have suspected that their actions may lead to the execution of the real Yorkist heir, Edward Plantagenet, 17th Earl of Warwick. Polydore Vergil later claimed that Warwick was 'born to misery' as a victim of the Wars of the Roses, effectively a blameless child.[14] He was an innocent victim, used as a pawn by others who sealed his fate, doomed by his royal blood.

Perkin Warbeck was eventually captured at Taunton in 1497. At the end of November, Henry VII returned to London with Warbeck as his prisoner, having questioned him at Exeter on 5 October where he made a full confession that he was not Richard, Duke of York, and that he was from Tournai, the son of John Osbeck who was a merchant. Initially Warbeck was treated leniently when he confessed that he was not in fact Richard of Shrewsbury and was allowed to remain at court, though not share a bed with his wife, Katherine Gordon, a Scottish noblewoman. A London chronicler wrote that Warbeck had freedom at court 'at lyberte with many other benefetis'.[15] Perhaps Henry VII used his own experience as a youth in exile in Brittany, as suggested by historian Nathen Amin, as a blueprint for how Warbeck should be treated; allowed some freedom of movement within the court, but not outside it.[16]

However, when Warbeck tried to escape, he was instead imprisoned in the Tower of London. The Spanish monarchs, Isabella I of Castile and Ferdinand II of Aragon, refused to conclude marriage negotiations between Henry VII's eldest son, Prince Arthur, and their youngest daughter, Katherine of Aragon, until both Perkin Warbeck and Edward, Earl of Warwick, were dead. This would eradicate two threats to the throne and make the future more secure for Arthur, who would not then have to worry about these threats, nor would any of his children and descendants. Ferdinand and Isabella had seen how the English throne could be destabilised by imposters and the existence of Yorkist heirs since the Battle of Bosworth in 1485 when Henry won his crown. Henry VII had been fixated on a Spanish match for his son since Arthur was born in 1486. The Tudor dynasty was a young one, and Henry was determined to unite his fledgling dynasty with the prosperous Spanish one. The proxy marriage between Prince Arthur and Katherine of Aragon took place in May 1499, which gave Henry VII the push to get Warwick out of the way. Henry's decision to act against Warwick had 'likely been heavily influenced by the demands of the Spanish monarchs'.[17] Warwick was a focus for malcontents and revolt. The treaty between the English and Spanish was ratified on 20 January 1500, just two months after the executions of Perkin Warbeck and the Earl of Warwick, saying that they 'hope that great advantages to both countries will flow from this matrimonial union'.[18]

England and Spain would be in alliance on and off largely due to Katherine of Aragon's influence, until Henry VIII's Great Matter in the late 1520s.

After the execution of another pretender, Ralph Wulford, in February 1499, who had also pretended to be Warwick, Henry VII was incredibly concerned about the threat posed by Warwick to his crown and throne. Wulford was encouraged by an Augustinian monk named Patrick to pretend to be the Earl of Warwick. It was claimed that Warwick had escaped from the Tower and was on the run, attempting to capture the throne which was rightfully his. Wulford was quickly arrested and confessed his true identity. He was executed by hanging on 12 February 1499.[19] The capture of Warbeck does not seem to have stopped the flow of belief that a Yorkist claimant was free and should be on the throne.

Henry VII was, as many in the Tudor period were, superstitious. He had heard of a priest who accurately foretold the deaths of both Edward IV and Richard III, and so invited him for a consultation. The priest warned the king that his life would be in danger all year as there were two parties in England with very different political alignments: one loyal to the Tudors, and one fighting for a Yorkist restoration, and that conspiracies would ensue.[20] This was after Perkin Warbeck was already safely imprisoned in the Tower. The king also consulted his astrologer, Dr William Parron, who expounded that 'it is expedient that one man should die for the people, and the whole nation perish not, for an insurrection cannot occur in any state without the death of a great part of the people and the destruction of many great families with their property'.[21] It is a pragmatic view, and one probably shared by Henry VII.

The Earl of Warwick had not done anything at this point that could justify a legal process against him. He had been imprisoned in the Tower of London since 1485 when Henry VII took the throne and had not had the chance to become involved in any kind of insurrection. His name, title, and claim had been used by others to incite rebellion against the Tudors, but Warwick himself held no blame for this. Henry VII did not have Warwick killed secretly in the Tower, as many believed about the Princes in the Tower at the hands of Richard III. Instead, he wanted Warwick to be seen to die, to head off any other rebellions in his name. Henry VII had learnt to his cost what could happen when an heir to the throne mysteriously disappeared. It was Warwick who would pay the price. But it had to be seen to be legal and right, so the only way was by process of law.

Perkin Warbeck was kept in a cell directly below that of the Earl of Warwick while in the Tower of London. The two could communicate through a hole in the ceiling or floor respectively, though they do not seem to have known each other prior to the summer of 1499. Warbeck was essentially imprisoned in the Tower in order to be forgotten. The initial intention was not for him to be executed, in my opinion. Henry VII would only execute once it became imperative for the security of the dynasty. It was alleged that the Earl of Warwick and Perkin Warbeck would escape the Tower, aided by a couple of their servants, and that Warwick had said that he would assist Warbeck in taking the throne for himself if Warbeck truly was the younger of the Princes in the Tower, Richard, Duke of York.[22] Discussions suggested that if Warbeck was not really Richard, then it was agreed that he would assist the Earl of Warwick to take the throne instead, as the rightful Yorkist heir. There were some divisions between the conspirators as to whether Perkin Warbeck really was Prince Richard, but they agreed that either Warwick or Warbeck were preferential to Henry VII.[23] Warwick seems to have assented to the plot, without truly realising what he was agreeing to, and understanding that he was committing treason, for 'whom the weary life of a long imprisonment, and the often and renewing fears of being put to death had softened to take any impression of counsel for his liberty'.[24] There is a suggestion that Warbeck required constant motivation, whether from Warwick in the room above or from servants within the Tower.[25] It seems strange given that it appears to have been Warwick who needed to be persuaded into the plan in the first place. On 3 August 1499, the alleged plot was betrayed, but no arrests were made for a further three weeks, suggesting that the plot had already been discovered, and perhaps had even been manipulated from the beginning.

The Treason Act of 1351 condemned both Warwick and Warbeck as it was considered treason if a man 'be adherent to the King's Enemies in his Realm, giving to them Aid and Comfort in the Realm'.[26] Warbeck was an enemy of the king as he had acted against him in raising armies and claiming his throne. The Earl of Warwick was then, after the fact, an 'adherent' to Warbeck when they were accused of plotting together in the Tower. Whether the plotting together in the Tower actually happened is up for debate, as there have been suggestions that it was entirely fabricated in order to condemn the pair and allow the Spanish marriage to go ahead. The extent of official involvement in the entrapment of Perkin Warbeck and the Earl of Warwick is unclear but is likely to be 'considerable'.[27] It was paramount for Henry VII to secure his crown and safeguard the Spanish alliance. He seized the chance to kill two birds with one stone.

* * *

As previously stated, the death of Edward Plantagenet, 17th Earl of Warwick, was necessary in the eyes of Henry VII because he had been negotiating a marriage for his eldest son, Prince Arthur, with a daughter of Isabella I of Castile and Ferdinand II of Aragon, the Spanish monarchs. However, Ferdinand and Isabella were reluctant to send their youngest daughter to a country under threat from pretenders to the throne who asserted that they had a greater claim and were the rightful rulers. Chronicler Edward Hall recounted that 'the fame after his [Warwick's] death sprung that Ferdinand, king of Spain, would never make full conclusion of the matrimony to be had between Prince Arthur and the Lady Catherine his daughter, nor send her into England, as long as this earl lived'.[28] The pressure was thus on Henry VII that, if he wanted the prestigious Spanish marriage to go ahead, he needed to find a way to rid himself of the Earl of Warwick. This was perhaps when the plot was conceived (if it was conceived) to entrap both Warwick and Warbeck together and kill two birds with one stone. It is possible that royal agents simply took advantage of a plot already brewing, although the idea that it was entirely guided by royal agents has also been suggested. We will likely never know either way. The king used the plot 'happening so opportunely to represent the danger to the king's estate from the earl of Warwick and thereby to cover the king's severity that followed'.[29] It seems almost too good to be true and too opportunistic that this plot emerged exactly when the king needed it to, in order to get rid of Warwick. Both Warwick and Warbeck, if they agreed to a plot to put one or other of them on the throne, were guilty of treason by the 1351 Treason Act.

On 12 November 1499, the king's council assembled at Westminster, including all of the bishops and prominent members of the English nobility including Henry Stafford, 3rd Duke of Buckingham, Henry Algernon Percy, 5th Earl of Northumberland, John de Vere, 13th Earl of Oxford, Thomas Howard, Earl of Surrey (later 2nd Duke of Norfolk), and Henry Bourchier, 2nd Earl of Essex. The gathering of so many important men made it clear how significant this case was to the king and country. Chief Justice Fineux had to show evidence before the council 'of certaine treasons conspired of Edward namyng himself of Warwick and Perkin and other within the Tower'.[30] Fineux believed the charges, that the pair intended to depose and kill the king, were true and that the case could proceed to trial. The trial date was set for just four days later for Warbeck and nine days later for Warwick, at Westminster in the heart of London. It was a public trial so that the people would hear about the crimes and believe that the king was justified in having Warwick executed. There was not really any question over the guilt of Perkin Warbeck.

Perkin Warbeck was tried on 16 November 1499 at Westminster Hall and was condemned to a traitor's death of hanging, drawing, and quartering. Just four days later, Warbeck, along with another conspirator, John Atwater, was taken through the streets of London to Tyburn for execution. Atwater was said to have aided the communication between Warwick and Warbeck when the pair were imprisoned in the Tower. This suggests that it was this particular plot that resulted in their deaths, and not Warbeck's original plot. On the scaffold before his death, Warbeck repeated his confession originally made two years earlier that he was not Prince Richard, Duke of York, younger of the famed Princes in the Tower, and that the entire conspiracy had been a sham. Warbeck died first, but it would not be long before the Earl of Warwick would follow. Warbeck had been tried and executed before the Earl of Warwick had been tried at all, though Warwick's case had the potential to be more complicated and controversial, given that he had not led a rebellion against the king, and there was a question mark over the way he had been trapped into colluding in treason while in the Tower of London. How were two young men allowed to communicate and plot while imprisoned? It left some unanswered questions. The king believed he had no choice but to condemn and execute Warwick but 'in this again the opinion of the King's greatest wisdom did surcharge him with a sinister fame, that Perkin was but his bait, to entrap the earl of Warwick'.[31] The general consensus seems to be, regarding Warwick's guilt, that he was trapped into some kind of agreement to his own escape, perhaps as a result of his imprisonment for so long, and a lack of human communication up to this point. He had been very isolated, and it is understandable that he wanted to be free, however that could be made to come about.

On 21 November 1499, Edward Plantagenet, 17th Earl of Warwick, the nephew of two Yorkist kings, cousin to the queen of England, and son of a traitor, was tried in front of a jury of his peers at Westminster on charges of treason. The trial was led by John de Vere, 13th Earl of Oxford, who was High Constable of England as Henry VII's most respected noble and his primary commander in the Battle of Bosworth fourteen years earlier. Warwick confessed to conspiring with Warbeck while in the Tower of London and committed himself to the king's mercy. Whether he was involved by the enticement of others, or of his own free will was not clear, though many doubted it was of his own free will because of his 'innocency'.[32] As previously stated, many believed that Warwick was 'simple' at the time of his death though perhaps he lacked usual life experiences due to his long incarceration. Warwick had been imprisoned in the Tower since 1485 (aside from when he was paraded in a propaganda stunt to disprove the identity of the pretender in the Lambert Simnel affair), so he had little experience with men and conspiracy. He was said by some to be naïve and even disabled, though the latter is a more modern interpretation. If this were true, it seems unlikely he would have been a conspiratorial mastermind and more likely that he was manipulated by others. Warwick was taken to Tower Hill on 28 November 1499 and beheaded. Not for him a private execution within the Tower of London like later Tudor nobles. Henry VII needed his death to be seen and believed.

Katherine of Aragon would later say, during divorce proceedings from her second husband, Henry VIII, that 'she had not offended, but it was a judgment of God, for that her former marriage was made in blood, meaning that of the Earl of Warwick'.[33] Katherine believed her and Henry VIII's problems in conceiving, carrying, and birthing a live son were a punishment from God, because her first marriage had been the catalyst to the execution of the Earl of Warwick in 1499. Her parents would not allow her to travel to England to marry her first husband, Prince Arthur, until Warwick was dead. Reginald Pole, Archbishop of Canterbury under Mary I, claimed that Katherine's father, Ferdinand II of Aragon, was averse to giving his daughter to one not secure in his own kingdom.[34] This would have given Henry the push to find a legal means to be rid of Warwick.

Katherine's first son born to Henry VIII, Henry, Duke of Cornwall, born 1511, died suddenly less than two months after his birth. She would not birth another surviving son. Katherine and Henry VIII had only a single surviving daughter, Mary, who would become Queen Mary I. Henry VIII believed that he needed a son to secure the Tudor dynasty. A daughter was not good enough; hence Henry wanted a divorce from Katherine in the 1520s. The Spanish ambassador in England, Rodrigo Gonzalez de Puebla, wrote to Ferdinand and Isabella after Warwick's execution that:

> 'England has never before been so tranquil and obedient as at present. There have always been pretenders to the crown of England; but now that Perkin and the son of the Duke of Clarence have been executed, there does not remain 'a drop of doubtful Royal blood,' the only Royal blood being the true blood of the King, the Queen, and, above all, of the Prince of Wales'.[35]

The undertone here was that it was safe for Ferdinand and Isabella to send their daughter, Katherine, to England to marry Arthur, Prince of Wales, because there was no longer any 'doubtful Royal blood'. This implies that Warwick's death came about because of his royal blood, and not actually through his links to rebellion. This is borne out by the fact that Perkin Warbeck was not executed or even really strictly confined after his initial capture, and he appears to have been used as a pawn to undo the Earl of Warwick.

The Simnel and, particularly, Warbeck conspiracies were used as an excuse. Henry VII could have safely kept Warwick locked up in the Tower of London as he had done for the previous fourteen years, but this may have meant that his son would not have been able to marry a Spanish princess and strengthen the English crown. This royal marriage was crucial for giving the new Tudor dynasty a sense of being the rightful dynasty, being able to make powerful diplomatic marriage alliances. This would continue with the marriage of Henry VII's eldest daughter, Margaret, to the Scots king, James IV, in 1503, and then his younger daughter, Mary, to the French king, Louis XII, in 1514. Warwick's death was a watershed in English history because:

> 'This was also the end, not only of this noble and commiserable person Edward the earl of Warwick, eldest son to the duke of Clarence: but likewise the male line of the Plantagenets, which had flourished in great royalty and renown, from the time of the famous king of England, King Henry the second … but it was neither guilt of crime not treason of state, that could quench the envy that was upon the king for this execution: so that he thought good to export it out of the land, and to lay it upon his new ally, Ferdinando, king of Spain'.[36]

Henry VII was certainly determined to portray Warwick's execution as something entirely necessary and legal but, like Elizabeth I when Mary Queen of Scots was executed in 1587, he was determined to lay the blame for the execution onto someone else. In Henry VII's case it was Ferdinand II of Aragon and the Spanish over the proposed marriage of Prince Arthur and Katherine of Aragon. Isabella I of Castile, Ferdinand's wife, is not mentioned, though possibly this speaks more to the perceived role of women than the reality of rule. Isabella was a queen in her own right, and of the more powerful part of Spain, but it is Ferdinand who seems to bear the brunt of blame. In the case of Elizabeth I and Mary Queen of Scots, it was her council who she claimed acted without her permission. Henry VII allowed the trial to go ahead and signed Warwick's death warrant. He could not have been executed without the king's signature. Had Henry VII really wanted to save Warwick, he could have done, though he would have sacrificed the Spanish marriage in the process. Henry VII most likely also had a hand in the plot that entrapped both Warwick and Perkin Warbeck in the Tower of London, knowing that he had to legally execute Warwick to allow the Spanish marriage to go ahead. That was the driving force behind the execution of a young man who did not really do any wrong.

The story of the Earl of Warwick could be seen as that of a young, innocent man, being caught up in conspiracy beyond his control and unable to step away from it, unable even, perhaps, to understand it. Alternatively, he could be seen as a man who manipulated a young and desperate pretender into assisting in his escape and both getting caught, though this seems less likely. What we know of Warwick suggests that he was not wily or educated in the ways of the world and was unwittingly caught up in something he did not fully comprehend. That he was caught up in the aftermath of conspiracy, with his royal blood and traitorous connections being used as a reason to justify his execution, in order to promote a Tudor dynasty still fairly new and unsafe on the English throne.

Chapter 2

Edward Stafford,
3rd Duke of Buckingham – 1521

E dward Stafford, 3rd Duke of Buckingham, was an intriguing character. He had noble and royal blood and connections, though he was the son of an attainted traitor. Under the reigns of Henry VII and Henry VIII, Buckingham regained some of the power lost by his father's execution in 1483, until he became suspected of treasonous activities himself and was arrested after an investigation. His pride and ambition was his downfall. Buckingham's execution marked the first of Henry VIII's noble executions and would set him on the path to many more.

Edward Stafford's father was Henry Stafford, 2nd Duke of Buckingham, and his mother was Katherine Woodville, who was the younger sister of Elizabeth Woodville; hence she was sister-in-law to the Yorkist king, Edward IV. Katherine Woodville was the daughter of Richard Woodville, 1st Earl Rivers, and Jacquetta of Luxembourg, who was related to the Burgundian royal family. It has been suggested that Buckingham resented being married to a Woodville upstart, despite their connections to the Burgundian royal family, but the two were married as children so he probably had no choice in the matter at all. Through Elizabeth Woodville's daughter, Elizabeth of York, Buckingham was thus first cousin once removed to Henry VIII. After the death of the 2nd Duke of Buckingham, his widow, Katherine, went on to marry Jasper Tudor, 1st Duke of Bedford, Henry VII's uncle. Henry Stafford was executed in 1483 for his involvement in a plot to overthrow Richard III and reinstate Edward V as king of England. The plot failed. Edward V was one of the infamous Princes in the Tower who disappeared, presumed murdered by Richard III in the aftermath of the plot to rescue them. Henry Stafford, 2nd Duke of Buckingham, had been a supporter of Richard III up to the rebellion, but after his death, his widow, a sister-in-law to the Yorkist king, Edward IV, married a staunch Lancastrian.

Edward Stafford, 3rd Duke of Buckingham, married Eleanor Percy around 1490, although the exact date is disputed, and they had four children together.

Eleanor was the daughter of Henry Percy, 4th Earl of Northumberland. The marriage united two of the most important noble families in England at the time. Eleanor was also the granddaughter of William Herbert, 1st Earl of Pembroke. Pembroke had the wardship of Henry Tudor when he was a child before he fled into exile in France with his uncle, Jasper Tudor, in 1471. Henry would return to England and became Henry VII after defeating Richard III at the Battle of Bosworth Field. The children of Edward and Eleanor were Elizabeth Stafford, who married Thomas Howard, 3rd Duke of Norfolk, Katherine Stafford who married Ralph Neville, 4th Earl of Westmorland, Mary Stafford who married George Neville, 5th Baron Bergavenny, and Henry Stafford, who became 1st Baron Stafford.

Buckingham, without a doubt had many noble connections through both of his parents, and associations with many prominent noble families through the marriages of his siblings. Of his siblings, his sister, Elizabeth Stafford, married Robert Radcliffe, 1st Earl of Sussex. His younger sister, Anne Stafford, married first Sir Walter Herbert, and secondly George Hastings, 1st Earl of Huntingdon. His younger brother, Henry Stafford, was created 1st Earl of Wiltshire within a year of Henry VIII succeeding to the throne, and he married Cecily Bonville, who was the niece of Richard 'the Kingmaker' Neville, 16th Earl of Warwick, and was an heiress in her own right.

A key thing to know about Buckingham, is his royal connections, further back than his connection to Edward IV through his mother. His mother had connections to the York kings, but his father's line went back to the old Plantagenet kings. Buckingham was a great-great-great-great-grandson of Edward III through his youngest son, Thomas of Woodstock, 1st Duke of Gloucester, and his wife, Eleanor de Bohun. This gave him a sense of pride and entitlement. However, this was through a daughter of Thomas of Woodstock rather than a direct male line from Edward III (as in the case of Henry VI, through John of Gaunt, 1st Duke of Lancaster, or Edward IV and Richard III through Edmund of Langley, 1st Duke of York). Thomas of Woodstock was also the youngest surviving son of Edward III so there were other more senior lines. Buckingham could also trace his descent back twice over to John of Gaunt, though through female lines, and through the same line to Edward I and Henry III. Henry VII came from an illegitimate line through John of Gaunt, so Buckingham's claim could be argued to be stronger than that of the Tudors. This would become very relevant in his fall and execution in 1521.

The Buckingham title would be lost forever to the Stafford family with Edward Stafford's execution in 1521. The title would be created again in 1623 for George Villiers, a favourite (and rumoured lover), of James I. Today there is no duke of Buckingham as the title died out in 1889 on its fourth creation. Edward Stafford, 3rd Duke of Buckingham, was the third holder of the title in its first creation. It was his ambition and pride in his lineage which would prove his downfall in many ways.

*   *   *

Buckingham was born at Brecon Castle, an 11th century stronghold in Wales, on 3 February 1478 as the eldest son and heir of Henry Stafford, 2nd Duke of Buckingham and his wife, Katherine Woodville. He was followed by two sisters, Elizabeth and Anne Stafford, and a brother, Henry Stafford. There was also another brother, Humphrey Stafford, who died young. Little seems to be known of Edward's childhood, although Brecon Castle would fall into a state of disrepair after Buckingham's execution, until it was renovated in the 19th century.

Edward's father, Henry Stafford, 2nd Duke of Buckingham, was executed in 1483 on the orders of Richard III, who had seized the throne from Edward V in June after the death of Edward IV in April that year. After his father's execution, it has been suggested that the young Edward was hidden in various houses across Herefordshire to stop Richard III taking him into custody.[1] Richard III had already, it was rumoured, killed his own nephews. What was to stop him killing the heir to the dukedom of Buckingham to stop him avenging his father's execution at a later date? The precise locations where the young duke was kept seem to be unknown. This threat was because the young Edward Stafford potentially had a claim to the throne by being a descendant of Edward III. In a less threatening scenario, it is possible that Richard III wanted to keep him close so that others could not use him to their advantage to topple the new king. It would not have been the first time or the last that a young boy was used as a pawn by those who wanted to remove the monarch from the throne to replace them with a new one.

When Henry VII defeated Richard III at the Battle of Bosworth Field on 22 August 1485, Buckingham's wardship was given to the new king's mother, Margaret Beaufort, Countess of Richmond and Derby. He probably stayed in several of her houses over the next few years and was educated there. Edward was restored to his estates and title of Duke of Buckingham when Henry VII reversed his father's attainder in November 1485, just a few months after coming to the throne. The 2nd duke, when he rebelled against Richard III in 1483, was acting either to restore Edward V or Henry Tudor to the English throne, depending on whether Edward V was still alive. Buckingham did attend court on 9 November 1494 when the future Henry VIII was created Duke of York (in a move designed to combat the claims of the pretender, Perkin Warbeck, who was in Burgundy claiming to be the younger of the Princes in the Tower, Richard, Duke of York). Buckingham himself was made a Knight of the Garter in 1495, at the age of 17. He was regaining the position lost by his father, and which he believed he was entitled to, slowly and steadily.

For the coronation of Henry VIII and Katherine of Aragon in 1509, Buckingham was appointed Lord High Constable for the day, usually a hereditary position, but one of great favour. He also served as Lord High Steward at the coronation and carried the crown. He was then made a member of the new king's Privy Council, though he was never particularly close to the king. Buckingham was also present at the proxy marriage of Henry VIII's sister, Princess Mary, to the aging Louis XII of France in 1514. However, the evidence suggests that he was never a part of Henry VIII's inner circle and exercised little political influence during Henry VIII's reign. He was more of a contemporary with Henry's brother, Prince Arthur, and was already 13 years old when Henry VIII was born. Had Arthur not died in 1502 and succeeded to the throne in 1509 on his father's death, Buckingham may have been more influential and powerful. Possibly this age gap with Henry VIII meant that Buckingham was too old to be in the king's close circle. This may have rankled with him as the senior peer in England and could have contributed to his gripes about the king towards the end of his life. But perhaps his pride meant that he did not want to be in the Tudor king's close circle as he considered himself above the upstart Tudors.

Buckingham also appeared to be allying himself to other noble families. He himself married Eleanor Percy, daughter of Henry Percy, 4th Earl of Northumberland in December 1489. Their son, Henry Stafford, married Ursula Pole in 1519, daughter of Margaret Pole, Countess of Salisbury, and granddaughter of George Plantagenet, Duke of Clarence, and thus great-niece to the Yorkist kings Edward IV and Richard III. Both of these marriages connected the Staffords to families with royal connections outside the Tudors.

It may have seemed to the Tudor king, Henry VIII, that Buckingham was allying himself with other noble families who potentially had more of a claim to the throne than he did. It was this latter marriage in 1519 which potentially gave rise to the possibility that Margaret Pole herself was involved in Buckingham's treason in 1521, as the mother of Ursula Pole, Buckingham's daughter-in-law. Margaret Pole was questioned on Buckingham's arrest.

Anne Hastings, sister to the Duke of Buckingham, was alleged to have been the first mistress of Henry VIII, though there is no real evidence to support this summation. Buckingham believed that he was a cut above the upstart Tudors and so this would really have angered him. His sister being someone's mistress would also have been seen as disreputable and staining the reputation of the Stafford family, which Buckingham was determined to restore and protect. There is no real corroboration for the affair from surviving contemporary sources, though it is thought to have happened while Katherine of Aragon was pregnant with her 'honeymoon' baby. This was a premature daughter who was stillborn on 31 January 1510, just over seven months after Katherine's wedding to Henry VIII. Henry's mistresses over the course of his life would be chosen from among his queen's ladies-in-waiting, a pattern which may have begun here with Anne Hastings.[2] Henry's second, third, and fifth wives, Anne Boleyn, Jane Seymour, and Katherine Howard, would be chosen from among his previous queen's ladies-in-waiting. Katherine Parr was in the household of Henry's eldest daughter, Princess Mary (later Mary I). So perhaps it is not too outlandish to suggest Buckingham's sister, Anne, was Henry VIII's first mistress, though there is no real proof.

Anne was married to Sir George Hastings in 1509 as her second husband, who would be created the 1st Earl of Huntingdon in 1529. Anne had been widowed in 1507 when her first husband, Sir Walter Herbert, died. It has been suggested that Anne was already engaged in an affair with the king's friend and Groom of the Stool, Sir William Compton, when the king himself approached her.[3] Gossip spread about Anne, Henry and Compton, and that Compton was acting as a go-between for Anne and Henry. Buckingham was enraged, not only over the affair itself, but because it appeared to be common knowledge and the subject of court gossip. On discovering Anne and Compton in a room together, Buckingham is said to have cried out 'Women of the Stafford family are no game for Comptons, no, nor Tudors neither'[4]; though this seems to have come from a later source rather than a contemporary one. Henry VIII seems to have confronted the Duke of

Buckingham over his comments and thoughts on the affair, but Buckingham did not appear to like what was said and left the court. Anne Hastings was seemingly put into a convent by her husband, and Katherine of Aragon also showed her distaste to Henry VIII.[5] This would be the only time that Katherine would confront her husband over an affair; when he took future mistresses she would take the moral high ground and endure, certain that he would come back to her in the end.

This event was a clear demonstration, whether you believe the affair really happened or not, of how people at court perceived Buckingham's pride, rancour, and ambition. He was determined to defend his family name and promote their position and wealth. He believed that he should have power and influence and would not give up on that idea very easily. His family survived his fall and execution, but the Buckingham title was lost to them forever through the actions of Edward Stafford.

* * *

What has been suggested about the fall of the 3rd Duke of Buckingham is that it may have been because of his royal blood. His claim to the English throne was arguably stronger than that of the Tudors, and this was a big worry to Henry VIII, particularly by the early 1520s when it looked more and more likely that he would not have a son by his wife, Katherine of Aragon. Buckingham was the premier noble in the kingdom with lots of properties, wealth, and the ability to raise a private army from his affinity. This was of huge concern to Henry VIII, combined with his royal blood, as he potentially had the power to overthrow the king. Henry VIII had been trying to reduce and restrict noble followings, so Buckingham's attempts to build his angered the king and made him suspicious of what Buckingham's intentions were.[6] Combined with his lack of circumspection and his folly in vaunting his royal blood and connections, Buckingham essentially doomed himself. The Venetian ambassador believed that the Duke of Buckingham would rule if Henry VIII died without a legitimate son.[7] Henry VIII did have a son, Henry Fitzroy, born in 1519 by his mistress, Bessie Blount, but he was illegitimate and thus ineligible to inherit the crown. Fitzroy would ultimately predecease the king, dying in 1536, aged just 17. The succession was a particularly sore point with Henry VIII.

Buckingham also claimed that the execution of Edward Plantagenet, 17th Earl of Warwick in 1499 (see Chapter 1) cursed the Tudor line. This was echoed in the words of Katherine of Aragon years later, that her first marriage to Prince Arthur was 'made in blood, meaning that of the Earl of Warwick'.[8] The execution of the Earl of Warwick seemed to hang over the Tudor Henrys. In the indictment issued against Buckingham in 1521, Buckingham was said to have claimed to Ralph Neville, 4th Earl of Westmorland, that:

'there be two new Dukes created in England, but that if anything but good should happen to the King, he, the duke of Buckingham, was next in succession to the crown of England'.[9]

This was dangerous talk. The two new dukes created in England were Thomas Howard, 2nd Duke of Norfolk and Charles Brandon, 1st Duke of Suffolk in 1514. Norfolk was regranted his family's title which had been forfeit in the aftermath of the Battle of Bosworth Field in 1485 because of his heroic actions at the Battle of Flodden Field in 1513 which had resulted in the death of the Scots' king, James IV. This was while Henry VIII was fighting in France. Henry VIII's childhood friend, Charles Brandon, was created 1st Duke of Suffolk possibly just as Henry's closest friend, though he had also fought with the king in France the year before, which may have influenced the precise timing of the creation. The new Duke of Suffolk would go on to marry Henry VIII's younger, sister, Mary, in 1515, and they would be the grandparents of the ill-fated Nine Days Queen, Lady Jane Grey.

It has also been proposed that Buckingham's downfall may have been, in part, because of his personality; he was full of pride and seemed contemptuous of the Tudors, arrested more for an abrasive personality than treasonous actions according to historian David Loades.[10] Whether this was because he truly believed that he had a better claim to the throne than they did is conjecture, but it is still interesting to consider. Possibly Henry VIII feared that his nobles were plotting against him. Buckingham had been made Constable of England for the coronation of Henry VIII and Katherine of Aragon in June 1509 and he believed that the position should be made permanent. He believed he had a hereditary claim to the Constableship of England, but Henry VIII refused to grant it to him.[11] It is possible that Henry VIII deliberately withheld it from him because he feared Buckingham's power and did not want his nobles to become too great. If there was a single noble at risk of this, it would have been Buckingham. The other two dukes in England in 1521 owed their titles to the Tudors. Buckingham thus had the oldest dukedom and the most royal connections in England.

Sir William Fitzwilliam was a servant of Cardinal Thomas Wolsey, Henry VIII's right-hand man, and he had visited the French court around the time that Buckingham was arrested in April 1521. Francis I of France asked Fitzwilliam's opinion of Buckingham and he said that he was a 'highminded man' and 'so full of choler that there was nothing could content him'.[12] This paints a picture of a man who was sure of his own vaunted position in the world, and wanted more power and riches, never content with what he had. His ambition was never-ending. His personality could thus explain a lot about what happened to cause his fall. In 1521, Buckingham seems to have had an abrasive personality and his sense of his own right would no doubt have rubbed Henry VIII up the wrong way, as he had the same sense of purpose about himself. Perhaps in a way they were too similar to get along and some kind of confrontation was inevitable.

Historian, Desmond Seward, recounts that in early 1520, one of the king's retainers, a man called William Bulmer, came to court wearing a Stafford badge. The king had him prosecuted in the Star Chamber, but he was eventually forgiven.[13] Star Chamber was part of the law courts that sat at Westminster, and it aimed to ensure fair use of the legal system, but it was noted for its abuse of power. It seems that Buckingham had a habit of employing royal servants himself. Buckingham had allegedly thought that he might be sent to the Tower for it. This demonstrated that he had experience of how the king reacted to his nobles overreaching, from this event over a year before Buckingham's own arrest, but that he did not seem to learn from his mistakes. He did not seem to understand the king's temperament and how he would not accept his nobles promoting their own affinities when they should be serving him. However, we cannot know if Buckingham was aware that Bulmer would do this, or whether he had a hand in it at all. It may be that the servant had taken it upon himself to state his support for the Staffords. The Tudors were an unstable dynasty, still only in the second generation at this point, who had seized the crown on the battlefield with only a weak claim. Any sense that people were trying to overturn the dynasty or usurp power from the Tudors would be treated severely.

Buckingham did make several mistakes in the months before his death, including flaunting his large retinue which may have worried the king. He also fell out with the king's chief minister, Cardinal Thomas Wolsey. Part of this falling out was over the expense of the Field of the Cloth of Gold diplomatic summit in 1520. This was a meeting planned by Wolsey for Henry VIII and Francis I of France to meet and conclude a peace treaty. Buckingham did not agree with the expense of the event which was extravagant and did not bring any real long-term peace. Within two years of the summit, Henry VIII declared war on France. Buckingham's hackles may also have been raised at the fact that the summit had been organised successfully by Thomas Wolsey, and it was to promote peace with France, which Buckingham did not approve of. He did not live to see the peace break down. It has also been suggested that Buckingham did not agree with or accept Wolsey's rise to the top of government.[14] Wolsey was the son of an Ipswich butcher and Buckingham likely did not consider him worthy to advise a king. The king asked Wolsey to keep an eye on Buckingham, perhaps fearing what he would do next.

William Shakespeare's *King Henry the Eighth* opens with the arrest of the Duke of Buckingham. Shakespeare suggests Buckingham's arrest and execution were due directly to Wolsey and the enmity between the two. Buckingham described Wolsey in the play as being involved in everything 'no man's pie is freed from his ambitious finger'.[15] King Henry spoke in his turn in praise of the duke but believed Wolsey's evidence against him, claiming that 'the mind growing once corrupt, they turn to vicious forms, ten times more ugly than ever they were fair'.[16] The insinuation being that Buckingham was corrupted by power, his own royal blood, unjust suspicion, and his own fevered imagination.[17] Whether Wolsey himself really was responsible for Buckingham's fall, as Shakespeare depicts, is debatable, as with so many other things regarding the erstwhile Duke of Buckingham.

Allegedly Buckingham spoke to his servants about kneeling before the king and stabbing him with a dagger concealed about his person. This was treason. Buckingham claimed that this was what his father, the 2nd duke, had planned to do to Richard III. As previously discussed, the 2nd duke was executed for treason by Richard III in 1483. A disgruntled ex-servant went to Wolsey with these threats.[18] Whether Buckingham's imagination had run wild, and it was a fantasy, or whether he had seriously considered doing this is unclear. It is possible that this disgruntled servant was Buckingham's surveyor, Charles Knyvet, who was sacked in 1520. It is worth contemplating whether he could have made up the claim. Historian, John Matusiak, claims that it was Knyvet who was the source of the rumour that Buckingham planned to stab the king as he knelt before him.[19] A variation of this scene is played out in season one of television show *The Tudors* (2007). However, in the television show Buckingham plays the scene out in front of Thomas Boleyn (later 1st Earl of Wiltshire and Ormond, and the father of Anne Boleyn), and Thomas Howard (later 3rd Duke of Norfolk). It was Thomas Boleyn who went to Wolsey, who then went to the king with the accusations, not one of Buckingham's servants as the sources demonstrate. The show is often called out for taking liberties with the truth, which it does for dramatic effect, but many of the events it depicts did take place, though perhaps not in quite the way portrayed. This is the case with Buckingham's threats against Henry VIII.

At the end of November 1520, Buckingham announced his intention to visit his Welsh estates with 300 to 400 armed retainers accompanying him. There were concerns at court that Buckingham had in fact raised his retainers because he feared danger from the court and that he believed that there was a plot against him. Buckingham had written to his chancellor, Robert Gilbert, on 26 November 1520, to say that he should inform Wolsey of his intention to take 300 or 400 men with him to Wales 'who will be his own servants, that he may be a mean to the King'.[20] He specified that they would be his own servants, so loyal to him, and appeared to suggest that he intended to make a show of power so that his lordships knew he was loyal to the king. Buckingham did not seem to be popular in Wales and there had been rumblings of discontent. The Welsh Marches were known to be a little unruly at times and Buckingham does not seem to have been very popular on his estates there, hence perhaps his excuse of raising armed men to accompany him. Whether he was planning rebellion against the king or not, he seemed to fear for his safety in Wales.

In spring 1521, Buckingham's servants were questioned by royal agents, looking for evidence of treason to use against the duke. In addition to the idea mooted about Buckingham stabbing the king with a knife, there appears to have been a suggestion from the servants that Buckingham had met with a necromancer who predicted that Buckingham would take the throne as Henry VIII would have no sons.[21] One suggestion is that this was in fact a Carthusian monk named Nicholas Hopkyns, who claimed that the

Tudors were cursed and that Buckingham would one day become king.[22] A daughter at this time was not considered a viable heir, though there was no salic law in England as there was in France, which excluded females from the succession completely. This was Henry's fear; that he would have no sons and leave the succession an open question, and England open to another Wars of the Roses. Whether this necromancer was actually Buckingham's confessor, Nicholas Hopkyns, is another option.

Hopkyns was said to have predicted that James IV of Scotland would die at the Battle of Flodden (which came true), and then that Buckingham would succeed to the throne as Henry VIII would die without sons.[23] The fact that Hopkyns had been correct about James IV would have worried those superstitious people of the sixteenth century, including the king. Henry VIII was known to consult astrologers, particularly during the pregnancies of his wives; an astrologer predicted that Anne Boleyn's first child would be a son, when of course it was a daughter, Elizabeth. John Delacourt, Buckingham's chaplain, was questioned and he recalled that he was sent to see Nicholas Hopkyns who 'pretended to have knowledge of future events' and that Hopkyns had told him that Buckingham 'should have all, and that he should endeavour to obtain the love of the community'.[24] Delacourt was made to take an oath not to reveal what was said except to Buckingham himself. The suggestion alone that the king would die without sons and Buckingham would succeed him, would have prompted Henry to act against Buckingham, especially given that we know how his paranoia seemed to develop later in life. Perhaps this was the first sign of what Henry VIII would become. It was after these interrogations that it was decided that they had enough evidence to act against Buckingham, on charges of treason.

On 8 April 1521 Buckingham was at his residence of Thornbury Castle in Gloucestershire when a messenger arrived to invite him to court. Buckingham had built Thornbury up from a manor house to a great noble residence, perhaps intended to rival some of the royal palaces in London. The chimneys at Thornbury are certainly similar to those that would later grace Hampton Court Palace, so perhaps Henry VIII took inspiration from Buckingham's own building works, jealous of the grandeur of his residence. Buckingham's own suspicions would have been aroused at Windsor Castle on 16 April 1521 when he was with the royal court and was told that a servant was watching him on the king's orders. Buckingham, was sailing on the Thames that same day, heading towards London Bridge, when he was intercepted by one hundred Yeomen of the Guard who told him he was under arrest. He was taken straight to the Tower of London. Whoever passed on the warning about a servant watching him on the king's behalf came too late to help him. He was already doomed.

Buckingham's former surveyor, Charles Knyvet, was already in the Tower, along with his confessor, Nicholas Hopkyns (who had made the prediction about the king dying without issue), his chancellor, Robert Gilbert, and his chaplain, John Delacourt. All had been questioned by the council and were being groomed as witnesses to speak against him at trial, and thus condemn him to death for treason. There was no escape once the king had decided he wanted you dead.

*   *   *

Edward Stafford, 3rd Duke of Buckingham, was the first noble to be executed under Henry VIII. Perhaps it is significant that there were no real noteworthy executions until this point, except that of Edmund de la Pole who was executed in 1513. He had at different times been known as Earl and Duke of Suffolk, though he had fled abroad, and began calling himself the 'White Rose'. He would return to England in 1505/6 and was imprisoned in the Tower. Henry VIII finally ordered his execution when the French king, Louis XII, began to pronounce Edmund as the 'rightful' king of England. Henry VIII only seemed to begin executing people when he began to doubt whether his wife, Katherine of Aragon, would produce a son to carry on his line. Henry only began to act against those close to the throne and with royal blood when he felt threatened, worried, or paranoid. Buckingham's royal blood was essentially a threat to the Tudor succession, in the same way that Margaret Pole and her son, Henry Pole, 1st Baron Montagu, were a threat to the Tudor succession in the late 1530s, even though Henry VIII did have a son at that point. He knew from experience, being a second son himself, that one was not enough to secure a dynasty. Henry VIII seemed determined to wipe out anyone whose claim could potentially supersede the claims of his own children to his throne. Buckingham's execution marked a turning point in the treatment of those closest to the crown.[25] This would later be seen in perhaps its most brutal form with the Pole family. Margaret Pole was actually suspected of colluding in the treasons of the duke of Buckingham, though nothing was proven, and no action was taken against her at this time.

Buckingham's high-mindedness and pride in his royal lineage was a key part of his downfall and execution. He liked to display his arms and boast of the fact allegedly. Buckingham used Woodstock's lily symbol as one of his own, emphasising his royal credentials. His lineage was unimpeachable, unlike that of the Tudors. Buckingham seemed to enjoy lauding his own superiority in the court, and making others feel small and insignificant in comparison. This could help to explain why no one stepped forward to defend him when he was arrested. Buckingham was not afforded the same level of trust as Suffolk and Norfolk by Henry VIII, probably because his claim to the throne was so much stronger than the other dukes, being descended from two sons of Edward III.[26] He had been mentioned as possible regent in 1502 when Henry VII was sick, should the king have died. This would have scared Henry VIII who had it drummed into him the importance of the succession and him feeling he had failed in 1521 with only a single living daughter. Buckingham was a serious threat, and the king would not allow him to live.

On 8 May 1521, Buckingham was indicted at the Guildhall for treason. The key charge was that he intended to take the crown from the king. He claimed that most of the English nobility would support the assassination of Henry VIII, although that seems unlikely given that it would probably plunge the country back into civil war. The Wars of the Roses had only ended with the accession of Henry VII in 1485 when he defeated Richard III at the Battle of Bosworth, though no one knew it at that point. By 1521, however, it was thought that the wars were over, and England was once again at peace. The Earl of Warwick, who had been the main threat to the throne after Richard III's death, had been executed in 1499, and Margaret Pole, Warwick's sister, was the widow of a Tudor supporter and raising the Princess Mary, heir presumptive to the English throne, in Wales. Threats had largely been nullified. Except Buckingham. Allegedly Buckingham had also intended to bribe the royal guards to assist him, and even retained royal servants in his own household. Buckingham also claimed that, if the king died, he would have Wolsey beheaded.[27] Wolsey was seen by many of the old nobility as an upstart, the son of an Ipswich butcher, and not worthy to advise the king and run the country. But the king relied heavily on him to get the business of the realm concluded and conduct diplomatic negotiations abroad.

There was even a claim that Buckingham had alleged that the death of Henry VIII's first son (Prince Henry, Duke of Cornwall, who was born in

1511 and lived for just 3 months), was revenge for the execution of Edward Plantagenet, 17th Earl of Warwick, in 1499 by Henry VII.[28] The infant duke of Cornwall was the first living child of Henry VIII and his first wife, Katherine of Aragon. This could be seen as another shot by Buckingham at the upstart Tudors, as Warwick was the son of George Plantagenet, 1st Duke of Clarence, brother of Edward IV and Richard III. Clarence was descended from Edward III through Edmund of Langley, 1st Duke of York. Warwick was descended down a legitimate male line and an excellent claimant to the English throne, where the Tudors were from an illegitimate female line. It is possible that this was Buckingham taking a dig at the weak claim of the Tudors to the English throne. The death of so many children born to Henry and Katherine would also later be used by the king as an excuse to request an annulment of his marriage from the Pope in the late 1520s. This would lead directly to the Break with Rome and the English Reformation.

Thomas Howard, 2nd Duke of Norfolk, was appointed as Lord High Steward to preside over Buckingham's trial, as the next senior peer to Buckingham himself. Buckingham and Norfolk were also related as Buckingham's daughter, Elizabeth, married Norfolk's son, another Thomas Howard, later the 3rd duke of Norfolk. This must have made the situation difficult for Norfolk, knowing that he was condemning his son's father-in-law to death. Norfolk was supported in his role by Charles Brandon, 1st Duke of Suffolk, and Thomas Grey, 2nd Marquess of Dorset, along with seven earls and twelve barons. Suffolk and Norfolk would be the ones who would benefit most from Buckingham's execution in terms of wealth, lands, and titles. The outcome was never in doubt. The king wanted Buckingham dead, and the jury of peers knew it, so found him guilty. Had they not acted as the king wanted, then they would have faced the wrath of the king and could have been imprisoned themselves, though Henry VIII's most malicious streak had not yet come out as the tyrant we often see him as in later years. Buckingham's execution was just the beginning.

The indictment is quite detailed, claiming that Buckingham intended 'to exalt himself to the crown' and that he did 'imagine and compass the deposition and death of the king'.[29] This was treason, for which the punishment was death, by the 1351 Treason Act. Buckingham had claimed 'he would rather die than be ordered as he was'.[30] This suggests the extent to which Buckingham was feeling hard done by, and that he wanted and deserved to be, in his eyes at least, in a more auspicious and powerful position than he was. He claimed that if the king died he intended to have the rule of kingdom whoever would speak against it. However, Buckingham knew that if the king learned of the predictions and the preparations he was making then 'he should be altogether destroyed'.[31] This is exactly what happened. He could not keep something of this magnitude to himself, especially with a number of servants who were privy to his plans and thoughts, and it was a massive error of judgement to sack a servant who was aware of what had been going on. This ensured that the plot would come to the notice of the king. Buckingham had understood the risks but had continued with his plotting anyway.

On 13 May 1521, Buckingham, was tried for treason in Westminster Hall. He denied the charges against him and defended himself well but as was usual in sixteenth-century treason trials, he was not allowed to cross-examine any of the witnesses himself. Buckingham stated that the charges against him were 'false and untrue and conspired and forged to bring me to my death'.[32] How many of the exact charges were true is a point of debate, but the popular saying 'there is no smoke without fire' can probably be applied here as the accusations must have come from somewhere, even if just from his abrasive personality and a few careless comments. Buckingham was found guilty by seventeen of his peers of imagining the death of the king. Norfolk allegedly wept, as he later would at his niece, Anne Boleyn's trial, as he pronounced the sentence of hanging, drawing, and quartering. Even after the death sentence had been pronounced, Buckingham proclaimed his innocence and said, 'the eternal God forgive you my death, and I do: I shall never sue to the king for life howbeit he is a gracious prince'.[33] Buckingham's pride would not even now allow him to beg for his life and for mercy. It was essentially a show trial where the king selected the judges and witnesses, and they were coached in how the trial was to go and what the outcome would be.

At the trial, Buckingham claimed that the charges had been conspired and fabricated to bring him down.[34] He believed that people were out to get him, like Cardinal Wolsey and the king. He seemed to refuse to accept that it could possibly be his own fault at all, despite all of the evidence gathered against him from witnesses including his own household staff. Perhaps Henry VIII did seek Buckingham's downfall once his folly in promoting his own claim to the throne, and debating over who would succeed to the crown if Henry VIII's line failed, came to light. Henry VIII saw Buckingham as too dangerous to be allowed to live. The king knew that Buckingham would keep being a thorn in his side because he firmly believed in his own rightness and claims. Some might argue that perhaps Henry VIII should have understood Buckingham's position as the king also had complete belief in his own claims, despite evidence against them. But perhaps this put them on a collision course instead. Nicholas Hopkyns, who had prophesised Buckingham's rise to the throne, had told Buckingham to gain the love of the people, but he does not seem to have done this, rather he bribed retainers to support him. Whether he would have had enough support to seize the throne had the king died is questionable. He certainly was not popular in Wales.

Edward Stafford, 3rd Duke of Buckingham was executed on Tower Hill on 17 May 1521 between 11am and noon. He had been escorted there from the Tower of London by 500 troops, and the Sheriffs of London, John Skevington, and John Kyme. Perhaps the king feared a rescue attempt. It was not until the execution of Henry VIII's second wife, Anne Boleyn (see Chapter 3), that high-ranking prisoners were sometimes granted a more private execution on Tower Green, within the Tower of London itself. Nobles who followed Buckingham to the block in the following decades would sometimes be granted this mercy and privilege. The sentence had been commuted from the full hanging, drawing, and quartering to a simple beheading with an axe, but it took three strokes to sever his head from his body. He was buried in the Church of Austin Friars in London, with the wooden coffin containing the corpse carried from the site of execution to the church by six friars.[35] The Stafford family would not rise so high again.

The Act of Parliament which confiscated his goods and lands was dated 31 July 1523, over two years after his death, and meant that his children lost not only the Buckingham dukedom, but also the likes of Thornbury Castle, the 3rd duke's big building project to create a dynastic home for his family. Mary I would later grant Thornbury Castle, though not the dukedom, to Buckingham's son, Henry Stafford, 1st Baron Stafford, in 1554. It fell into disrepair during the English Civil War of the 1640s but was eventually restored in the 1820s by the Howard family and is now a Grade I listed building and hotel.

In the death of the duke of Buckingham in 1521, perhaps Katherine of Aragon lost a natural ally who would have supported her in her divorce proceedings to come. He was very powerful and had good connections. Although where he would have fallen on the religious issues of the time is unknown. From what we can glean of his personality, he probably would have supported the undoubtedly royal Katherine of Aragon over the upstart Tudors who he believed had an inferior claim to the English throne than his own. Buckingham's insight into the Boleyns could also have been intriguing; would he have seen them as upstarts like the Tudors? They did come from an old family, though not a noble one, and had connections going back centuries; in a way the family was older than the Howard dukes of Norfolk! There is another interesting 'what if' to consider; how might the divorce have played out differently if Katherine had the support of the most powerful noble in England? The events of 1521 meant that we would never get the chance to find out.

Buckingham was one of three dukes in England in 1521, the others being Norfolk and Suffolk. His strong claim to the throne meant that Buckingham was the most dangerous of the three, descended from two sons of Edward III: John of Gaunt and Thomas of Woodstock. His royal blood, claim to the throne, and his folly in openly proclaiming and promoting his royal blood made him the perfect target for Henry VIII. The king had it drummed into him by his father how important it was to provide an heir and a spare but was struggling to provide a single son for England. Buckingham was a powerful alternate to the Tudors and Henry VIII was not willing to allow him to build his power and prestige in the way that Buckingham wanted to.

Chapter 3

Queen Anne Boleyn & George Boleyn, Viscount Rochford – 1536

Anne Boleyn is one of the most famous (or infamous) figures in English history. The second wife of Henry VIII, she is often seen as the catalyst for the English Reformation as Henry sought to annul his marriage to his first wife, Katherine of Aragon, in order to marry Anne. Her violent fall from power and execution just three years into her marriage, and after Henry spent seven years trying to marry her, is one of the most shocking events in English history and has made Anne notorious. As historian, Amy Licence, describes it, the execution of Anne Boleyn was a 'brutal departure from the long-standing chivalric tradition of mercy towards women'.[1] Her brother, George, became entangled in her fall, possibly because he was too powerful an advocate for his sister to be left alive, or that he had made formidable enemies at court who wanted him gone. Both promoted the reformed religion which contributed to alienating many in the wider population. Historian, Eric Ives, summed up Anne's career as 'the court made Anne Boleyn, and it would be the court which destroyed her'.[2] There is no more apt description.

It is often assumed that Anne Boleyn and her brother were commoners. They were in comparison to the pedigree of Henry VIII's first wife, Katherine of Aragon, the daughter of the King of Aragon, and Queen of Castile, who united Spain. Anne certainly was not royal, but she was the most well-born of Henry VIII's domestic queens. Her mother, Elizabeth Boleyn, was the daughter of Thomas Howard, 2nd Duke of Norfolk, and sister of Thomas Howard, 3rd Duke of Norfolk. Anne's great-grandfather, John Howard, 1st Duke of Norfolk, had been slain with Richard III at the Battle of Bosworth Field in 1485. The family had long associations with loyalty to the crown, though it would take the 2nd duke until 1513 to regain the dukedom after his victory against the Scots at Flodden Field. As will be seen in later chapters, the Howard family would go on to lose several more members over the coming years to the executioner's axe.

Anne's father, Thomas Boleyn, was created 1st Earl of Wiltshire and Ormond by Henry VIII in 1529 when Henry had decided to marry Anne. He had previously been created Viscount Rochford in 1525, probably due to Henry's affair with Anne's older sister, Mary Boleyn. When Thomas was made an earl in 1529, his son, George, gained the courtesy title of Viscount Rochford. Thomas Boleyn was descended through his mother, Margaret Butler, from the Butler earls of Ormond. There were some disagreements between Thomas Boleyn and the head of the Butler family, Piers Butler, 8th Earl of Ormond, as Boleyn believed that he was the rightful Earl of Ormond, even though he descended through a female line. There was a plan to resolve the dispute by marrying Anne Boleyn to her cousin, James Butler, heir to the earldom, thus uniting the two claims, but this marriage never happened. Why the marriage fell through is not known, but possibly there was a dispute over a dowry, or the fact that neither party really wanted the marriage in the first place. Thomas Boleyn's father, William Boleyn, had served as Sheriff of Kent and his grandfather, Geoffrey Boleyn, was the Mayor of London. Geoffrey Boleyn married Anne Hoo around 1437/8, the daughter of Sir Thomas Hoo. The noble advancement of the Boleyn family did not begin with Thomas Boleyn as is so often supposed.[3] His mother's lineage, however, is certainly more illustrious and noble.

There cannot be a dispute over the fact that Anne and George Boleyn were descended from nobility from both their mother and father. Of Henry VIII's domestic queens – Anne, Jane Seymour, Katherine Howard, and Katherine Parr – Anne Boleyn had the most noble connections and was the closest to the English court. She had also grown up in some of the most sophisticated European courts, including the court of Margaret of Austria in the Netherlands, and that of Francis I and Queen Claude in France, before her return to England in 1522. In 1532, Anne was raised to the peerage in her own right as Marquess of Pembroke in preparation for a visit to France and her impending queenship. She was one of only two women in the Tudor period to be created a peer in her own right; notably the other was Margaret Pole, Countess of Salisbury, who was of royal blood as niece to Edward IV and Richard III and would also end up under the executioner's blade.

* * *

Anne Boleyn was the second of three surviving children born to Thomas Boleyn and Elizabeth Howard, probably at Blickling Hall in Norfolk. Her elder sister, Mary, was likely born around 1499 and her younger brother, George, around 1503. We do not have concrete dates of birth for any of them, though it is generally accepted that Anne was the middle child, born around 1501. Historian, Eric Ives, offers plausible evidence of a birth date around this time, based on a letter written by Anne circa 1513.[4] There is also the fact that Henry Carey claimed the earldom of Ormond in 1592. He was the son of Mary Boleyn and would have had the best claim as the son of the eldest daughter, rather than the younger, especially given that his cousin was the queen. Within three years of the execution of Anne and George in 1536, both Thomas and Elizabeth would also die, leaving Mary as the sole survivor of her immediate family. Court life had destroyed the Boleyns, and Mary survived because she left the court behind her when she married her second husband, William Stafford, in 1534. Legend says she never saw her brother or sister again.

Anne spent most of her childhood at Hever Castle in Kent after the family left Blickling around 1506, until her father secured her a position as maid of honour to Margaret of Austria, Regent of the Netherlands, at Mechelen, in 1513 after he had been sent there on embassy. It was from Mechelen that the first surviving letter we have written by Anne was sent to her father back in England. Anne acknowledged that her father desired her to be 'a worthy woman when I come to the court' and that 'the Queen will take the trouble to converse with [her]'.[5] This implies that there was already a plan to introduce Anne to the English court, and probably into the household of the English queen, Katherine of Aragon. This would not have been an unusual path for a young English noblewoman, though we know with hindsight that the path of Anne's life would be far from usual.

At Mechelen, Anne was exposed to female role models who wielded power. She was also introduced to Renaissance culture. Anne seems to have embraced culture and ideas at Margaret's court and would emulate her in her own queenship years later.[6] Anne appears to have received a glowing report from Margaret, who wrote to Thomas Boleyn describing Anne as 'of such good address and so pleasing in her youthful age' and claiming that she was more indebted to Thomas for sending Anne to her than he was to her for taking Anne in.[7] When Henry VIII's sister, Mary Tudor, married the ageing Louis XII of France in 1514, Anne was sent to wait on her at the French court. It was originally intended for Anne to arrive in France in time for the wedding but her name does not appear on the list of attendees so it is possible she was delayed from Mechelen.[8] Anne would also have been present at the meeting in 1520 of Henry VIII and the new French king, Francis I, at the Field of the Cloth of Gold as she transferred into the service of Queen Claude, wife of Francis I, after the death of Louis XII in 1515. It was possible she acted as a translator at the event. This may also have been the first time that the Boleyn family had been together since Anne had left for the court of Margaret of Austria at Mechelen seven years earlier.

Anne would return to England in 1521 or 1522 as a marriage was being arranged for her with James Butler, heir to the Earl of Ormond. This was supposed to settle a conflict between Piers Butler, 8th Earl of Ormond, and Thomas Boleyn, over who was the rightful heir to the Ormond earldom. The marriage of Anne Boleyn and James Butler was intended to unite the two claims and end the debate. This marriage would never actually take place, though the exact reason why is unclear. Anne would instead become embroiled in a relationship with Henry Percy, heir to the Earl of Northumberland. It was rumoured that the pair had become secretly betrothed, but this was broken by Cardinal Thomas Wolsey, Henry VIII's right-hand man. This would have been a great marriage for Anne, to be Countess of Northumberland one day, and potentially a love match to boot. Once the match was broken, Anne was sent back to Hever Castle and Percy was married off to Mary Talbot, daughter of the Earl of Shrewsbury, though it would be an unhappy, childless, marriage. Anne's time abroad shaped her into the sophisticated woman that Henry VIII fell in love with in the 1520s. It also exposed her to the reformist ideas that were being discussed by the likes of Margaret of Austria in the Netherlands and Marguerite of Navarre in France. She likely re-entered the English court after time rusticating at Hever after the end of her relationship sometime in 1524 or 1525, although this is conjecture.

Once she returned to England, Anne Boleyn appeared in the 1522 Chateau Vert pageant alongside her sister, Mary, who had caught the king's eye. Mary played the role of 'Kindness' and Anne 'Perseverance', a foreshadowing of what was to come, although obviously nobody could have guessed this at the time. This relationship between Henry VIII and Mary Boleyn explains why Henry VIII needed a dispensation to marry Anne Boleyn, as the two were thus related within the forbidden degrees of affinity. Henry VIII would request a dispensation on the grounds that he had slept with one of her relatives. But before Henry made his interest in Anne known, there was a rumoured relationship between her and the poet, Thomas Wyatt, and certainly some kind of involvement between her and Henry Percy. Thomas Wyatt would be one of the men arrested during Anne's fall in May 1536, though he was never charged and was released after Anne's execution. Henry Percy would swear before Henry VIII married Anne Boleyn that there was never a betrothal between them; 'the same may be to my damnation, if ever there were any contract or promise of marriage between her and me'.[9] We cannot take this as gospel that there was never a precontract between them as the letter was written in May 1536 when the king was looking for a reason to annul his marriage to Anne. Percy may have feared reprisals or even execution if he admitted to it, given the number of men already imprisoned in the Tower.

Aside from her dramatic fall and execution, the thing that Anne Boleyn is most noted for is her role in the 'divorce' of Henry VIII and Katherine of Aragon; a divorce that was really an annulment. Henry VIII wanted the marriage annulled on the grounds that it was not valid in the first place due to Katherine's first marriage to his brother, Arthur. A passage in Leviticus in the Bible stated that 'if a man shall take his brother's wife, it is an unclean thing ... he shall be without children'.[10] Henry considered his marriage to Katherine childless, in spite of the birth of a daughter, Mary, in February 1516, because they did not have any surviving sons. He believed that when the Bible said 'children' it meant 'sons' who could inherit. Henry VIII started proceedings towards annulment in 1526, having fallen deeply for Anne Boleyn.

Henry VIII's love for Anne is expressed in a series of love letters he wrote to her. Henry's dislike for writing has been documented, which makes these letters all the more important as a sign of his love and devotion. The exact chronology of the letters is unknown, and historians have put forward several different suggestions for this. One of the most memorable letters Henry wrote to Anne is where he wrote that he was 'wishing myself (especially an evening) in my sweetheart's arms, whose pretty dukkys I trust shortly to kiss'.[11] Dukkys meaning breasts, so there was obviously some kind of physical intimacy between them, though probably stopping short of intercourse. It seems to be alluded to in one of the letters where Anne submits to Henry and agrees to marry him, as Henry writes of the gift he received from her of a diamond and a ship with a solitary damsel on it, 'for the fine interpretation and the too humble submission'.[12] The fire would burn for seven years and their marriage would last for three, but it would come crashing down.

* * *

The commonly held belief over Anne Boleyn's fall from power is that it happened because she had failed to provide Henry VIII with the son and heir that he so desperately wanted. He believed he needed a son as England could not be ruled by a woman. This would be disproved by his own daughters, Mary and Elizabeth. Though the success of Mary I's reign is certainly more debated than that of Elizabeth I. We can perhaps understand Henry's concern when we realise that the only example of a female ruler in England before this was the Empress Matilda in the 12th century. The people of London refused to allow her entry to the city to be crowned. It had been drummed into Henry VIII by his father that he needed to secure the future of the dynasty with a son, or preferably two. Henry himself was a second son who only became heir to the throne when his elder brother, Arthur, unexpectedly died in 1502. Anne had promised Henry a son when he was wooing her, but her first child, born 1533, was a daughter called Elizabeth. She then suffered at least two, maybe three, miscarriages (depending on which accounts you believe), the last of these was in January 1536 and 'seemed to be a male child which she had not borne 3½ months'.[13] This led Henry VIII to claim that 'he had made this marriage, seduced by witchcraft, and for this reason he considered it null; and that this was evident because God did not permit them to have any male issue'.[14] This was reported by the Spanish ambassador, Eustace Chapuys, who was opposed to Anne Boleyn and a great supporter of Katherine of Aragon; he always called Anne the 'whore' or 'Concubine' in his letters.

Chapuys reported back to Charles V, Holy Roman Emperor, who was Katherine's nephew. Charles wanted his aunt to remain queen of England rather than Anne, who was known to favour the French over the Spanish. Anne Boleyn was never actually accused of witchcraft in the indictment against her as has been suggested by some, likely prompted by Henry's comment after Anne's 1536 miscarriage. However, it is a persistent myth, along with the claim that Anne had six fingers on one hand; physical deformities were considered to be the sign of a witch. Catholic polemicist, Nicholas Sander, wrote that Anne Boleyn 'had a projecting tooth under the upper lip, and on her right hand six fingers'.[15] Sander would only have been a small child when Anne was executed and never met her, so would have been reliant on speaking to those who did know her, or on rumours and speculation. Even Chapuys, who was one of Anne's greatest enemies, never reported any physical deformity in Anne, and certainly would have reported it to Charles V had it been true. Chapuys did report that 'there are some who murmur at the mode of procedure against her' and 'already it sounds ill in the ears of the people'.[16] This implies that the people doubted the veracity of the evidence against Anne and the accused men and wondered whether the evidence was at least in part concocted so that Henry could marry Jane Seymour and produce a male heir.

The lack of a son may not in fact have been Anne's fault as the king believed. Today with modern science we know that it is the sperm which decides the gender of a child. Of course, women can still have problems conceiving or carrying a child to term, but there has been a suggestion of a medical problem due to being Kell positive or negative. If Henry VIII was Kell positive and Anne Boleyn was Kell negative, then Henry's Kell positive blood status could have caused problems for any of his wife's pregnancies after the first one.[17] Surviving children born to Anne Boleyn and Jane Seymour were the result of first pregnancies, so Henry's Kell positive status would not have been an issue. It would only have affected later pregnancies; hence Anne Boleyn never birthed another live child after Princess Elizabeth in September 1533. Jane Seymour never got a chance of another pregnancy as she died as a result of her first childbirth experience, so we cannot know whether she would have followed the same pattern as her predecessor. We cannot be sure of Henry VIII's Kell status as testing was not available in the sixteenth century or any real understanding of genetic conditions, so all we can do is suggest, question, and wonder. How far Henry VIII's repudiation of Anne Boleyn was due to her seeming inability to produce a male heir is uncertain. Some historians believe it was the main reason for her downfall but there are other things that acted against her as well. It took Henry a decade or more of miscarriages to start proceedings against Katherine of Aragon, and only once she had gone through the menopause. He was married to Anne for only three years and could not have known that she would not have another child.

Another key aspect leading to the deaths of Anne and George Boleyn were their religious inclinations. Both were advocates of the new reformed religion and this made them many enemies at court, particularly from those who supported Katherine of Aragon and Princess Mary, who were staunch Roman Catholics. The way in which Anne Boleyn had supported and promoted the reformed religion and advocated the Break with Rome in order to marry Henry VIII meant that Katherine of Aragon was seen as the victim and Anne as the supplanter, rather than Henry VIII as the instigator of the divorce and England's religious divisions. Anne certainly was not innocent in the proceedings and seems to have introduced Henry to books that would bring him round to her way of thinking, like William Tyndale's *The Obedience of a Christian Man*. This book advocated the idea that the king was the head of the church in his country and not the Pope, and it promoted the idea of divine right. Legend says that Anne gave the book to Henry who read it and declared 'this is a book for me and all kings to read'.[18] He wanted to believe in what Tyndale wrote because it gave him a way out of the deadlock of divorce and reinforced his belief in his own power and right. Anne helped to provide an alternative route to divorce rather than waiting for the Papal decision. Henry, however, was the driving force. If he did not want to marry Anne and break with the Roman Catholic Church then nothing she did or said would have pushed him to act in the way that he did.

Factional politics were a huge part of court life in the sixteenth century, as different groups fought for power, titles, wealth, and the attention of the monarch. The factional fighting around Katherine of Aragon and Anne Boleyn in the late 1520s and early 1530s is perhaps the most violent and polarised example of this. From the moment it became known that Henry VIII intended to annul his marriage to his first wife, Katherine of Aragon, and marry Anne Boleyn, the courtiers began to choose sides. Many of those who were staunch Roman Catholics supported Katherine of Aragon and those of the new reformist or Protestant persuasion supported Anne Boleyn. However, there were exceptions as those who wanted power attached themselves to the rising star, but those who truly believed that Katherine of Aragon was Henry VIII's true wife remained loyal to her. So, there were two different aspects to the factionalism: religion and succession. Chapuys summed the situation up in a letter written to Charles V, Katherine of Aragon's nephew, that 'he could not separate from the Concubine without tacitly confirming, not only the first marriage, but also, what he most fears, the authority of the Pope'.[19] Henry VIII would not want to do that as it would mean admitting that he was wrong, that everything he had done to marry Anne, including the Break with Rome, was incorrect, and he would have lost face not only in England but abroad as well. Factionalism would continue to be a part of the court after Anne's fall and would contribute to the fall of other nobles after her.

The Boleyn faction, headed by Anne, also contained the men who were accused alongside her of adultery and treason – her brother, George, Sir Henry Norris, Sir William Brereton, and Sir Francis Weston. Thus, when Anne was charged with adultery many of those around her were also caught up and accused in order to decimate her support network. Thomas Cromwell had been a big supporter of Anne, but he appears to have turned against her sometime in late 1535 or early 1536. The Imperial ambassador, Eustace Chapuys, wrote to Charles V on 2 May 1536, the day of Anne's arrest, referring to a conversation he had at the beginning of April 'with Cromwell about the divorce of this King from the Concubine'.[20] This suggests that Cromwell was right at the heart of the plot to bring down Anne, though when it changed from divorce to execution is difficult to determine. The Aragonese faction supported Katherine of Aragon and then, when she died in January 1536, the support moved across to Katherine's daughter, Princess Mary, as the Catholic figurehead and rightful heir to the English throne. The Aragonese faction also supported Jane Seymour in supplanting Anne Boleyn as queen of England, knowing that she was sympathetic to the Roman Catholic cause and would promote Princess Mary's claim as heir to the throne. The factional politics tended to be polarised by religion, with the Aragonese faction favouring Roman Catholicism and Papal authority; and the Boleyn faction favouring reform and the Royal Supremacy. This naturally put them at odds. It also meant that, when Anne Boleyn fell from grace and was executed, the course of reform in England was also slowed.

There has been much importance by historians placed on the fact that Henry VIII already had another wife in mind in 1536 in the person of Jane Seymour, who Henry would go on to marry just eleven days after Anne's execution, on 30 May 1536. When the Imperial ambassador, Chapuys, wrote to his master, Charles V, after Anne Boleyn's January 1536 miscarriage, he wrote that some thought that the miscarriage was due to her being unable to bear children, some to fright over the king's fall in a jousting accident, and others to a fear that Henry would treat her as he had Katherine of Aragon 'especially considering the treatment shown to a lady of the court, named Mistress Semel'.[21] It seems Jane Seymour had already come to the notice of foreign ambassadors at the English court as early as January and February 1536. Chapuys also reported on the day of Anne's execution, that Henry VIII had been saying publicly that he had 'no desire in the world to get married again' unless he was 'constrained by his subjects' to do so.[22] This suggests that Henry VIII knew that there were rumours he was only getting rid of Anne because he had fallen in love again, with Jane Seymour, and he wanted to make sure that Jane's name and reputation were not stained by Anne's death. Jane was not at court at the time of Anne's fall, with Henry having sent her away to stay at Beddington, downriver.

Anne Boleyn was arrested on 2 May 1536 at Greenwich Palace, questioned by the council, and then taken down the river to the Tower of London. Mark Smeaton, a court musician, had already been questioned by Cromwell at his house in Stepney on 30 April before being transferred to the Tower. There were rumours his confession to adultery with Anne was obtained by torture. On 1 May 1536, Henry VIII suddenly left the May Day jousts at Greenwich, accompanied by his Groom of the Stool, Sir Henry Norris. Henry told Norris he would get mercy if he confessed to adultery with Anne, but Norris refused, declared his innocence, and was also sent to the Tower. When he left the May day jousts, this was the last time that Henry saw Anne. She was arrested the following day. Interestingly, when Chapuys reported the arrests to Charles V on 2 May, it seems that he believed Smeaton was accused of adultery with Anne and Norris was arrested for having covered it up and not having revealed it to the king.[23] Anne's brother, George Boleyn, was arrested the same day. Two days later, on 4 May, Francis Weston and William Brereton were also arrested, after Anne had implicated them during some rambling comments she made in the early days of her imprisonment. On 5 May 1536, Thomas Wyatt and Richard Page were both arrested and sent to the Tower, but they were never indicted with the other men for adultery with Anne Boleyn and were released after her execution.

While imprisoned in the Tower of London, Anne seemed to ramble, possibly from the shock of her life crumbling around her. Her ramblings and comments were reported by the Constable of the Tower, William Kingston, to Thomas Cromwell, who was compiling the case against Anne. When she first arrived at the Tower, Anne asked Kingston if she would go into a dungeon, but the lodgings she had occupied before her coronation had been prepared for her. She replied, 'it is too good for me, Jesu have mercy on me' and wept. She went on to say, 'I am as clear from the company of man as sin'.[24] Why she thought these lodgings too good for her has never been satisfactorily explained; unless she believed herself guilty of some other sin or was actually guilty as charged in spite of her claims of innocence throughout her ordeal. The latter seems unlikely when you begin to look at the evidence against her. Kingston's letter, however, does offer a piece of evidence of treason, by the 1534 Treason Act. While in the Tower, Anne recounted a conversation she had with Henry Norris where she asked him why he did not marry, and he said he would tarry a time. Anne then replied, 'you look for dead men's shoes, for if ought came to the king but good, you would look to have me'.[25] Imagining the king's death in word, thought, or deed, was treason. The insinuation being that if the king died, Norris hoped to marry Anne. It was an accusation made at trial, that Anne and her lovers had plotted the death of the king so that she could marry one of them and rule England as regent for her daughter, Elizabeth.

At the trial of Anne and George Boleyn, it was said that Thomas Boleyn, their father, was willing to sit in judgement against them, as he had done in the trial of the accused men.[26] In the end, he did not. Perhaps it was thought to be too much in bad taste for a father to sit in judgement against his own children. The men accused alongside Anne were tried first; once they had been found guilty, Anne's fate was sealed. Anne's trial, before that of her brother, inevitably found her guilty, and she was sentenced to be burned or beheaded at the king's pleasure. George Boleyn's trial had a more uncertain outcome, and 'to all he replied so well that several of those present wagered ten to one that he would be acquitted'.[27] However, he condemned himself by reading out a charge which was written down for him regarding the king's virility and a comment he had made about a lack of it. All he had to do was nod or shake his head but instead he chose to read this out; in doing so he damned himself.

*   *   *

The execution of Anne Boleyn on 19 May 1536 was a turning point in English history. It marked the first time that an anointed queen had been judicially executed, though it would not be the last. Henry VIII would execute another wife, and Anne's cousin, Katherine Howard, also for adultery in 1542. Historian, Lacey Baldwin Smith, said that 'the closer the proximity to the crown, the greater the danger' and that the law was used as an instrument to remove those who became too powerful.[28] This certainly proved true in the case of Anne Boleyn. She was as close to the crown as you could get and was perceived to have great power and influence over the king, even when it waned. The account of the executions of Anne and George Boleyn from the Vienna Archives says that 'according to old writings, he has seen the prophecy of Marlin fulfilled'.[29] This actually refers to the prophecies of the wizard Merlin, who predicted that a queen of England would be burnt at the stake. The prophecy did not precisely come true in the case of Anne Boleyn, as she was actually beheaded. However, when she was found guilty at her trial, she was sentenced to be burned or beheaded according to the king's pleasure, as was traditional for a woman. Henry VIII could have chosen to burn her, but instead opted for the more merciful death.

George Boleyn, Lord Rochford mounted the scaffold first, as the highest ranking of the men, on 17 May 1536. His speech on the scaffold seems to have had several purposes, as he spoke about deserving death, and sinning, linking it to religion and the word of God. Of course, religion played a large role in death in the sixteenth century, as the dying wanted to enter heaven and avoid hell and shorten their time in purgatory if possible. Several versions of George Boleyn's execution speech survive. *The Chronicle of Calais* quotes George Boleyn on the scaffold as saying the below:

'Christian men, I am born under the law, and judged under the law, and die under the law, and the law has condemned me. Masters all, I am not come hither for to preach, but for to die, for I have deserved to die if I had twenty lives, more shamefully than can be devise, for I am a wretched sinner, and I have sinned shamefully. I have known no man so evil, and to rehearse my sins openly, it were no pleasure for you to hear them, nor yet for me to rehearse them, for God knoweth all … and beware, trust not in the vanity of the world, and especially in the flattering of the court … and yet, my masters all, I have one thing for to say to you: men do common and say that I have been a setter forth of the Word of God, and one that have favoured the Gospel of Christ; and because I would not that God's word should be slandered by me, I say unto you all, that if I had followed God's word in deed as I did read it and set it forth to my power, I had not come to this. I did read the Gospel of Christ, but I did not follow it.'[30]

George made the longest recorded execution speech out of the men accused of adultery with Anne Boleyn and who followed him to the scaffold, exhorting those watching to read and listen to the word of God and follow the reformed religion which had been promoted by himself and his sister. George openly admitted on the scaffold that he was 'a wretched sinner', but what those sins were, he declined to say. He told the people to 'trust not in the vanity of the world, and especially in the flattering of the court' as it was essentially a false place where you could not trust people, and it had only brought him to his death for reaching high and putting his trust in others, like the king.

George was followed onto the scaffold by Francis Weston, Henry Norris, William Brereton, and Mark Smeaton. Smeaton went last as the lowest in status and had to watch the others die. Francis Weston ended his short execution speech by saying 'I thought little it would come to this'.[31] No one expected the marriage of Henry VIII and Anne Boleyn to end this way. It was a shock to the court and the country that the woman Henry had fought to have for seven years and broken the church apart for, was ending on the scaffold. It was to be the first execution of an anointed queen, and she was bringing down five innocent men with her. Mark Smeaton merely asked the people to pray for him and admitted 'I have deserved death'.[32] He had not retracted his confession of adultery with Anne Boleyn even on the scaffold. If you believe Anne to be guilty as charged, Smeaton's confession could be just a straightforward admission of guilt. If, however, you believe that Anne was innocent and Smeaton was coerced or tortured into making a false confession, then Smeaton could have implied that he deserved death for making said false confession and sealing Anne's fate. Even without Smeaton's confession, Henry VIII and Cromwell would have had Anne found guilty anyway. All were executed with a single blow of the axe, even Smeaton as a commoner, who traditionally would have been hung, drawn, and quartered for treason.

On the same day that the men were executed, 17 May 1536, Anne's marriage to Henry VIII was declared null and void in a convocation led by Thomas Cranmer, Archbishop of Canterbury. He had declared the marriage of Henry VIII and Katherine of Aragon null and void and that of Henry and Anne legal and valid just three years earlier. The reason given for the annulment was not recorded but could be either Anne's earlier betrothal to Henry Percy, 6th Earl of Northumberland, or Henry VIII's prior relationship with Anne's sister, Mary. Both had been potential obstacles to Henry and

Anne's marriage but had been pushed aside. They were re-examined at this point to find a reason to annul the marriage and bastardise Princess Elizabeth.

Anne Boleyn was initially to be executed on 18 May, but this was delayed a day when the executioner had not arrived from Calais. Anne was not to be executed with the cumbersome English axe, but by a French swordsman. Perhaps this was a favour from the king to the woman he had once loved, as she had an affinity with the French. However, it is worth noting that the swordsman had been sent for even before the trial and guilty verdict, so certain was the king that she would be found guilty. Anne spent the night before her execution in prayer, and took Holy Communion in the morning, swearing her innocence on the sacrament with the Constable of the Tower, William Kingston, in attendance as a witness. She was then escorted to the scaffold on the morning of 19 May 1536 which had been erected, not where the monument to the dead now sits within the Tower of London, but actually between the White Tower and what is now the Waterloo Barracks according to more recent research; to the north of the White Tower, rather than the west.[33] She was beheaded with a single blow from the executioner's sword.

Anne Boleyn's execution speech that she made on the scaffold just before her death has been quoted and discussed in so many different contexts over the years, but it is really worth analysing because it offers insight into her state of mind and what was utmost in her thinking as she approached her death. The speech quoted below comes from John Foxe's *Acts and Monuments*, better known as the *Book of Martyrs*, first published in the 1560s. Although Foxe was determined to present Anne Boleyn as Protestant martyr, the speech is quoted in a similar vein in other places as well, so we can surmise that it is pretty much what was said.

'Good Christian people! I am come hither to die, for according to the law, and by the law, I am judged to death; and therefore I will speak nothing against it. I am come hither to accuse no man, nor to speak of the thing of that whereof I am accused and condemned to die; but I pray God save the king, and send him long to reign over you, for a gentler, or a more merciful prince was there never; and to me he was ever a good, a gentle, and a sovereign lord. And if any person will meddle of my cause, I require them to judge the best. And thus I take my leave of the world, and of you all, and I heartily desire you all to pray for me. O Lord have mercy on me! To God I commend my soul.'[34]

The general sense of the speech is that Anne was determined not to add any more fuel to the fire over the accusations made against her. Most likely, her main reasoning for this was to protect her daughter and her surviving family. It was too late for her to save her brother, George, but she likely did not want her parents, her sister or, most importantly, her daughter, to suffer. She had already been sentenced to death so speaking out now against the king would not save her but could lead to sanctions against those closest to her, hence her saying 'therefore I will speak nothing against it'. The line which stands out is 'if any person will meddle of my cause, I require them to judge the best'. This suggests that Anne knew people would examine the charges against her, and it was as close as she dared come to declaring her innocence. She asked history to be kind to her, subtly saying that what happened to her was not what it seemed. Even before Anne was dead, there appeared to be some muttering that Anne may not have been entirely guilty of what she was accused. Anne also refused to speak against the king, calling him 'good' and 'gentle', possibly mindful of how he had raised her to be queen, but not mentioning how he had pulled her down. Her entire speech seems to have been crafted to protect those she was leaving behind.

After quoting Anne's final speech, John Foxe went on to give his thoughts on her and her death. Bearing in mind that Foxe was determined to paint Anne as a Protestant martyr, his almost eulogy spends time expounding on her 'desire unto the truth and setting forth of sincere religion' and how under her reign 'the religion of Christ most happily flourished'.[35] Foxe also wrote about how Anne promoted Nicholas Shaxton to the bishopric of Salisbury, and Hugh Latimer to the bishopric of Worcester, both notable reformers. Latimer was later burned under Mary I for heresy. Foxe also claimed Anne was innocent of the charges against her, saying that the king 'the third day after' her execution 'was married in his whites to another'.[36] The timing was slightly wrong as it was actually eleven days after Anne Boleyn's execution that Henry VIII married Jane Seymour, but the point still stands. Foxe essentially claimed that Henry VIII had Anne executed because he wanted to marry another. This is still part of the accepted argument today about Anne Boleyn's fall from power. Even at the time, the speed of Henry's remarriage made people question what they had been told about Anne's guilt.

Most historians nowadays agree that Anne Boleyn was innocent of the charges against her. However, one historian, G.W. Bernard, has written quite a controversial book where he claimed that Anne was in fact guilty of at least some of the charges against her. He writes that 'Anne had indeed committed adultery with [Henry] Norris, probably with [Mark] Smeaton ... and was then the victim of the most appalling bad luck'.[37] Her bad luck was being caught. Bernard believes that the elaborate theories other historians have come up with to explain her life could more easily be explained by the simple fact that everything was exactly as it seemed, though he seems alone in this view. She was certainly unlucky in the way that her own nature was used against her in order to bring about her overthrow.

The favoured view of most historians seems to be that Anne Boleyn's flirtatious nature and her playing the game of courtly love was to her detriment. She played it so well that she managed to catch the love of the king and become his queen, but she overplayed her hand and let her guard down to have damaging conversations with Henry Norris and Mark Smeaton, which gave her enemies evidence to use against her. The conversations alone were not enough to condemn her, but her poor reputation in England and abroad contributed to factional politics being able to bring her down. Innocent men were caught up with her because they were too dangerous to leave alive. Men like Anne's brother, George, or the Groom of the Stool, Henry Norris, could have spoken up in Anne's defence, or sought revenge after her death. Perhaps the charge of incest against George Boleyn was intended to add an additional sense of disgust to the proceedings; if she would do that, how many other men would she have had sex with?

Anne Boleyn's execution was 'one of the greatest miscarriages of justice'.[38] In today's courts of justice, it is very unlikely that Anne or her alleged lovers would have been found guilty as there was not the evidence needed. We can only surmise this from the surviving sources as some sources were no doubt destroyed after Anne's death. As Anne Boleyn's marriage to Henry VIII had been annulled by Archbishop Thomas Cranmer on 17 May 1536, two days before she died, she could not technically have been guilty of adultery. Historian Helen Castor describes the annulment and execution as 'a legal nonsense of the trumped-up charges of adultery on which she had just been tried and convicted'.[39] Anne would certainly not be the last woman under the Tudors to suffer; her cousin and others would follow her path to the scaffold. Anne's case demonstrated that even the beheading of an anointed queen was acceptable if the circumstances were right.

Chapter 4

Margaret Pole, Countess of Salisbury – 1541

Margaret Pole is an intriguing figure in Tudor history, but does not seem to be widely written about, despite her extraordinary life. Her brother was Edward Plantagenet, 17th Earl of Warwick, who was executed by Henry VII in 1499. Hence, both brother and sister were executed 42 years apart when Margaret was put to death in 1541. Margaret's father was also executed for treason by his brother, Edward IV, on 18 February 1478. He was allegedly drowned in a butt of malmsey wine, his own choice of execution method if you believe the legends. Margaret was born into the ruling Yorkist royal family in 1473.

Margaret was the niece of both Edward IV and Richard III, so was considered very close to the Yorkist regime as well as a potential heir to the throne. This could have caused some major problems for her when the Lancastrian Henry VII defeated the Yorkist Richard III at the Battle of Bosworth Field in 1485 and her uncle was overthrown and killed. Margaret had a claim to the English throne, which was stronger than that of Henry VII, though tainted by the treason of her father. The treason of George, Duke of Clarence, meant that Margaret and her brother, Warwick, were barred from the succession to the throne. The children of those accused of treason automatically lost their rights of inheritance.

Margaret was married by Henry VII to Sir Richard Pole, a noted Tudor supporter, and they had five children together, four of them sons. Henry VII may have intended the marriage to neutralise Margaret's succession threat, as Richard Pole was not noble and had no real power. The most famous of their children was Reginald Pole, who became Papal legate and a Cardinal, and spoke out strongly against Henry VIII's divorce from Katherine of Aragon and the Break with Rome in the 1530s. He was staunchly Roman Catholic and would become Archbishop of Canterbury under Mary I, dying just hours after his Queen. Margaret's elder son, Henry Pole, 1st Baron Montagu, was executed in 1539 for treason, when the whole family, including Margaret, were arrested. Margaret was kept in the Tower of London for the following two years before her own execution. Henry VIII had initially seemed to favour the family when he acceded to the throne, with Margaret being his mother's cousin. Henry VIII's mother, Elizabeth of York, was the eldest daughter of Edward IV. Thus, the Poles became relatives of the Tudors through the marriage of Henry VII to Elizabeth of York. Of Margaret's other sons, Arthur Pole died in 1528 so did not live to see the destruction of his family. Geoffrey Pole survived as he spoke out against his mother and brother, though he did admit to burning some incriminating letters. Geoffrey fled England for Rome in 1548 after the accession of Edward VI, knowing that England would embrace further Protestant reform under his rule. Geoffrey would only return to England on the accession of Mary I in 1553 when she returned the country to the Roman Catholic fold. Margaret's only daughter, Ursula, lived well into the reign of Elizabeth I, dying in 1570. She married Henry Stafford, 1st Baron Stafford, the son of the 3rd Duke of Buckingham, who had been executed in 1521 (see Chapter 2). Ursula did not appear to become embroiled in the destruction of her family, though her royal blood was passed down to her children.

The Poles were a part of the White Rose faction; those with a connection to the Yorkist royal family that remained in the Tudor court. The White Rose was the badge of the York family, and Margaret had a right to use it as part of her symbolism as niece to two Yorkist kings, and cousin to another deposed Yorkist king, Edward V. The White Rose came to pose a big threat to the Tudors, as the execution of the Earl of Warwick in 1499 showed, and then the Exeter Conspiracy and execution of the remains of the Pole family in 1539 and 1541.

Margaret Pole was one of only two women to be made a peeress in her own right in the sixteenth century without benefit of her husband. The other was Anne Boleyn who was ennobled as Marquess of Pembroke in 1532 to pave the way for her to marry Henry VIII. Margaret was made Countess of Salisbury by Henry VIII in 1512, while she was serving Katherine of Aragon at the royal court after her husband had died. The earldom of Salisbury descended from Margaret's great-grandfather, Richard Neville, 5th Earl of Salisbury. On 29 December 1886, centuries after her death, Margaret would be beatified by Pope Leo XIII as a martyr for the Roman Catholic Church.

* * *

Margaret Pole was raised as part of the royal court during the reign of her uncle, Edward IV. She was born on 14 August 1473 to George Plantagenet, 1st Duke of Clarence, brother of the king, and Isabel Neville, elder daughter of Richard Neville, 16th Earl of Warwick, known as the 'kingmaker'. As such, she was at the centre of the Yorkist royal court and had a claim to the English throne. She was the eldest surviving child. Her parents did have a child in April 1470, born in a ship off Calais when her father had fled England due to his involvement in rebellion, but the child lived only a day or two. Some sources say it was a girl and others a boy. Her younger brother, Edward, 17th Earl of Warwick, was born in 1475. Margaret's mother, Isabel Neville, died in December 1476 after giving birth to another short-lived son. Her father, George Plantagenet, 1st Duke of Clarence, believed that his wife had been poisoned, though it is now generally accepted that she died from childbed fever after the birth, as Elizabeth of York, wife to Henry VII would in 1503, or Jane Seymour, third wife of Henry VIII, would in 1537. Childbirth was very dangerous for women in the sixteenth century. Many died as a result of infection.

Clarence accused one of Isabel's ladies, Ankarette Twynho, of poisoning her and had her hanged after a kangaroo court. Clarence had challenged the king's justice by acting as judge, jury and executioner himself, rather than taking the issue through the official channels. Edward IV did not like Clarence questioning his power and authority, especially when there were suggestions that Clarence was plotting against the king when Edward IV challenged him over Twynho's execution and had him questioned by the council. An Oxford astrologer, John Stacy, was also arrested and, under torture, confessed to having cast horoscopes on Clarence's behalf predicting the death of the king and his son and heir, Prince Edward.[1] This was indisputably treason under the 1351 Treason Act which declared that it was treason to 'compass or imagine the Death of our Lord the King, or of our Lady his Queen or of their eldest Son and Heir'.[2] In 1478 in front of a session of parliament, Edward IV accused Clarence of crimes against the throne, acting as the prosecutor against his own brother, and called witnesses to speak against him. Clarence was inevitably found guilty of treason and sentenced to death. It was said that he had claimed Edward IV was illegitimate so he in fact was the rightful king of England. Edward IV claimed in response that, to pardon Clarence and allow him to live, would endanger the peace and security of the whole realm.[3] On 18 February 1478, George Plantagenet, 1st Duke of

Clarence, brother to the king of England, was executed within the Tower of London. He was buried at Tewkesbury Abbey alongside his wife, Isabel.

After Clarence's execution, his children, Margaret and Edward, became royal wards until 1480, when Edward IV granted the wardship to Thomas Grey, 1st Marquess of Dorset, his stepson. When Richard III became king, the pair were put into the care of Anne Neville, Richard's wife and their aunt. Both were raised alongside Richard and Anne's son, Edward of Middleham, largely at Middleham Castle in North Yorkshire. When Edward IV died in 1483 and Richard III succeeded to the English throne, having overthrown his nephew, Edward V, Margaret and Edward were sent instead to Sheriff Hutton Castle in Yorkshire. Clarence's execution meant that Margaret and Edward were barred from succeeding to the English throne, so when Richard III declared Edward IV's marriage to Elizabeth Woodville to be null and void, Warwick was not granted the throne as the next in line. The marriage of Edward and Elizabeth was annulled on the grounds that Edward IV had been precontracted to Eleanor Butler before their marriage, so Richard III was offered the throne rather than Clarence's children as their father's attainder meant that they could not inherit.

Had Clarence not been executed and attainted, Margaret and Edward would have been in line for the crown ahead of Richard, as Clarence was the elder brother. Warwick would have been ahead of Margaret as a boy and potentially crowned as Edward VI, or even Edward V if parliament truly did not believe that Edward IV's sons should be king, but Margaret technically would have followed him in line. As a girl, Margaret probably would have had to fight against the likes of her uncle Richard, and her de la Pole cousins to gain the throne. Margaret's life under Richard III was fairly uneventful by all accounts. She remained in the country, away from court, and remained unmarried. Richard potentially did not want to risk passing her royal blood down to any heirs. Or perhaps she was thought too young, only aged 10 in 1483, though a betrothal at that age would still have been considered normal and allowable. However, there is no evidence of a betrothal being sought for Margaret at this time.

When Henry VII defeated Richard III at the Battle of Bosworth Field on 22 August 1485 he took the English throne and married Margaret's cousin, Elizabeth of York, the eldest daughter of Edward IV and thus niece to Richard III. Margaret and Edward, Earl of Warwick, were taken into the custody of Henry and Elizabeth. Towards the end of 1487, though there seems to be some disagreement on the exact date, Margaret was married off to Sir Richard Pole, a Tudor supporter. Henry VII did not want Margaret to make a powerful marriage to a noble as this would increase the danger from her as a woman with royal Yorkist blood in her veins. She was married to someone with strong Tudor loyalties; steady, and without any royal or noble blood. Margaret and Richard's marriage, however, seems to have been a happy one and they had five children together: Henry, who would become 1st Baron Montagu, Arthur, Reginald, who would become a Cardinal and the last Catholic Archbishop of Canterbury, Geoffrey, and Ursula, who would marry into the Stafford family. Sir Richard Pole would die in 1505, leaving Margaret a widow who would not remarry, despite living for another thirty-six years. She would devote herself to her family and serving the Tudors.

Margaret's son, Reginald Pole, would benefit hugely from Margaret's association with the Tudor royal family, although he would also suffer from the connection. Henry VIII paid for Reginald's schooling at Oxford, the Sorbonne in France, and Padua in Italy, as Margaret wrote to remind him in 1536 after he had spoken out about Henry's church reforms and the Break with Rome. The letter will be discussed in more detail later in the chapter, but Margaret asked Pole 'for who hath brought you up and maintained you to learning but his Highness?'.[4] The implication being that Pole would not have been sufficiently educated enough to write against Henry VIII's divorce from Katherine of Aragon, remarriage to Anne Boleyn and church reforms without Henry himself having financed his travels and education. How ironic for the king, that someone he had helped and hoped would then work for him, turned against him so publicly, only returning to England on the accession of the Catholic Mary I, daughter of Henry VIII, in 1553. He chose to go into self-imposed exile on the Continent, leaving his mother and siblings behind in England to face the king's wrath. They would suffer for his actions and beliefs.

Margaret Pole had, crucially, supported Katherine of Aragon in Henry VIII's annulment proceedings against her, known as 'The King's Great Matter'. Margaret had known Katherine since she arrived in England from Spain in 1501 to marry Henry VIII's elder brother, Prince Arthur. Margaret had served Katherine during her time as Princess of Wales at Ludlow Castle, alongside her husband, Richard Pole. Margaret had also helped Katherine through her grief after Arthur's death in 1502 and her own sickness from which she recovered when Arthur did not. Margaret also assisted Katherine to acclimatise to English manners and customs. No doubt this forged a bond between the two women, and this bond would be strengthened when Margaret was chosen as a sponsor and godmother for Katherine of Aragon's daughter, Princess Mary, who was born in February 1516. Margaret would later become Mary's governess, asking to continue serving her out of her own pocket once Mary's household was dissolved in 1533 when her parents' marriage was annulled, and she was declared illegitimate. Margaret Pole was also implicated in supporting the Nun of Kent, Elizabeth Barton, who prophesised that Henry VIII would die within a few months if he divorced Katherine of Aragon and married Anne Boleyn. Henry VIII's determination to annul his marriage to Katherine and marry Anne instead marked the beginning of the end of the Pole family, as they set themselves against the king. Once set in opposition to Henry VIII few appear to have survived.

*   *   *

It has been suggested that Margaret's chief crime was to be the mother of Henry VIII's enemy, Cardinal Reginald Pole, and that her execution was not, in fact, the result of her royal blood, which seems to be the largely assumed position of many historians.[5] Reginald Pole had fled England for Rome in 1536 after a final severing of relations with Henry VIII over the latter's marriage to Anne Boleyn and the Break with Rome, which embraced church reforms Pole did not agree with, along with banishing the Pope's authority from England. Pole published a treatise called *Pro ecclesiasticae unitatis defensione* in 1536 which he sent to Henry, and which prompted the decisive break between the pair. The title translates as 'In Defence of the Unity of the Church' or 'In Defence of Ecclesiastical Unity'. In his work, Pole directly tackled the Break with Rome and Henry's assertion that he was now Head of the Church, which meant that his Roman Catholic religion was no longer acceptable in England. Pole defended vigorously the authority of the Pope as head of a unified Catholic church. He wrote, quite powerfully, on this matter:

'Therefore, I maintain and repeat, that I can conceive of no greater injury you could inflict upon the Church than to abolish the head of this Church from the face of the earth. You do exactly this when you deny that the Roman Pontiff is the one head of the Church on earth, the vicar of Christ. Another injury follows immediately from this when you set yourself up as supreme head of the Church in England … therefore, your self-appointment depends upon your denial of the existence of one head of the Church.'[6]

Pole saw Henry VIII as doing a great injury to the church in refusing to accept that the Pope was Head of the Church on earth, and that the monarch could not usurp that power, as Henry VIII had done. Conversely to Pole, Henry VIII saw it as his right to assume the headship of the Church in his country, seeing it as a right that had been usurped from the monarch by the Pope in times past. Henry had come to believe that the Pope was a foreign leader who should never have had any rights in England, even though he did not believe entirely in church reform and Protestantism. On Henry VIII's death in 1547, the English church was still essentially Catholic, though without the figurehead of the Pope and Henry himself still followed many tenets of the Catholic faith. The Pole family were known to be Roman Catholics in their hearts, which maybe seemed more of a threat to Henry VIII because of their royal blood in addition to their beliefs. Margaret Pole forbade her servants to read the Bible in English; reformers believed that everyone should be able to read the Bible in the vernacular, meaning their mother tongue. To not allow it was a statement of traditional Catholic beliefs and thus opposition to royal decree, and to the wishes of the king.

Pole certainly was not afraid of tackling issues head-on in this treatise, though as he was outside England at this time, really there was very little Henry VIII could do to punish him. He continued to speak out in opposition to Henry VIII and had even travelled across Europe to Italy, Spain, and France, to try and raise support for the Pilgrimage of Grace in 1536. The Pilgrimage of Grace was a rebellion against Henry VIII in the north of England to try and halt the dissolution of the monasteries, restore Catholicism to England, and reinstate Princess Mary to the succession. The rebellion was ruthlessly put down and hundreds executed. By 1537, Reginald Pole was seen as a threat to England acting from Continental Europe, and Henry VIII began to see his mother and wider family as a threat from within England. Henry VIII eventually reacted against Pole's family violently. Within three years of the publication of his treatise, *Pro ecclesiasticae unitatis defensione*, Pole's family in England would be arrested, his brother, Henry, 1st Baron Montagu, would be executed, and his mother confined in the Tower of

London. Pole's family paid a high price for his stand against the English king when he himself was out of danger.

Contrary to the idea that Margaret Pole's execution was due to being the mother of Reginald Pole, another reason which generally seems to be more accepted is that Margaret was killed as a result of her Yorkist royal blood. The Tudors were usurpers, as Henry VII took the throne after victory on the battlefield, and they latterly struggled with insecurity. Henry VIII was especially worried when he struggled to produce living sons; he'd had it drummed into him by his father that they needed to secure the throne with sons and deal with anyone who threatened the Tudor claim to the throne. Henry only had a single son in 1539; the future Edward VI. However, he knew that one son was not enough to ensure a Tudor succession. Henry VIII himself was a second son, originally destined for a life in the church, until his older brother, Arthur, died in 1502 and he became the heir. Margaret Pole, however, had a sense of self-preservation and married as directed by Henry VII, raised her children, and served the Tudors. After so many years of loyal service, would Margaret have acted against the Tudor royal family which included Princess Mary, whom Margaret had seen and raised as a daughter of sorts almost since her birth? This seems unlikely unless she was hoping to replace Henry VIII potentially with Mary. There had been a suggestion that Mary would marry Margaret's son, Reginald Pole, and the pair could rule together.

Margaret Pole had also been a big supporter of Katherine of Aragon during Henry VIII's divorce from her in the late 1520s and 1530s, a controversy which lasted around six years between 1527 and his marriage to Anne Boleyn in 1533. Margaret had been with Katherine from her arrival in England in 1501, through her marriage to Prince Arthur at Ludlow Castle and her widowhood between 1502 and 1509. They were probably more like friends and Margaret would also look after Princess Mary, Katherine's daughter, after her birth in 1516. This friendship with Katherine of Aragon would not have endeared Margaret to Henry VIII either after 1527. Anyone who chose Katherine over Henry was seen as an enemy, like John Fisher, Bishop of Rochester, and later Cardinal, who would be executed in 1535 for failing to accept the Acts of Supremacy and Succession of 1534. Katherine was stubborn and would not agree to annul her marriage to the king, declaring that she was the king's true wife and her daughter his heir. Margaret would back her to the end, and when Katherine died in 1536, alone at Kimbolton Castle, in exile, Margaret's allegiance would transfer to her daughter, Mary.

The Exeter Conspiracy, as it became known, was a plot involving members of the Courtenay family and the Poles, amongst others. The plot was supposedly designed to overthrow Henry VIII and replace him with Henry Courtenay, 1st Marquess of Exeter, who was a cousin to the king. Exeter was a grandson of Edward IV through his daughter, Catherine, who had married William Courtenay, 1st Earl of Devon. He was thus nephew to Elizabeth of York and first cousin to Henry VIII with royal blood running through him, as Margaret had. The alliance of the two families must have worried an increasingly paranoid Henry VIII. There was another suggestion that the aims of the conspiracy were actually for Reginald Pole to marry Princess Mary and for them to take the throne together once Henry VIII was overthrown. They would together then restore Roman Catholicism to England, undo the Royal Supremacy and re-establish the Pope as Head of the Church in England rather than the monarch.[7] This is precisely what Mary would do on her accession to the throne in 1553. A contemporary of Reginald Pole's in Italy, Ludovico Beccadelli, later Archbishop of Ragusa, reported the idea of a marriage between the two in his *The Life of Cardinal Reginald Pole*.[8] There certainly seems to have been enough royal blood around for Henry VIII and his advisers to be worried about the conspiracy and this can help to explain the violent reaction to it when it was discovered in 1538.

William Fitzwilliam, 1st Earl of Southampton, along with Bishop Goodrich of Ely, arrived at Warblington on 12 November 1537 to question Margaret Pole, who denied writing to her son, Reginald, or burning compromising letters and, two days later, Southampton reported to Thomas Cromwell that they could get nothing from her. She was kept under house arrest at Southampton's house at Cowdray Park in Sussex until May 1538, but still she gave nothing away that would implicate herself or her family in treasonous activity or conspiracy of any kind.[9] However, an Act of Attainder was passed against her on 12 May 1538, and others involved in the Pilgrimage of Grace in 1536 as well as the Exeter Conspiracy in 1538, including Margaret's eldest son, Henry Pole, 1st Baron Montagu, and Henry Courtenay, 1st Marquess of Exeter. However, no details were given of the crimes they were supposed to have committed in the attainder. This suggests that there was not actually enough evidence against them and can help to explain why there was no trial.

Sir Nicholas Carew was another man executed as a result of the plotting in the Exeter Conspiracy.

In November 1538, Thomas Cromwell struck and brought down the remainder of the White Rose faction, of which the Poles were a major part.[10] Cromwell is implicated in a lot of actions taken during the 1530s after Wolsey's downfall in 1529 and before his own execution in 1540, though his exact involvement is still questioned in many of them. Henry Courtenay, 1st Marquess of Exeter, was arrested and sent to the Tower of London on a charge of conspiring the king's death and plotting to usurp his throne, which was treason. He would pay the ultimate price and be executed. Exeter's wife, Gertrude Courtenay, was also arrested for corresponding with the Imperial ambassador, Eustace Chapuys. Henry Pole, 1st Baron Montagu, Margaret Pole, Countess of Salisbury, and Sir Edward Neville were also arrested for conspiring with Exeter. Most had been in contact with Reginald Pole who was on the Continent. Even the young sons of Exeter and Montagu were imprisoned in the Tower of London alongside their fathers. Edward Courtenay, Exeter's son, would not be released until 1553 on the accession of Mary I, when she created him 1st Earl of Devon. He would go on to become involved in Wyatt's Rebellion in 1554. Montagu's son, Henry, seems to have vanished from the historical record, likely dying either of natural causes or being mysteriously put to death. There does seem to have been a conspiracy of sorts, but those who conspired were 'incompetent and indiscreet' and it seems 'unlikely' that the conspiracy was as malicious and organised as it was made out to be by the government.[11] It was likely used as a way to bring down those with royal blood who could potentially threaten the throne, though there does seem to have been some kind of conspiracy going on, blown out of proportion perhaps.

A search was made of Margaret Pole's house, based on the evidence of her son, Geoffrey Pole. He had been arrested initially for corresponding with his brother, Reginald. He gave evidence against his mother and brother, Lord Montagu, in order to save his own skin. Margaret's servants were also questioned. A piece of cloth was found depicting the five wounds of Christ, which had been the symbol of the Pilgrimage of Grace in 1536. It was a potent symbol of rebellion and religious conservatism. On the banner found in Margaret's house, the five wounds were encircled with marigolds and pansies, to symbolise the marriage of Princess Mary, daughter of Henry VIII, with Reginald Pole.[12] Marigolds were for Mary, widely used as her emblem, and the pansies were a noted symbol of the Pole family.

This marriage had been spoken of in 1533 in a letter from the Spanish ambassador, Eustace Chapuys, to Emperor Charles V, saying that Katherine of Aragon 'would like to bestow the Princess on him in marriage rather than any other; and the Princess would not refuse'.[13] The marriage would unite two potential claims to the throne and prevent Mary from being married to a foreigner who might drag England into foreign wars or put her under the dominion of a foreign country, threatening her independence and raising English xenophobia. It would also have guarded against the prospect of Henry VIII not producing a son, which was a real fear by 1536, but was resolved the following year by the birth of Prince Edward to Henry's third wife, Jane Seymour. English xenophobia would not allow a foreign marriage of an English princess and heir, as would be seen with the Wyatt Rebellion in 1554 over Mary I's proposed marriage to Philip II of Spain. The banner could be seen as seditious and treasonous, a plan to overthrow the line of succession, or even the current king. When letters were found to and from Reginald Pole, the contents were twisted to try and suggest treason, even if they were completely innocent. This implies that many of the accusations made against the Pole family were spurious at best, based on rumour rather than facts or evidence, or even possibly completely fabricated, though a complete fabrication seems unlikely given that there is some evidence of a conspiracy of sorts.

On 9 December 1538, the Marquess of Exeter, Lord Montagu, and Sir Edward Neville were all beheaded for their parts in the conspiracy against the king on charges of treason. Lady Exeter would later be pardoned, though her son, Edward Courtenay, would remain imprisoned in the Tower of London. Soon after the executions, news arrived in England that Pope Paul III, who was shocked by Henry VIII's treatment of the Catholic Pole and Courtenay families (who were, after all, his kin), ordered the Bull of Excommunication to be put into effect, which had been drawn up by his predecessor, Pope Clement VII, in 1533. This meant that the Catholic kings of Europe were being called upon to dethrone the English king and left Henry VIII isolated in Europe. There were suggestions that Henry VIII had tried to have Reginald assassinated. Reginald's death would certainly have made the king feel safer, without him meddling and promoting an invasion of England on the Continent. Rumours said that Henry VIII only arrested

Margaret Pole and Henry, Lord Montagu, once his plans for Reginald's assassination had failed. Acting against Reginald's family was perhaps a way to force Reginald to give himself up. He didn't, and his family suffered the consequences.

In June 1539, Margaret Pole was moved to the Tower of London with two of her ladies and without any changes of clothes. It was only when Henry VIII's fifth wife, the teenage Katherine Howard intervened, that Margaret received new clothes.[14] Katherine Howard seems to have tried to intercede for Margaret's life as well as her standard of living in the Tower, but it did not work. Henry VIII seemed to be determined to get rid of anyone who was suspected of the slightest whiff of treason or were deemed to be too close to the throne by blood. There appears to have been some kind of plot to rescue Margaret from the Tower of London in 1540 as Reginald Pole wrote about it, but details are scarce. Margaret's attainder, which was passed by parliament, read as follows:

> 'And where also Margaret Pole, Countess of Salisbury, and Hugh Vaughan ... by instigation of the devil, putting apart the dread of Almighty God, their duty of allegiance, and the excellent benefit received of his Highness, have not only traitorously confederated themselves with the false and abominable traitors Henry Pole, Lord Montagu, and Reginald Pole, sons to the said countess, knowing them to be false traitors, but also have maliciously aided, abetted, maintained, and comforted them in their said false and abominable treason, to the most fearful peril of his Highness, the commonwealth of this realm, &c., the said marchioness and the said countess be declared attainted, and shall suffer the pains and penalties of high treason'.[15]

There is little that amounts to evidence in the attainder, mainly that Margaret Pole was guilty of aiding and abetting those accused of treason like her sons, Henry and Reginald. There is nothing really said against her specifically. Perhaps that is why the government chose to proceed against her by attainder rather than a trial which would have exposed the weak case against her.

Margaret had previously written to her son, Reginald, denouncing him as a traitor, but this may have been because she knew she was being watched and her letters intercepted and read, and wanted to protect herself and her family from being linked with Reginald's treason. Perhaps the letter was in fact dictated for her by Thomas Cromwell or another royal agent to try and trap Reginald. In July 1536, Margaret Pole responded to a letter written to her by her son, Reginald, though we cannot trust the contents of the letter as to Margaret's true feelings about her son's actions. Letters were being intercepted and read before leaving the country, so Margaret had to be careful what she wrote to a man who was seen by Henry VIII as an ungrateful traitor. In her letter she told Reginald 'my trust to have comfort in you is turned to sorrow' and asking that 'upon my blessing I charge thee to take another way and serve our master'.[16] Outwardly in this letter Margaret pleads with Reginald to stop speaking out against Henry VIII and find a way to serve him, letting disappointment ring through in the tone. However, she was a Roman Catholic, in spite of outward conformity to Henry VIII's Church of England, and her letter may have been a way for her to communicate with her son without raising the suspicions of the king and government, seeming to try and reconcile the king and her errant son. Though just communicating with a known traitor would have raised suspicions anyway. There is the possibility that the letter was dictated by someone like Cromwell to try and force Reginald back to England, though there is no evidence for this.

* * *

Margaret Pole denied all charges against her right to the end. She would always deny being a traitor and plotting against the king. Reginald Pole, who was in Italy when he heard of his mother's execution in 1541, was upset over what the king had done to his family. The later Archbishop of Ragusa in Italy, Ludovico Beccadelli, who was a contemporary of Pole, would claim that Reginald said:

'It has now pleased the Almighty to honour me still more ... I am now the son of a martyr whom the King of England hath brought to the scaffold although she was seventy years old and his own near relation, for her perseverance in the Catholic faith'.[17]

Pole believed that Margaret had died for being a Catholic, and the mother of a Roman Catholic Cardinal, as Reginald had been created a Cardinal on 22 December 1536, though Pole himself allegedly objected to his elevation.

It was Pole's activities on the Continent against Henry VIII and the Break with Rome that pushed Henry VIII to act against the entire Pole family.[18] Henry wanted to take revenge on Pole but could not get hold of the man himself so took his revenge out on his family instead. The Pole family were also the last potential claimants to, and rivals for, the English throne from the old Yorkist line, aside from the Marquess of Exeter, executed in 1538, and his son, Edward Courtenay, 1st Earl of Devon.

The action against the Poles, however, does not seem to have been part of a deliberate aim in this way. However, the historian David Loades does believe that it was Margaret's Yorkist royal blood rather than any actual offence which led to her execution after the Exeter Conspiracy.[19] This is similar to the execution of Edward Stafford, 3rd Duke of Buckingham, in 1521, who had claimed that he had a better claim to the throne than the Tudors and was executed, at least in part, for his royal blood (see Chapter 2).

Henry VIII had become paranoid in his fear of a Catholic attack on England and decided to clear the Tower of London of potential supporters of a foreign invasion and any notable Catholics before his progress to the north in 1541. This was so that, if there was an invasion, the prisoners in the Tower could not be released to act against him, particularly nobles who could potentially rely on a large power base and plenty of retainers to serve them. This was perhaps not such a paranoid delusion when we consider that Reginald Pole was in Europe trying to persuade France and Spain to join together against Henry VIII. Margaret Pole was one of those unfortunate people in the Tower who was sent to her death at this time, although Reginald's actions on the Continent no doubt played a role in Henry VIII acting against her. She was woken early on 27 May 1541 and was told that she would die that morning at 7am.[20] Margaret did not seem to know her crime but walked to the block within the Tower walls on Tower Green, with no scaffold. She sent a blessing to Princess Mary before her execution, as Mary had been like a daughter to her in many ways, and she had seen her grow up. She had cared for Mary through the adversity between her parents and the annulment of their marriage, which had led to Mary's own bastardisation and ostracisation from the royal court, and her father's affections, for many years.

Henry VIII did grant Margaret Pole the privacy of an execution on Tower Green rather than on the more public Tower Hill, potentially because he knew that the people would not agree to the execution of such an old lady, aged 67, for seemingly committing no crime other than having royal blood. She was pitied and respected by many in England. The French ambassador to England, Charles de Marillac, reported to Francis I that Margaret was not killed publicly because of the potential for an outcry against it; he wrote 'those here are afraid to put to death publicly those whom they execute in secret'.[21] The suggestion being that if someone was not executed in public, there was probably a reason why; most likely due to the potential for public outcry, a rescue attempt, or a doubt in their guilt. Realistically there was not enough evidence to convict Margaret, and had she been tried in an English court today, she would not have been convicted. But the sixteenth century was very different when it came to royal justice, especially for the nobility for whom it depended often on the whim or desire of the monarch, particularly when that monarch was Henry VIII. When led to the block, Margaret reportedly said that she would not put her head on the block as she had received no trial and was not guilty.[22] No trial meant that she had not had the chance to prove her innocence, which was probably exactly what Henry VIII had intended by condemning her through an Act of Attainder rather than an open trial. Attainder meant that a trial was not required for the finding of guilt. It just needed the monarch's signature and seal.

Eustace Chapuys, the Imperial ambassador, reported that the usual executioner was not available and so an inexperienced youth was chosen, who hacked at Margaret's head and shoulders, taking several attempts to sever the head from the body.[23] It was completely botched. Chapuys went on to say that Margaret did not know her crime, but desired those present to pray for the king, queen, prince, and princess; but no mention was made of Princess Elizabeth; the princess she asked the people to pray for was Mary. Margaret Pole had not forgiven Anne Boleyn for usurping Katherine of Aragon and considered Elizabeth a bastard, as did most of Catholic Europe. It has been proposed that it took as many as eleven strokes to sever Margaret's head from her body, after the first strike hit the shoulder, and it has even been suggested that the executioner had to chase Margaret around the block before she would submit to death.[24] There was also a suggestion that she had to be held down for the executioner to strike and that it took several minutes for her to die.[25] It was not instantaneous or merciful in the end.

Lord Herbert of Cherbury in his account, which was written decades after it happened, claimed that Margaret was told to lay her head on the block, but she refused, saying that 'so should traitors do, and I am none' and 'if he would have her head, to get it as he could'.[26] This perhaps shows Margaret's spirit and her assertion that she was innocent, rather than what actually happened. Eustace Chapuys, actually writing at the time, described none of this battle of wills between Margaret Pole and the executioner, with him writing that she seemed to submit, pray, and lay her head on the block. Margaret had been dignified throughout her life, even when her brother was executed, and Katherine of Aragon was having her marriage annulled. There is no reason to think she would have behaved any less dignified at the end of her life.[27] Margaret knew what was expected of royals and would have known how to act in the most difficult of situations. Therefore, it is difficult to believe Herbert of Cherbury's account of Margaret's last moments.

Marillac, the French ambassador, reported that she was executed in the presence of so few people that the veracity of rumours that she was dead were doubted most of the day until the news was confirmed.[28] However, Chapuys reported that Margaret was executed in the presence of the Lord Mayor of London and around 150 people.[29] There is no surviving record of who was actually present. These accounts from several sources suggest that Margaret's final minutes were awful for her and for people witnessing the execution who may have included family or friends. The execution of Margaret Pole is one of the most difficult to read about; an older woman who had given so much to the dynasty and had already lost her father to the executioner's axe in 1478, her brother in 1499, as well as her son in 1538. Her own end was ignominious, protracted, and in all likelihood painful, a 'blundering youth … was chosen, who literally hacked her head and shoulders to pieces in the most pitiful manner'.[30] She died in a truly awful way, a poor end to a distinguished life.

Margaret Pole was buried, like so many other nobles executed by the Tudors, in the Chapel of St Peter ad Vincula within the Tower of London near the remains of Anne Boleyn, who had been so critical to the overthrow of the Roman Catholic Church in England. There have been alleged sightings of the ghost of Margaret Pole being chased by a phantom executioner at the Tower of London, and even that a spectral axe has been seen to fall at the scene of her death.[31] There seem to be ghosts linked with quite a few of the executions in this book, though the best known are linked to the women, like Anne Boleyn and Katherine Howard. During restoration work on the Chapel of St Peter ad Vincula, on 11 November 1879, remains were found of a 'tall and aged female' assumed to be Margaret Pole.[32] They were reinterred where they had been found.

With Margaret's execution, and that of her son and heir, Henry, Lord Montagu, the family lost their lands and titles. Reginald Pole, as previously mentioned, survived and served Mary I as her Catholic Archbishop of Canterbury, dying just hours after the death of his queen. Geoffrey Pole did plead guilty to treason in December 1538 at his trial, but was pardoned the following year, probably for the evidence which led to the executions of his brother and mother. He tried to commit suicide several times while in the Tower before his release. Geoffrey did receive some of his family's lands back in 1544 but fled England in 1548 to beg the forgiveness of his brother, Reginald. Geoffrey returned to England in 1553 on the accession of Mary I. Margaret's only daughter, Ursula, lived into the reign of Elizabeth I, dying in 1570. She does not seem to have been involved in the treason of the Pole family, and her daughter, Dorothy Stafford, would go on to serve Elizabeth I, so she does not seem to have suffered unduly as a result. As she was more closely linked to the Stafford family at this point rather than the Poles, there would have been no evidence against her if she were at home raising her children.

After Margaret Pole's beheading, these words were found carved into the wall of the cell in which she was kept in the Tower of London; according to legend, a memorial in stone to the fact that she declared her innocence to the last, and would not submit to the executioner's axe:

> 'For traitors on the block should die;
> I am no traitor, no, not I!
> My faithfulness stands fast and so,
> Towards the block I shall not go!
> Nor make one step, as you shall see;
> Christ in Thy Mercy, save Thou me!'[33]

Margaret, it seemed, did not just want the people to know of her innocence, but for a statement of it to live in stone. 'Towards the block I shall not go' is haunting, given rumours that the executioner had to chase her around the block before she would submit to the axe, although how much credence we can give these rumours is unknown. It is difficult to know where this came from as it is quoted in several works but with no contemporary citation. She is remembered today on the glass memorial within the Tower of London, alongside the likes of Anne Boleyn, Katherine Howard (who had tried to make conditions better for her during her imprisonment), and Lady Jane Grey, the Nine Days Queen.

Margaret Pole went from one difficulty to another in her life, enjoying pockets of happiness in between. But she ended her long life ignominiously, as a condemned traitor under the executioner's axe, declaring her innocence to the last.

Chapter 5

Queen Katherine Howard & Jane Boleyn, Viscountess Rochford – 1542

Katherine Howard was the second niece of Thomas Howard, 3rd Duke of Norfolk, to marry Henry VIII, but the only one to bear the Howard name. The first was, of course, Anne Boleyn. If we take Katherine Howard's birth to be around 1523/4 then she was aged just 16 or 17 when she married the king, and just 18 or 19 when she was executed for adultery and treason in 1542. Her actual birthdate or birth year are unknown, as are Anne Boleyn's, though it is generally accepted that she was born sometime between 1521 and 1525. However, 1524 seems to be the favoured year by many historians, meaning she would be around age 17 or 18 when she was executed. She was young and did not have the chance to live her life. Katherine's story is tragic and 'like a butterfly, her existence was ephemeral', leaving 'a memory of her that is both charming and tragic'.[1] Katherine's downfall and execution is, in a way, difficult to understand because she was so young and, in a manner of speaking, innocent and naïve in the ways of the court and world, yet appeared to have plenty of sexual experience from a tender age. This experience would completely undo her.

Katherine Howard was born the daughter of Edmund Howard, who was himself the son of Thomas Howard, 2nd Duke of Norfolk, and Joyce Culpeper. She was one of six children and had three brothers and two sisters. She was the fourth child and second daughter. Through her father, Edmund, Katherine was related to Anne Boleyn who was her cousin, and the future Elizabeth I who, as well as being her stepdaughter through her royal marriage, was also her first cousin once removed. Most noble families were interrelated somehow in the sixteenth century, no matter how distant the connection. The Howards seemed to be connected to most noble families at the English court, through many clever dynastic marriages to bolster their line.

Katherine's mother, Joyce Culpeper (also sometimes called Jocasta), had already been married once before and had six children by her first husband, so the family was not very well off raising so many children, and Edmund would have had to make his own way in the world without expecting an inheritance. As the third son of his father, he could not expect any significant bequest as, by the laws of primogeniture, everything went to the eldest son, Thomas Howard, who would become 3rd Duke of Norfolk. Through her mother, Katherine was the fourth cousin once removed of Thomas Culpeper, who would be executed just a couple of months before Katherine for having committed adultery with her. Their relationship would mean that in future it would be treason for a woman to conceal her sexual history before marrying the king. That was one of Katherine's legacies.

In comparison, Jane Boleyn, Viscountess Rochford, had been the wife of George Boleyn, Viscount Rochford, and thus sister-in-law to Henry VIII's second wife, Anne Boleyn. She had been widowed when her husband was executed along with his sister in May 1536 for incest and treason. She was the daughter of Henry Parker, 10th Baron Morley and Alice St John. Through her mother, Jane was a great-great-granddaughter of Margaret Beauchamp of Bletsoe, who was the mother of Margaret Beaufort and thus the great-grandmother of Henry VIII. Jane Boleyn was therefore a half-second cousin to Henry VIII, as Jane descended from Margaret Beauchamp of Bletsoe's first marriage to Oliver St John, and Henry VIII descended from her second marriage to John Beaufort, 1st Duke of Somerset. Jane Boleyn was also a second cousin to Reginald Pole, the son of Margaret Pole who was discussed in Chapter 4, through his father, Richard Pole. Both were descended from the children of Margaret Beauchamp of Bletsoe and Oliver St John.

Through her marriage to George Boleyn, Jane Parker was also related to the powerful Howard Dukes of Norfolk, just as Katherine Howard was. The two women were cousins by marriage, though Jane was more tainted than Katherine, as she was said to have given evidence against her husband and sister-in-law, George and Anne Boleyn, which led to their executions. Whether Katherine Howard knew this when she married the king and Jane became one of her ladies-in-waiting, is unknown, though it is entirely possible she at the very least had heard rumours at court of what had happened to her cousins and Jane's supposed role in it.

Both Katherine Howard and Jane Boleyn (née Parker) were noble women, descended from great families, who had places at the English court right at the centre of power. But that power and position would be their downfall, combined with their reckless behaviour, secret relationships and adultery.

* * *

Katherine Howard was not raised by her parents. She was likely born around 1523/4 as the fourth of six children. Her mother died around 1528 when Katherine was aged 4 or 5, and she was sent to live in the care of her step-grandmother, Agnes Tilney, dowager Duchess of Norfolk. The dowager duchess had large households at Chesworth in Horsham and at Norfolk House in Lambeth. She had several young ladies under her care and Katherine lived alongside them for many years whilst growing up. The ladies were usually the poor relatives of aristocratic families. It was usual for aristocratic children to be sent away to be brought up by others, but the supervision at Lambeth and Horsham seems to have been lax, with many of the ladies having male partners who were let into the chamber by said young ladies who had stolen the key to the locked door at night. The young ladies all slept together in the same room so Katherine would have been exposed to this side of the household likely from very early on during her stay there.

Katherine Howard is often seen as being not very intellectual or well-read, unlike her cousin Anne Boleyn, or Katherine of Aragon, the first two wives of Henry VIII. However, she was also considered to be vivacious, giggly, and quite child-like, even naïve. It is recorded that she really enjoying dancing and, on her arrest, was told it 'is no more the time to dance'.[2] This implies that perhaps Katherine did not realise the danger she was in on her arrest and maybe believed it would soon blow over without any serious consequences and her life would continue as before. It is actually quite upsetting that a young life could fall apart so utterly and completely.

Around 1536, Katherine had started music lessons with a man named Henry Manox and they appear to have begun some kind of relationship, though just how far their relationship went is unclear. Confessions from both Katherine and Manox suggest that it did not go as far as intercourse. Manox was older than Katherine, though his exact age is unknown; he was probably in his early to mid-20s in 1536, when Katherine would have been around aged 12 or 13, if we take her birth date as 1523/4. It has been suggested that the relationship was abusive rather than consensual, even at a time when girls could marry young, and that Manox was grooming her, expounded on by historians such as Conor Byrne who said that Katherine 'had not necessarily consented to, or welcomed, the sexual experiences she had undergone between the ages of 13 and 15'.[3] We cannot be sure of the nature of these sexual occurrences. We only really have the evidence of Katherine's own confession in 1541 along with that of Manox and those of the other girls who shared the dormitory with her, but it is certainly interesting to consider. Manox claimed that he never had intercourse with Katherine and that her affections were taken by another before their relationship reached that point. Katherine's confession, and Manox's, could have been an attempt to save themselves rather than a truthful recollection, though the evidence of the other ladies does seem to prove their stories which did match up with each other. Perhaps that is why Manox avoided execution even though he was arrested and questioned in 1541. He never had sexual intercourse with Katherine.

Katherine knew that she wanted to go to court. Her family connections meant that this was completely feasible and even probable. She received her first stipend in December 1539 when the household was being set up to receive Anne of Cleves as queen on her arrival. Katherine would receive an annual stipend of £10 along with lodgings, provision for a servant and food for her servant and herself, as well as stabling for one horse and a provision of wax candles.[4] Money for her clothes and bedding was provided by the dowager Duchess of Norfolk. Her duties were to obey the queen and serve her to the best of her ability, although it was also understood that she would advance the interests of her family.

By May 1540, Henry VIII's marriage to Anne of Cleves was pretty much doomed, and Henry was in love, or lust, with Katherine Howard. Traditionally, Henry could have remained married to Anne, and taken Katherine as his mistress. However, Henry VIII, like with Anne Boleyn and Jane Seymour previously, wanted the woman he loved to be his wife. Hence, he put in motion plans for another marriage annulment. His marriage to Anne of Cleves would be his shortest, at just six months, when it was annulled in July 1540. Henry married Katherine just weeks later.

Katherine Howard, aged around 15 or 16, married the 49-year-old Henry VIII at Oatlands Palace in Surrey on 28 July 1540. She adopted the motto 'No other will but his' from the French *Non autre volante que la sienne.* The marriage was made public on 8 August and Katherine was prayed for as queen of England in the Chapel Royal at Hampton Court Palace that day. The wedding took place on the very same day that Henry VIII's former chief minister, Thomas Cromwell, was executed, and just sixteen days after the annulment of Henry's previous marriage to his fourth wife, Anne of Cleves. It was said that Henry was so enamoured of Katherine that he could not keep his hands off of her, even in public.[5] A question that has been asked since Katherine Howard's history came to light in 1541, was how did Henry VIII not notice that his fifth wife was not a virgin on their marriage? As historian David Loades puts it 'perhaps enthusiasm made him unobservant'.[6] Henry was furious when this information came to light over a year after their wedding. Probably angry at himself for not realising, but he tended to blame anyone else rather than apportion blame on himself.

Katherine's queenship is interesting. She appears to have promoted the release of Margaret Pole, Countess of Salisbury, from the Tower of London, where she had been imprisoned since 1538 when her son, Henry Pole, 1st Baron Montagu, was executed for treason. Katherine failed to save Margaret, as discussed in Chapter 4, but did manage to get her some new clothes when hers were falling apart during her imprisonment.[7] Katherine also seems to have intervened when Thomas Wyatt was again imprisoned in the Tower. The first time was in 1536 when he was implicated in Anne Boleyn's downfall, though he was not charged and survived. This time Katherine was successful, unlike with Margaret Pole, and Thomas Wyatt was released. This is a traditional role for a queen, interceding on behalf of others in calculated acts of mercy. Sometimes they were used as a public demonstration of a king's mercy, where the queen knelt before her husband in front of the court and begged for the lives of those condemned. This happened after Evil May Day in 1517, when Katherine of Aragon and her sister-in-law, Mary Tudor, Duchess of Suffolk, knelt publicly before the king and begged for the lives of the condemned. This was a piece of theatre planned in advance. We have no evidence of Katherine Howard's intercessions being in this public form, however. Perhaps she just asked the king when they were dining together and he wanted to please her, as he seemed to constantly want to do.

Katherine had gone from serving a queen to being queen of England herself, and many of her household had transferred from serving Anne of Cleves to serving her. These included her half-sister, Isabel, and brother-in-law Sir Edward Baynton, Mary Howard, Duchess of Richmond and Somerset, who was Katherine's cousin. and Lady Margaret Howard, Katherine's aunt. She had plenty of family around her. But the lady who would become tied up the most with Katherine and in her fall was her cousin-by-marriage, Jane Boleyn, Lady Rochford. Jane had served Anne of Cleves before transferring to Katherine's household in 1540. It was later alleged that it was Jane who promoted Katherine's affair with Thomas Culpeper, and she would be executed alongside Katherine in 1542.

While queen, Katherine also appears to have promoted a relationship between her brother, Charles Howard, and the king's niece, Lady Margaret Douglas. Margaret Douglas was the daughter of Henry VIII's sister, Margaret Tudor, Queen of Scotland, and thus in the line of succession to the English throne. Any relationship she entered into needed the permission of the king and council. She did not have this permission and Ralph Sadler wrote to Cranmer and others on behalf of the Privy Council on 12 November 1541 after Katherine Howard's arrest that they were to 'show [Margaret Douglas] how indiscreetly she has acted, first with lord Thomas and then with Charles Howard, and bid her beware the third time'.[8] Margaret had already been punished for an indiscreet relationship with Lord Thomas Howard, brother to the 3rd Duke of Norfolk. There were rumours that they had actually married in secret, but that Henry VIII had declared it invalid and separated the couple by imprisoning them both in the Tower of London. Perhaps the council were suspicious of Katherine's involvement and promoting her own family into royal circles.

*   *   *

Katherine Howard's fall from power after less than two years of marriage and queenship rested on her past, as it was discovered that she had at least two and possibly three relationships with men before her arrival at court and marriage to the king. On All Soul's Day, 2 November 1541, the Archbishop of Canterbury, Thomas Cranmer, left a note for the king on his pew at Mass at Hampton Court Palace. This letter revealed to the king what Cranmer had discovered about Katherine Howard's past and that she was not entirely his 'rose without a thorn'; there were indeed some thorns. The suggestion is that he was too scared to reveal it to the king face to face, hence the letter. This is understandable as it was known that Henry VIII had slapped Thomas Cromwell about the head when he was the king's chief minister if he was angry. The letter implicated both Katherine's music teacher, Henry Manox, and the dowager Duchess of Norfolk's secretary, Francis Dereham, of carnally knowing her from when she was very young and in the dowager duchess's care. This relationship with Dereham seemed to follow on quite quickly from that with Henry Manox from the confessions we have.

The Northern Progress of 1541 was a milestone of Henry VIII's reign. It was the furthest north he ever travelled, and it had been hoped that he would meet the Scottish king, James V in York. It was months in the planning and finally began on 30 June 1541 and by 18 July the court had reached Grafton in Northamptonshire, then on 9 August they entered Lincoln. On 19 August they arrived in Yorkshire, reaching Pontefract five days later, where Katherine would be reunited with a face from her past: her former lover, Francis Dereham. Dereham wanted a position in Katherine's household. Television drama *The Tudors* which sees Katherine Howard played by Tamzin Merchant suggests that Dereham effectively blackmailed Katherine to give him a position in her household by threatening to reveal their past indiscretions. Whether this is what really happened is unknown, but whatever the truth of it, Katherine took Dereham into her household on 27 August. Dereham seems to have begun making trouble in Katherine's household soon after he was admitted to it and seemed to be making enemies. He appeared cocky over the fact that he had known Katherine before she was at court and declared regarding one of the queen's gentlemen ushers, 'I was of the queen's Council before he knew her and shall be when she hath forgotten him'.[9] Dereham was flaunting his previously close relationship with Katherine in the faces of those who had the power to bring them both down. Katherine heard of Dereham's comments and warned him to be careful of what he spoke.

While the king and queen were on the Northern Progress in summer 1541, a man called John Lascelles had approached the Archbishop and revealed that his sister, Mary Lascelles, had been with the queen at Lambeth under the dowager duchess's care. Mary claimed that Katherine was 'light, both in living and conditions'.[10] She claimed that Manox had known a secret mark on Katherine's body, and that Dereham had laid with Katherine between the sheets a hundred nights. At first, the king did not believe the accusations against his queen and asked for the accuser to be re-examined, but John Lascelles stuck to his story, and his sister, when questioned, backed up his story. Thomas Wriothesley, later created 1st Earl of Southampton under Edward VI, was sent to question both Henry Manox and Francis Dereham. Manox confessed that he had touched her body, but no sexual relations ensued though claimed 'I know her well enough, for I have had her by the cunt, and I know it among a hundred'[11], and Dereham confessed that he 'hath had carnal knowledge with the Queen, lying in bed by her in his doublet and hosen divers times and six or seven times in naked bed with her'.[12]

There was a suggestion made by those questioned that Katherine Howard's sexual misdemeanours may not only have occurred before her marriage, as she had given Francis Dereham a job in her service after she married the king. Several of the ladies who had been with her in the dowager Duchess of Norfolk's household had also been given positions in Katherine's household as queen. Potentially Katherine could have been blackmailed to give these women positions for them to keep their mouths closed about what they knew of her past indiscretions. This would suggest that Katherine understood that keeping this from the king was wrong and could land her in trouble with him. But perhaps she was scared of what would happen if she told, so gave in to the blackmail, knowing that she should have told the king before they were married, and that the consequences would be worse when she was already proclaimed queen.

Katherine was confronted with the accusations and the statements of those who had been questioned and she initially denied everything despite the evidence gathered against her. Eventually she made a confession to Thomas Cranmer. Katherine confessed regarding Francis Dereham that 'there was Communication in the House that we Two should Marry together' and that:

> 'as for Carnall Knowledge, I confess as I did before, that diverse Times he hath lyen with me, sometimes in his Doublet and Hose, and Two or Three Times naked: But not so naked that he bad nothing upon him, for he had al wayes at the least his Doublet, and as I do think, his Hose also, but I mean naked when his Hose were putt down. And diverse Times he would bring Wine, Strawberryes, Apples, and other Things to make good Cheer, after my lady was gone to Bed … and sometime Dereham hath come in early in the Morning, and ordered him very lewdly, but never at my Request, nor Consent'.[13]

Perhaps Katherine realised that there was no use in hiding it any longer when there were so many witnesses who had testified to it. Or perhaps she was so scared that it came out without her meaning it to. Conceivably, initially she may have panicked and just denied it automatically, without thinking it through. Either scenario is entirely possible. An important line of the confession is the last one quoted above 'never at my Request, nor Consent'. Katherine is effectively accusing Dereham of abuse or rape, saying that she did not consent to what went on between them. It does not seem that

Cranmer or the council believed her accusations, possibly in part because of the evidence given by the other ladies who were in the dormitory with Katherine when they were teenagers, who did not appear to mention any words spoken by Katherine to suggest she did not want it. The suggestion of making 'good Cheer' also does not imply that Dereham in any way forced himself on Katherine, but that he was welcomed by the ladies to the dormitory. However, Katherine would only have been very young at the time, and sources suggest she was naïve in many ways. Having sexual relations at such a young age would certainly nowadays be seen as abuse but we cannot judge by twenty-first century standards what happened 500 years ago. For example, Henry VII's mother, Margaret Beaufort, was married at age 12 and gave birth at age 13. This is perhaps an extreme example, but it did happen.

The French ambassador, Charles de Marillac, reported in his letter of Tuesday 11 November 1541 that the council had met around midnight on Sunday 9 November, but did not disperse until 4 or 5am on Monday and that the councillors seemed very troubled, particularly Thomas Howard, 3rd Duke of Norfolk. However, Marillac did not seem to know what was happening or why the council had been called, although later in his letter he said that 'he hears the Queen is newly accused of being entertained by a gentleman while she was in the house of the old duchess of Norfolk'.[14] This was the beginning of Katherine Howard's downfall, when her behaviour before the marriage to the king was uncovered. Though any question of adultery during her marriage does not yet seem to have entered the equation, or at least not reached the ears of foreign ambassadors. Just a few days after this initial letter, Marillac again wrote to Francis I to say that Katherine had 'prostituted herself to seven or eight persons'.[15] Who these seven or eight people are, Marillac does not say, and possibly can be put down to rumour and speculation flying around the court, rather than anything concrete from someone in the know. Norfolk might well have looked particularly troubled, given that Katherine was his niece, and that he had promoted the marriage in the first place. Katherine would be the second of his nieces to be executed by Henry VIII, the first being Anne Boleyn, which must have been a horrible example for Katherine to have in front of her. This must have raised concerns for Norfolk over whether he would be indicted for his involvement in encouraging the marriage, though he seemed to be very good at getting out of potentially dangerous situations and saving himself, often at the expense of others.

Archbishop Thomas Cranmer visited Katherine Howard to question her as to the accusations made against her, initially at Hampton Court Palace before she was taken by boat along the river Thames to Syon Abbey, closer to central London and the council and court at Whitehall. In a letter written by Ralph Sadler on behalf of the Privy Council on 12 November 1541, it was decided that Katherine would be moved from Hampton Court Palace to Syon Abbey where she would be questioned further.[16] She was allowed to take a couple of attendants with her and was told to pack dresses without any jewels or embellishments. By this time, it was fairly certain that the accusations against Katherine were at least partly true, and she would not be remaining as queen of England. Her exact fate at this time was undecided, though I imagine execution was not on the cards. She had not been entirely honest, but at this point there was no real crime, and her possible adultery had not been uncovered yet.

Katherine's ladies were all questioned as to what they knew about Katherine's behaviour during her marriage to the king, and it soon became clear that Katherine and Jane Boleyn, Lady Rochford, were hiding something. Both had been secretive and exchanging messages. One of Katherine's ladies, Katherine Tylney, said that sometimes she was sent from Katherine to Lady Rochford with cryptic messages such as 'ask her when she should have the thing she promised her' and that the answer was 'she sat up for it, and she would next day bring her word herself'.[17] It was obvious that they had some kind of secret that they did not want getting out, though using her other ladies as go-betweens was reckless, given the nature of the court and how people used what they knew to gain power and influence. Those who served Katherine who were questioned included Joan Bulmer, Katherine Tylney, Edward Walgrave, Mary Lascelles, Margaret Morton, and Alice Wilkes, formerly Alice Restwold. Servants from the household of the dowager Duchess of Norfolk were also questioned and revealed what they knew.

Thomas Culpeper would be Katherine's downfall. He was born in Kent and while still a boy he entered the royal court as a page. By 1533 he had a position as a gentleman of the privy chamber. Historian, Josephine Wilkinson, describes Culpeper as having an 'aura of arrogance about him and a tendency towards pretentiousness coupled with burning ambition' and describes he and Katherine as entering into some kind of relationship in early 1540 once she came to court.[18] Culpeper retreated once it became obvious that the king was interested in Katherine. It is unclear exactly when Katherine and Culpeper began to meet secretly again after Katherine's marriage, though they were certainly meeting during the Northern Progress of 1541. The state of their relationship is also debated; did they have sexual relations, or did they not? Katherine's fate was reminiscent of charges brought against Anne Boleyn, Katherine's cousin, in 1536. Two of Surrey's cousins had married the king, and both were executed on charges of adultery. Adultery in a queen was considered treason as it threatened the succession. Any pregnancy could not be confirmed to be from the king, so the legitimacy of any child born to an adulterous queen could be questioned.

Katherine's lady, Margaret Morton referenced Thomas Culpeper specifically, saying she 'never mistrusted the Queen until at Hatfield she saw her look out of her chamber window on Mr. Culpeper after such sort that she thought there was love between them'.[19] Morton probably never thought, even if there was love between them, that they would ever act upon it, knowing the consequences if they were caught. Morton continued that if ladies had left Katherine Howard's service, she thought that Katherine would have replaced them with ladies of Lady Rochford's choosing, as they spend so much time alone together.[20] It appeared suspicious that Katherine spent so much time locked away with just one of her ladies, and the others never knew what they were up to. The only way a queen could commit adultery was with the connivance of her ladies, as she was surrounded all day every day and was never really alone. Jane Boleyn, Viscountess Rochford, was that woman by all accounts, who enabled Katherine to have a relationship with Thomas Culpeper while married to the king.

When Francis Dereham was questioned he confessed to being familiar with Katherine before her marriage to the king. She had taken him into her household after her marriage, but he appears to have been careless and Katherine had to warn him 'take heed what words you speak'.[21] Dereham admitted that Katherine had also given him money, which could be seen as a bribe or a response to him blackmailing her. Katherine was in a difficult position with Dereham as he knew her past, and he could easily blackmail her, holding her past against her. Although some of Katherine's ladies knew about her past indiscretions, Dereham was in another league, and did not seem to know how to hold his tongue and be discreet, which was very important when in the cut and thrust of Henry VIII's court.

With Katherine Howard's arrest, there were rumours spreading that Henry VIII would take back his fourth wife, Anne of Cleves, after annulling his marriage to Katherine. Anne had only been Henry's wife for six months, from January to July 1540, before Henry had the marriage declared null and void. He married Katherine Howard just two weeks later. The French ambassador, Charles de Marillac, said that Anne had 'conducted herself wisely in her affliction, and is more beautiful than she was'.[22] Anne seems to have settled well in England and showed no inclination to return home to Cleves. In England, Anne had a measure of freedom living in her own establishment and able to fill her days as she pleased, whereas in Cleves she would be at the mercy of her brother, William (sometimes seen as Wilhelm), Duke of Jülich-Cleves-Berg, who would probably have arranged another diplomatic marriage for her. She was content to remain in England and would die at Chelsea in 1557.

There does not, however, seem to have been any serious suggestion that Henry would take back Anne of Cleves. That would mean that he would have had to admit that he was wrong to have annulled the marriage in the first place. This would go against Henry VIII's belief in his divine power and would hurt his ego. This was a similar situation to where he found himself in 1535/6 with Katherine of Aragon and Anne Boleyn. In order to annul his marriage to Anne, Henry would have had to acknowledge his error and likely return to Katherine. However, when Katherine died in January 1536, this protection for Anne was removed and she herself was removed just four months later. In 1540, however, Henry VIII did not feel that he would be expected to return to Anne of Cleves if he annulled his marriage to Katherine Howard. He was more confident and secure in his own power and divine right to rule by this point in his reign.

The Privy Council wrote to the English Ambassador to France, William Paget, 1st Baron Paget of Beaudesert, saying that the king had thought 'now in his old age to have obtained a jewel for womanhood. But this joy is turned to extreme sorrow'.[23] Henry VIII's discovery of Katherine Howard's infidelity showed him without a shadow of a doubt that he was no longer the young and desirable king who could have any woman he wanted, like he was when he married to Katherine of Aragon and wooing Anne Boleyn in the 1520s. The downfall of Katherine Howard marked the end of Henry VIII's quest for another son and his acceptance that he was ageing. He became aware, possibly for the first time, that he was old and that siring another son was very unlikely. His final marriage to Katherine Parr, was intended to bring him companionship rather than another child.

* * *

Katherine Howard and Jane Boleyn, Viscountess Rochford, would be executed on Tower Green within the Tower of London itself in a private death, rather than the public death of nearby Tower Hill. In this they would follow in the footsteps of Katherine's cousin and Jane's sister-in-law, Anne Boleyn, as well as Margaret Pole, rather than Jane's husband, George Boleyn. The current glass monument to those executed within the Tower of London outside the Chapel of St Peter ad Vincula is seemingly not the actual site where the scaffold was actually erected for executions within the Tower grounds. Recent scholarship suggests that the scaffold site was actually north of the White Tower rather than further to the west where the glass monument to the victims is now, between the White Tower and what is now the Waterloo Barracks but was once the royal armoury.[24] This private execution within the bounds of the Tower rather than the public Tower Hill, a short distance away, was a small mercy from the king for a wife he had adored, his 'rose without a thorn'.

The Imperial ambassador, Eustace Chapuys, wrote on 9 February 1542 that two days before, the Comptroller of the king's household went to Syon to break up Katherine's household and dismiss her servants.[25] This was a crucial moment which demonstrated that Katherine Howard would not be remaining as queen of England so had no need for a royal household. There would no longer be a queen to serve so her servants could all be sent home. The evidence had been gathered and the decision had been made. Katherine Howard would not survive her past, or her deception of the king, as innocent as she may have thought it was. Within days, she would be transferred to the Tower of London and then executed. Things from here began to move quickly.

Katherine Howard was moved from her imprisonment at Syon to join Jane Boleyn, Viscountess Rochford, in the Tower of London on 10 February 1542. Jane Boleyn had already been in the Tower for several months since her initial arrest. It was likely at this point that Katherine knew for sure that she would die. There would be no pardon from the king, her husband. Henry VIII was putting a second wife to death. The Imperial ambassador, Eustace Chapuys, reported that Katherine was taken to the Tower 'with some resistance'.[26] Precisely what form this resistance took is unclear. Historian, Conor Byrne, records that Katherine broke down and had to be forcibly put into the barge to convey her to the Tower.[27] On her way to the Tower from Syon, Katherine would have passed under London Bridge where the heads of her lovers, Francis Dereham and Thomas Culpeper, were displayed on spikes. Henry Manox had escaped execution and was released after questioning, as he claimed he had not actually had sex with Katherine and was believed. Knowing how paranoid Henry VIII had become by 1541, this was a very lucky escape for Manox.

The French ambassador, Marillac, reported that the execution was delayed for several days for Katherine to compose herself as she 'weeps, cries, and torments herself miserably, without ceasing'.[28] The aim was for Katherine to recover from her bouts of weeping, compose herself, and prepare her soul and conscience for death. This Katherine appears to have done, for there was little sign of her being weepy on the day of her execution. She had submitted herself to the king's will and his mercy and he desired that she die for her sins. She knew that there was little point in hoping for clemency. The night before her execution, on 12 February 1542, Katherine Howard asked to have the block brought to her room, 'that she might know how to place herself'.[29] She practised her own death, to make sure that she would do it right, and leave the world with a good impression. Her previous actions had not done that, so maybe the manner of her death would.

Katherine Howard was the first to die, on 13 February 1542. As she was lower in rank, Jane Boleyn, Viscountess Rochford, would have to wait to see her mistress die, though they would die within minutes of each other just after 9am. This was confirmed in letters from both the French and Imperial ambassadors.[30] The French ambassador, Marillac, wrote that Katherine 'was so weak she could hardly speak, but confessed in a few words that she had merited a hundred deaths for so offending the king who had so graciously treated her'.[31] This was traditional form for a scaffold speech; to confess to unnamed sins and praise the monarch who had condemned you. Not everyone admitted to deserving death, but were accepting of it, seeing that there was no other option. Katherine's uncle, Thomas Howard, 3rd Duke of Norfolk, was absent from her execution. Perhaps he could not bear to see another one of his nieces, who had again married the king, die under the executioner's blade.

Katherine Howard also did not die a queen; her title of queen was stripped from her in November 1541 when it became obvious that the accusations against her were at least in part true. She was not worthy of being queen. It is Martin Hume's *The Chronicle of King Henry VIII of England* which cites the infamous line, used in Showtime's television drama *The Tudors* of

'I die a Queen, but I would rather die the wife of Culpeper' as Katherine Howard's final speech.[32] This seems unlikely to actually have happened as observers and foreign ambassadors would have reported these words, and both Chapuys and Marillac, the Imperial and French ambassadors, reported that both Katherine and Jane Boleyn said little on the scaffold except to acknowledge their sins and ask forgiveness. Hume also reports Katherine as having said that 'long before the King took me I loved Culpeper, and I wish to God I had done as he wished me, for at the time the King wanted to take me he urged me to say that I was pledged to him. If I had done as he advised me I should not die this death, nor would he'.[33] In this account of Katherine's final moments, she feels guilt for Culpeper's death and is antagonistic almost on the scaffold, though in a slightly naïve way it feels. But the authenticity is seriously in doubt. Chronicler, Edward Hall, said that they died repentant.[34] 'I die a Queen, but I would rather die the wife of Culpeper' is hardly repentant and actually quite antagonistic. It certainly makes good drama!

Jane Boleyn, Lady Rochford, had shown signs of madness during her imprisonment, whether real or faked is unclear. The Imperial ambassador, Chapuys, reported that Jane had 'shown symptoms of madness till they told her she must die'.[35] The insinuation here is that Jane was faking madness to get out of being executed. However, Henry VIII changed the law in 1542 to make it legal to execute mad people, previously not being able to do that, just so that Jane could be killed. The insinuation of 'till they told her she must die' is that Jane was faking madness to avoid execution, but once the law was changed to allow the execution of mad people there was little point in carrying on with the charade. Jane Boleyn, according to Marillac, 'said as much in a long discourse of several faults which she had committed in her life'.[36] Some historians have taken these 'several faults' to encompass her accusations against her husband and sister-in-law, George and Anne Boleyn, in 1536. Sources suggest Jane was the source of the accusations of incest against the pair, as discussed in Chapter 3. Both Katherine Howard and Jane Boleyn were buried in the Chapel of St Peter ad Vincula within the Tower of London, close to the remains of Anne and George Boleyn.

Thomas Howard, 3rd Duke of Norfolk had been instrumental in his niece's marriage to Henry VIII. He must have feared that the shadow of Katherine's condemnation and death would fall on him, as it had many of his family, including his stepmother, Agnes Tilney, the dowager Duchess of Norfolk, who had been questioned about Katherine's behaviour and imprisoned in the Tower. The French ambassador, Marillac, reported to Francis I that Norfolk 'dare not show that the affair touches him, but approves all that is done'.[37] He could not be seen to approve of Katherine's actions, or those of the dowager duchess, or admit that he had any knowledge of them. If it were thought that he had been involved in hoodwinking the king into marrying his unsuitable niece, he could also have found himself imprisoned, or worse. Like with the execution of his other niece, Anne Boleyn, six years earlier, Norfolk condemned Katherine and approved the measures taken against her in order to save himself. He was deeply self-serving and would again be embroiled in the treason of a family member, this time his son, Henry Howard, Earl of Surrey, in 1546. Norfolk would be saved from the executioner's axe himself only by the death of the king in January 1547 (see Chapter 6).

Elizabeth I was too young to remember the execution of her mother, Anne Boleyn, at the hands of her father, Henry VIII. However, she was old enough at the age of 8 to remember that of her third stepmother, Katherine Howard, nearly six years later. Katherine's death is cited as one of the reasons why Elizabeth I refused to marry many years later as 'she was acutely aware, as she could not have been in her mother's case, of what it meant to be executed for treason'.[38] Elizabeth was old enough to remember Katherine's execution and the repercussions where she likely had very few memories of the execution of her mother. This awareness must then have been enhanced by the Thomas Seymour affair of 1548/9 which Elizabeth was embroiled in and Seymour was executed for (see Chapter 7). Katherine's marriage to Henry VIII was another poor example to Elizabeth of marriage. Katherine Howard's death did have a personal effect on more than just the king and his realisation of loss of youth, but on a young girl beginning to understand her place in the world. And that is almost as tragic as Katherine's death.

With Katherine's death, rumours abounded as to whether Henry VIII would marry again. The French and Imperial ambassadors seemed to have very different views on the subject. The Imperial ambassador, Chapuys, had been at the English court since 1529 (apart from a few brief absences) and saw Henry VIII through the end of five marriages. He believed that the king would not be in a hurry to marry again, unless parliament asked him to take another wife.[39] However, the French ambassador Marillac, who had only been at the English court since 1538, believed that the king would 'not be long without a wife' as he hoped to have more children.[40] By 1542, Henry VIII was 50 years old and must have realised that he would be unlikely to sire any more children. In fact, when he did remarry in 1543 he chose a wife in Katherine Parr who had been married twice before but had no children and seemed to value her companionship rather than a sexual relationship. Chapuys reported that few ladies would wish to marry the king given his history with wives, and that a law was passed in the wake of Katherine's condemnation that any woman whom the king would think to marry must reveal any potential charges of misconduct and previous sexual relationships on pain of imprisonment and forfeiture of goods.[41] Perhaps Chapuys believed that there were few women at the English court who would be willing to meet these conditions, or virginal enough to meet the king's standards. A widow, by definition, was different, and could be assumed to already have had sexual experience, so in a way had more leeway.

Katherine's reputation did not seem to suffer in the same way Anne Boleyn's did, possibly because she was much younger, naïve, and had not torn apart an established marriage of over twenty years, replaced a much-loved and admired queen, and changed the entire religion of England to achieve a marriage which did not produce a son and heir. Anne was more controversial than Katherine. Katherine Howard's story is disturbing in many ways; accusations of child abuse and grooming, marriage to a man old enough to be her father or potentially her grandfather, and execution before she was out of her teens. Henry VIII's 'love for Katherine was intense, matched only by the anger and hatred that overwhelmed him when he thought his beautiful jewel had betrayed him'.[42] Katherine never really had a chance to live her life, being always subject to the whims and ambitions of others, and her short life ended in ignominy.

Chapter 6

Henry Howard, Earl of Surrey – 1547

The Howard family do not seem to have had the best luck when it came to treason and the executioner's axe. As we have seen already, Anne Boleyn and Katherine Howard were executed for treason in 1536 and 1542 respectively by Henry VIII. The women were cousins; Anne's mother, Elizabeth Boleyn, was the sister of Katherine's father, Edmund Howard. Henry Howard, Earl of Surrey, would be Henry VIII's final execution, as the king himself died just days later, saving the patriarch of the Howard family, Thomas Howard, 3rd Duke of Norfolk, from the same fate. The duke himself would remain in the Tower until the accession of Mary I in 1553 and would die the following year, not long surviving his release. He was a devout Catholic where the new king, Edward VI, was a staunch Protestant. Although it was Surrey who was executed, this is the tale of both Surrey and Norfolk.

Henry Howard, Earl of Surrey, was a member of the influential Howard family and son of Thomas Howard, 3rd Duke of Norfolk. Henry would have been the 4th Duke of Norfolk had he managed to outlive his father and avoid being executed by Henry VIII. In the event, it was Henry's son, Thomas, who became the 4th Duke of Norfolk, and was also executed for treason in 1572 for his treasonous activities against Elizabeth I in the Ridolfi Plot (a reckless plan to marry Mary Queen of Scots and take the English throne – see Chapter 10). Henry was also cousin to executed English queens Anne Boleyn and Katherine Howard as their parents were siblings. Henry Howard was aged around 19 or 20 at the time of Anne's execution and aged around 25 or 26 at the time of Katherine's execution, more than old enough to understand the implications and dangers of being involved in treasonous activities and how even those closest to the throne were not immune from the threat. It begs the question, why did Surrey himself became involved in treason with the first-hand experience of his cousins before him? It obviously did not work as a deterrent. His pride was greater than his fear.

Henry Howard, Earl of Surrey, was born as the eldest son to Thomas Howard, 3rd Duke of Norfolk, and his second wife, Elizabeth Stafford, daughter of the 3rd Duke of Buckingham, who would be executed in 1521 (see Chapter 2). Norfolk had been married previously, but there were no surviving children from his first marriage to Anne Plantagenet, daughter of Edward IV and Elizabeth Woodville, as all died in infancy or early childhood. Norfolk's children from his first marriage, had they survived, would have been Yorkist royals. Surrey was therefore descended from two distinguished, noble, and even royal, lines; from Edward I on his father's side, and Edward III on his mother's side. He was followed by a younger brother, Thomas, and two sisters, Mary and Katherine. Thomas would be created 1st Viscount Howard of Bindon, by Elizabeth I in 1559. Katherine would briefly be married to Edward Stanley, 3rd Earl of Derby. Mary would make what would be a very illustrious marriage, to Henry Fitzroy, Duke of Richmond and Somerset, the illegitimate son of Henry VIII by his mistress, Bessie Blount. They would not have any children, however, before Fitzroy died in 1536. Whether the marriage was consummated is also a topic for debate. The Howards managed to marry into some of the most respected families in England, but it did not stop them from falling victim to the Tudors.

John Howard, 1st Duke of Norfolk, Henry Howard's great-grandfather, had been slain fighting for Richard III at the Battle of Bosworth Field in 1485 against Henry Tudor. The family had always seemed to be loyal to the crown itself, rather than the person who was sitting on the throne, whoever that might be. As such, Thomas Howard, later created 2nd Duke of Norfolk when the family dukedom was restored to him, was soon released from imprisonment after Bosworth and allowed to begin to climb the ladder of favour at the Tudor court under the new king, Henry VII, and continued under Henry VIII. He would regain the Norfolk dukedom after his success against the Scots in 1513 at the Battle of Flodden Field, which resulted in the death of the Scots' king, James IV. This would pave the way for the long career of Thomas Howard, 3rd Duke of Norfolk, Henry Howard's father, and the accession of two of his nieces, Anne Boleyn, and Katherine Howard, to the English throne as queen consorts as two of the six wives of Henry VIII.

Henry Howard married Frances de Vere, daughter of John de Vere, 15th Earl of Oxford, and together they had five children. All would make solid noble marriages and increase the prestige of the Howards through them, though Henry's own fate and that of his eldest son, Thomas, would diminish the family's prospects somewhat.

* * *

Henry Howard, Earl of Surrey, was born around 1516 or 1517, and was nearly the same age as Princess Mary, later Mary I, who was born in February 1516. His family were at the centre of the King's Great Matter in the 1520s and early 1530s, as it was Henry's own cousin, Anne Boleyn, who was the king's intended and eventual second wife. The Howard family supported the rise of Anne Boleyn and the annulment of Henry VIII's marriage to Katherine of Aragon because they believed it would bring them greater power and prestige at court, as Anne would be in a position to advance the family as a whole, not just her Boleyn relatives. However, Thomas Howard, 3rd Duke of Norfolk, was known to be a staunch Roman Catholic, whereas Anne Boleyn and her immediate family favoured the reformed religion, though how far they wanted the English Reformation to go is a subject of hot debate, especially in recent years. Like his cousin and unlike his father, Henry Howard also appears to have favoured reform over conservatism in religion.

Surrey was raised alongside Henry VIII's illegitimate son, Henry Fitzroy, and the two would become brothers-in-law when Fitzroy married Surrey's sister, Mary, in 1533. Surrey himself would not have been very involved in the early stages of the Great Matter, being only a child at the time, but as he got older he would have understood the wider implications for his family. For part of his early childhood, Surrey lived in Ireland, where his father was lord lieutenant in 1520/1, but when in England, the family moved between several Howard properties including Lambeth and Tendring Hall in Stoke-by-Nayland in Suffolk, as well as Hunsdon in Hertfordshire and Framlingham Castle in Suffolk.[1] The Howard heartlands were based largely in the southeast and Surrey would have been familiar with many of their lands and properties from an early age. He understood the inheritance he stood to gain as heir to a dukedom and that is likely where his pride stemmed from.

Surrey seems to have had repeated run-ins with the law for rash behaviour, which would characterise his later actions and would then lead to his arrest and execution in 1546/7. For instance, in July 1542, Surrey was taken to the Fleet prison, supposedly for challenging a John Leigh to a duel within the bounds of the royal court. When he wrote to the council after his arrest in December 1546, Surrey referred to the confrontation, proclaiming his innocence, declaring 'wherein God knoweth with what danger I escaped notwithstanding mine innocency'.[2] Referring to this incident four years later when he was arrested on much more serious charges of treason suggests that Surrey had acknowledged that he had a rash streak which may have led to his current situation. His spell in the Fleet prison does not seem to have done anything to temper his behaviour. He appears to have enjoyed indulging in drink and gambling which probably enhanced his already volatile personality.

He had a history of doing things which would put him in tricky positions that he would try and talk his way out of. Surrey admitted his recklessness and said he would change his ways. But he would not be able to talk his way out of the treason charges in 1546. Edmund Knyvet, a cousin of Surrey's, would later claim that Surrey had retained a servant who had been with Reginald Pole in Italy.[3] Pole was persona non grata with Henry VIII and had been declared a traitor. Pole continually wrote against the king and bade the English people to act against him. Surrey himself continued to provoke comment with both his words and actions, though he would draw the line at actually rebelling openly against the king. Whether through choice or fear from his arrest is unknown. His temperament suggests that open rebellion may have been something Surrey would engage in.

Surrey married Frances de Vere, the daughter of John de Vere, 15th Earl of Oxford. Oxford was a staunch supporter of the Tudors. His second cousin, the 13th earl, had been in exile with Henry VII before he took the throne and fought for Tudor at Bosworth against Richard III. Henry and Frances would have five children together: Thomas Howard, 4th Duke of Norfolk, who would be executed for treason in 1572; Henry Howard, 1st Earl of Northampton; Jane, who would marry Charles Neville, 6th Earl of Westmorland, who fled to the Continent after being involved in the Northern Rising against Elizabeth I; Katherine, who married Henry Berkeley, 7th Baron Berkeley; and Margaret, who was born after her father's execution, and would marry Henry Scrope, 9th Baron Scrope of Bolton. Surrey's line would live on after his disgrace and death through his children. After Surrey's execution, Frances would remarry to Thomas Steyning in 1553, with whom she had a further two children: Henry and Mary. They would not have the royal blood of which Surrey was so proud and would prove his downfall. Frances would outlive Surrey by thirty years and would be buried beside him.

Henry Howard, Earl of Surrey, was a notable Tudor poet. Several of his works were published alongside those of Sir Thomas Wyatt and others in the likes of the Devonshire Manuscript, which is currently held in the collection of the British Library. Surrey and Wyatt were the first English poets to write in the sonnet form, paving the way for William Shakespeare nearly fifty years later. Shakespeare is often credited with being the first

Englishman to write a sonnet, but it is not true. When Surrey completed a translation of Virgil's *Aeneid* he was also the first English poet to write in blank verse, which is unrhyming metric rhythmic verse. Poetry is often thought to have to rhyme to maintain the rhythm, but Surrey's verse proves that poetry can still maintain its rhythm without needing to rhyme. Though one of his most intriguing poems does in fact rhyme. Surrey's poetry was hugely inspired by real people and events, like 'Eache beast can choose his fere' which portrays the feuding friendship between the Howards and the Seymours, and lamented the tragedies which befell the Howards, even before Surrey's own arrest and execution.

> A lion saw I late, as white as any snow,
> Which seemed well to lead the race, his port the same did show.
> Upon the gentle beast to gaze it pleased me,
> For still methought he seemed well of noble blood to be.
> And as he pranced before, still seeking for a make,
> As who would say, 'There is none here, I trow, will me forsake',
> I might perceive a Wolf as white as whalèsbone,
> A fairer beast of fresher hue, beheld I never none;
> Save that her looks were coy, and froward eke her grace:
> Unto the which this gentle beast gan him advance apace,
> And with a beck full low he bowed at her feet,
> In humble wise, as who would say, 'I am too far unmeet'.[4]

A white lion was the symbol of the Howard family, whereas the white wolf was a symbol of the Stanhope family. Anne Stanhope was Countess of Hertford, wife to Edward Seymour, 1st Earl of Hertford, who would later become Lord Protector to the young Edward VI. The poem implies that Surrey had approached Anne to dance with her, finding her beautiful but aloof, and it goes on to recount her stinging rebuke of him, which appears to have influenced the formation of the poem itself. In the course of the poem Surrey went on to express his own views about himself and his place in the world:

> While that I live and breathe, such shall my custom be
> In wildness of the woods to seek my prey, where pleaseth me;
> Where many one shall rue, that never made offence:

Thus your refuse against my power shall boot them no defence.
And for revenge thereof I vow and swear thereto,
A thousand spoils I shall commit I never thought to do.[5]

What comes from these six lines in particular is that Surrey claimed he would seek his prey 'where pleaseth me', implying he would do so without permission or acceptance, even from the king. He appears to be railing against those who did not believe in or accept his power and his rightful place, saying that he would get revenge against those who try to stop him. It is almost a foreshadowing of what is to come, that would lead to his death. Understanding Surrey's poetry can help to give an insight into his character and state of mind as it is his own voice coming to us from the past.

* * *

In essence, the Earl of Surrey's downfall came from flaunting his royal blood in an ill-conceived attempt to control the minority of Edward VI.[6] It was known by 1546 that Henry VIII was nearing the end of his life, and that Edward VI would come to the throne in his minority, needing guidance and either a council or a protector to govern in his name. Possibly the arrests of Norfolk and Surrey, execution of Surrey, and intended execution of Norfolk, were Henry VIII trying to remove what he perceived as the last dynastic threat to his son, knowing that he was dying and had limited time left to act to protect him. Henry VIII would have known of the last Lord Protector of a king in his minority; Richard of Gloucester who acted as protector for the young Edward V in 1483. Richard usurped the young Edward V within months of his acceding to the throne and claimed the throne himself as Richard III. Edward V and his brother, Richard of Shrewsbury, were imprisoned in the Tower of London, and vanished, assumed murdered by Richard III, although this has never been proven. They became known to history as the Princes in the Tower. Richard was killed by Henry's father, Henry VII, on the battlefield at Bosworth. Perhaps Henry VIII feared that, if he appointed a protector, the same thing that happened to the princes could happen to his young son who was around the same age.

The Imperial ambassador in England, François Van der Delft, wrote to Charles V on 14 December 1546 regarding the arrests of Surrey and Norfolk that 'people assert confidently that it is because of a secret discourse between them concerning the King's illness six weeks ago, the object being to obtain the government of the Prince'.[7] In a letter to Mary of Hungary, Charles V's sister and governor of the Netherlands, Van der Delft wrote that they 'are said to have entertained some ambiguous designs when the King was ill'.[8] The letter to Mary of Hungary implies some uncertainty regarding Surrey and Norfolk's plans, where the letter to Charles V suggests that their plans are well-known, though that is only a rumour. In treasonous situations rumours abounded and could sometimes be used as additional ammunition against the accused.

There were concerns from both Catholics and Protestants in England over who would have control when Henry VIII died. Surrey believed that his father, the Duke of Norfolk, should be either protector or head of the council as the foremost noble in the country and that, if his father died, he would take his place at the head of government. Surrey resented the rise of the Seymour family, particularly Edward Seymour, 1st Earl of Hertford, as the elder uncle of Prince Edward. The Howards had little regard for 'new men' like the Seymours without much noble blood in their veins. Surrey had called Thomas Cromwell a 'foul churl' and William Paget a 'mean creature'.[9] He claimed that the new men would 'by their wills, leave no nobleman on life!'.[10] There would be fewer high-ranking nobles at the end of the Tudor century, but that was not because of the new men, but because of accusations of treason brought against the nobility, whether rightly or forged.

The position of the Howard family had been greatly damaged by Henry VIII's failed marriage to his fifth wife, Katherine Howard. Henry had married Katherine just weeks after the annulment of his fourth marriage to Anne of Cleves in July 1540. After the Northern Progress in summer 1541, it was found that Katherine had sexual experiences prior to her marriage when she was in the household of the dowager Duchess of Norfolk, her step-grandmother. While this was being investigated, it was then discovered that Katherine may have had relations with a member of the king's Privy Chamber, Thomas Culpeper, while she was married to the king. This was reminiscent of charges brought against Anne Boleyn, Katherine's cousin, in 1536. Two of Surrey's cousins had married the king, and both were executed on charges of adultery. Adultery in a queen was accounted treason as it threatened the succession. Any pregnancy could not be confirmed to be from the king, so the legitimacy of any child born to an adulterous queen could be questioned.

These two failed royal marriages damaged the Howard family's standing. Both Katherine Howard and Anne Boleyn were nieces to Thomas Howard, 3rd Duke of Norfolk, and Norfolk managed to distance himself from them when they fell, but the king's trust in the Howards was nevertheless damaged. In the aftermath of Katherine Howard's fall and execution, many of her Howard relatives were questioned and arrested, including the dowager Duchess of Norfolk, who it was thought had neglected her charge in allowing the girls in her care to run free and entertain men in their rooms at night. On 15 December 1541, Norfolk wrote to Henry VIII that he had learnt of the arrests of 'mine ungracious mother-in-law, mine unhappy brother and his wife, with my lewd sister of Brydgewater'.[11] Norfolk's stepbrother, Lord William Howard and his wife, Margaret, along with Lady Katherine Bridgewater (who was Katherine Howard's aunt), Anne Howard (Katherine's sister-in-law), and her step-grandmother, Agnes, Dowager Duchess of Norfolk, were all arrested, tried, and found guilty of misprision of treason. Their estates and possessions were forfeited, and they were sentenced to life in prison. But within a year all were released and pardoned.

Norfolk followed on from mentioning the arrests and crimes by wanting to know if he was still in favour with the king. He had survived Anne Boleyn's downfall so there was no reason to think he could not do the same here. However, the king was not as forgiving as he had been before. Norfolk and Surrey were not arrested as part of this investigation, but they must have felt like they were losing any power they had because of the actions of others and 'Norfolk was soon to discover that his influence at court had waned for ever'.[12] For his son, Surrey, especially, this seems to have led to resentment. Norfolk was absent from Katherine's execution at the Tower of London on 13 February 1542, though Surrey was present to see his cousin die.

Some of the controversy surrounding Katherine Howard's fall does not come from the actions of Katherine herself, but from the Howards, of which Norfolk was the head. It has been suggested that reformers like the Seymours and Archbishop Cranmer acted against Katherine because Norfolk was known to be a religious conservative, quite possibly against the royal supremacy, or at least it was rumoured that was the king's view. This then feeds into the possibility that Surrey and Norfolk were brought down in 1546/7 because the king wanted to protect the royal supremacy. He wanted those around the young Edward VI to be men such as the Seymours who would protect England's independence from Rome, though I doubt

Henry VIII realised that those around the young prince were more radical than he wanted. Henry VIII was still essentially Catholic when he died, believing in the Mass and the sacraments, though without the figurehead of the Pope. Edward VI's reign would abolish a lot of these Catholic rites. This religious divide can help to explain why Norfolk and Surrey's enemies brought the pair down as it became obvious that the old king was dying. When Henry VIII remarried in 1543 to Katherine Parr, she was known to be a supporter of reform rather than the traditional Catholic rites, and Henry VIII chose to leave her as regent while he travelled to France within a year of their marriage.

Henry VIII had campaigned in France in 1544, and his armies had seized control of the city of Boulogne. The original plan had been to march on Paris in conjunction with Emperor Charles V, but Henry VIII decided instead that his main objective would be capturing besieged cities, especially Boulogne. Charles was furious but Henry argued that he would not be able to supply his army without taking Boulogne.[13] Henry entered Boulogne in triumph on 18 September 1546. The king spent less than two weeks in Boulogne before returning home. Charles V had made peace with Francis I of France, so Henry had to maintain his French possessions without Imperial support. Surrey had been appointed marshal of the army sent to capture Montreuil and was wounded on 19 September 1546 after a failed attempt to storm the city. He assisted in evacuating the retreating army to Calais, so did not cover himself in glory with a great victory.

In summer 1545, nearly a year after the capture of Boulogne, Surrey was sent to command the vanguard of the army to defend Boulogne from French attacks to try and re-take the city. By 9 August he had marshalled 5,000 men and on 15 August he sailed to Calais where he gathered a further 3,000 men. In early September 1545 Surrey was appointed lieutenant-general of the king for all of England's continental possessions.[14] Surrey, however, encouraged the king to pursue further conquests in France against the advice of the council who were trying to persuade the king to cede Boulogne back to the French. Surrey appears to have been reprimanded by Henry VIII for becoming involved in skirmishes around Boulogne and needlessly endangering himself. On 7 January 1546, Surrey 'suffered an ignominious and portentous defeat' at St Étienne. Captains were killed and troops fled. On 19 February 1546, Sir William Paget sent Surrey the news that Edward Seymour, 1st Earl of Hertford, would replace him as lieutenant-general, and on 21 March Surrey was summoned home as the king had received reports of treachery. Surrey left, believing he would clear his name and return. He would not regain his position or military honour, but in recognition of his service he was granted the rent of estates and buildings at Wymondham Priory in Norfolk.[15] The fact that Surrey was not allowed to return to France suggests some kind of poor management, and the fact that he initially was not allowed access to the king on his return demonstrates the king's anger with him. This anger would build as more evidence against Surrey came to light back in England after his return.

A key piece of evidence against Surrey came from the fact that he had changed his coat of arms to reflect his royal origins, based on a shield carved in stone in his house in Norfolk. Surrey had reassumed the arms of his grandfather, Edward Stafford, 3rd Duke of Buckingham, who was executed in 1521 (see Chapter 2), which included the royal arms and lilies inherited from Thomas of Woodstock, son of Edward III. By implication, this reversed Buckingham's attainder and reinstated a claim to the throne for himself and his descendants. Surrey also, controversially, included the arms of Edward the Confessor.[16] He could not be a direct descendant of Edward the Confessor as Edward had not had children. This was a direct challenge to royal authority, as only the king and a few other members of the royal family, like the queen and prince of Wales, were allowed to use the royal arms. This was not just Surrey asserting his noble pedigree, but also his royal connections and a potential claim to the throne. It was seen as a sign he actually intended to usurp the throne for himself and his heirs. Henry VIII would have been eager to nip this in the bud and make the throne as safe as possible for the young Edward VI. This would certainly be considered treason as it was attempting to undermine the line of succession, as per the Treason Act 1534 in acting against the king, queen, or their heir, 'to deprive them or any of them of their dignity, title, or name of their royal estates'.[17] From the evidence we have, Surrey certainly seems to have been guilty of treason under the law as it stood at the time.

An intriguing part of the evidence against Surrey was the testimony of his sister, Mary, Duchess of Richmond, the widow of Henry VIII's illegitimate son, Henry Fitzroy, who died in 1536, not long after Anne Boleyn. Mary herself would not remarry after Fitzroy's death and her presence at court dwindled after her brother's execution and Henry VIII's death in January 1547. Mary would claim that Surrey saw Edward Seymour as 'his enemy' and was 'so much incensed' against him.[18] He struggled to countenance a proposed marriage between his sister, Mary, and Edward Seymour's brother, Thomas. Mary also claimed that she was not inclined towards the marriage, though the Duke of Norfolk, the Seymour family and the king seemed to favour it. Gawain Carew would later testify that Mary was told by Surrey to dissemble when speaking of the matter to the king,

> 'that the King's Majesty should take occasion to speak with her again; and thus by length of time it is possible that that King should take such a fantasy to you that ye shall be able to govern like Madame d'Étampes. Which should not only be a mean to help herself, but all her friends should receive a commodity by the same. Whereupon she defied her brother, and said that all they should perish and she would cut her own throat rather than she would consent to such a villainy'.[19]

Anne de Pisseleu d'Heilly, Duchess of Étampes, was the chief mistress of the French king, Francis I. She wielded great political power in France, and her brothers all gained good positions due to her influence with the king. Surrey's reference to her suggests that he hoped his sister could have similar influence with Henry VIII if he took her as his mistress. Mary, however, was the Henry VIII's daughter-in-law and there was a twenty-eight-year age gap. It would create a problem of affinity as the pair were too closely related. This perhaps was not completely unusual in the sixteenth century, but it is easy to understand why Mary did not want what her brother suggested. The king was also ill with an ulcerated leg and had executed two of his wives. Surrey hoped that, if his sister became the king's mistress, she could persuade him to make either himself or their father head of a regency council, or even protector of the realm during Edward VI's minority. Mary's evidence would be used against Surrey at his trial, leading to his execution.

Surrey's pride and inbred arrogance of his position as a member of one of the most powerful families in England led to complacency.[20] He came to believe that, as he and his father were the top peers in the country, they should have control of Edward VI during his minority. Norfolk's mistress, Bess Holland, reported Norfolk's words that the king was sick and could not survive long, leaving the country divided over religion. Imagining the king's death was treason by the 1534 Treason Act, so in this respect Norfolk was also guilty according to the law. There was a rumour that Surrey had taken to riding around London with a group of mounted retainers and this sparked fears that he would use them to mount a rebellion against the king to seize control by force. Whether Norfolk knew of Surrey's plan is unclear, but he may well have heard rumours spreading in London.

One of Surrey's own servants had been on the Continent with the 'traitor' Reginald Pole, who was a staunch Catholic and supporter of the Pope, so this was also used against Surrey and his father as proof of their complicity in a Catholic plot to overthrow the English Church and seize control. Imperial ambassador Van der Delft wrote 'their hope of liberation is small'.[21] Van der Delft had replaced Eustace Chapuys as ambassador in 1545 due to the latter's worsening health. Treason was the most serious of all possible charges against a person, and very few managed to escape once it was brought against them.

*   *   *

Surrey was arrested by Anthony Wingfield, a member of the Privy Council, on 2 December 1546 after the Privy Council received some damaging information about him from Sir Richard Southwell, one of Surrey's former friends.[22] He was taken to Ely Place at Holborn (the London residence of Thomas Goodrich, Bishop of Ely) for questioning, rather than directly to the Tower of London. He remained there for five or six days before then being marched through the streets of London from Holborn to the Tower. He would only leave the Tower for his trial at the Guildhall in London, and then for his execution. Odet de Selve, who was a French diplomat on embassy to England in 1546 and 1547 and saw the king's final year in person, wrote to Claude d'Annebault, the Admiral of France, on 12 December 1547 that he had only been told that morning, ten days after Surrey's arrest, that he was in the Tower on two principal charges 'one that he had the means of attempting the castle of Hardelot, when he was at Boulogne, and neglected it, the other that he said there were some who made no great account of him but he trusted one day to make them very small … many hold that Surrey will suffer death'.[23] The 'some who made no great account of him' may have referred to the Seymours and other 'new men' who Surrey believed were not worthy to have power, but whom Henry VIII relied upon to govern the country. Selve also reported that Southwell had been arrested but released. The belief that Surrey would die would prove entirely correct.

A list of questions had been drawn up before Surrey's interrogation and survives in the archives, so it is easy to see what Surrey was suspected of, and what the council wanted to try and gain evidence of. The first ten questions are regarding whether Surrey bore the arms of Edward the Confessor, so this was obviously of prime importance to the king and council. Did he believe that he had the right to bear them, and did it give him the sense that he was an heir to the English throne? Number eleven on the list has been edited and reads 'if the King should die in my lord Prince's tender age, whether you have devised who should govern him and the realm' which was corrected from 'who ought within the realm to be protector and governor of him during nonage'.[24] This is interesting because the original question asked Surrey directly his thoughts where he might refuse to answer, where the edited version asks for his opinion on the matter which leaves more room for embellishment, where Surrey might be more likely to incriminate himself. Questions twelve and thirteen are along similar lines. Surrey was brash and prideful so asking an open-ended question used his personality against him in a way.

Question fourteen asked whether Surrey 'procured any person to dissemble in anything with the King's Majesty to th'intent the same might grow in his favour for the better compassing of your purposes' which was changed from 'procured your sister or any other woman to be the King's concubine or not'.[25] This is perhaps what the Duchess of Richmond took umbrage to. Mary was a noble woman, well-brought up, and was a daughter-in-law of the king that her brother was trying to persuade her to sleep with. The fact that this question reached the council suggests that the questions were potentially drafted after they had spoken to the duchess, and she told them what Surrey had asked her to do, or that it was known around court, implying that Surrey himself may have been the source in speaking so freely, as he was wont to do. The rewording of the question again indicates that the council wanted Surrey to be free to elaborate and incriminate himself, and not just giving him yes or no answer questions, or anything he might take exception to. It is a good read on Surrey's character and his prideful ambition.

Thomas Howard, 3rd Duke of Norfolk, was arrested on his return to London on 12 December 1546. He had been at one of his many properties but travelled to the capital on hearing of his son's arrest. When he had heard that Surrey had been arrested, Norfolk wrote letters which were used against him, and he was taken down the Thames to the Tower. Both men wrote to the king to beg for clemency. Norfolk requested that 'he may know what is laid to his charge and have some word of comfort from his Majesty', proclaiming that 'some great enemy has informed the King untruly; for God knows, he never thought one untrue thought against the King or his succession'.[26] Norfolk eventually admitted on 12 January 1547 that he had committed misprision of treason by concealing the wrongdoing of his son, Surrey, but refuted any charges of treason he himself committed. When he was questioned Surrey would claim that 'my matter is prejudicial to no creature, unless to myself'.[27] As his cousin, Anne Boleyn, attempted to do before him, Surrey is taking all the blame for the charges onto his own shoulders, trying to save his father. Norfolk would survive, though not through Surrey's efforts. Norfolk would have shared his son's fate if not for the death of Henry VIII himself. The king would not forgive Norfolk this time.

Norfolk's, statement to the council does not touch on Surrey's treason, but on separate questions concerning Norfolk's own actions. Perhaps Norfolk had not been told at this point exactly what Surrey was accused of, so he could not answer those specific questions. Or maybe the council wanted Norfolk to talk and not knowing the specific charges he might unwittingly reveal something useful against either himself or Surrey. Norfolk was asked whether he used a cipher, to which he replied that he only used a cipher when given one by the king for correspondence. There was nothing suspicious there. He was also questioned over his religious beliefs, as Norfolk was known to favour the Catholic religion, to which he replied, 'as for the Bishop of Rome, if I had 20 lives I would rather have spent them all than that he should have any power in this realm'.[28] Whether these were Norfolk's true beliefs, or something he was saying to try and save himself is unclear, but he also said that the Pope was the king's enemy, and Norfolk had been notably loyal to the crown so perhaps he spoke his own truth; he chose the crown over his religion. Norfolk had been trying to arrange marriages for his children – his daughter, Mary, Duchess of Richmond, to Thomas Seymour, uncle to the future Edward VI, and one of his granddaughters (Surrey's daughter) to the son of the Lord Great Chamberlain, Edward Seymour, 1st Earl of Hertford, later Duke of Somerset. He was looking to create great alliances with those who had the power in England. This could be read as furthering Surrey's own plans, though Surrey had railed openly against the Seymours.

It is the final section of Norfolk's statement that is the most interesting, however. He seemed to create a rollcall of his greatest achievements and acts of loyalty to the Tudor crown. His father, Thomas Howard, 2nd Duke of Norfolk, sat as a judge in the treason trial against Edward Stafford, 3rd Duke of Buckingham, in 1521. He goes on to mention his two nieces married to the king (Anne Boleyn and Katherine Howard) and how they disliked him, though it is not clear how this would help his case. He distanced himself from them during their falls and managed to survive, maintaining his position at court, though he had taken advantage of their power while they had it to try and gain greater power and riches. Norfolk then wrote of his role in the putting down of the Catholic rebellion, the Pilgrimage of Grace, in 1536/7, and of how he turned against his mother-in-law who was convicted of misprision of treason in the aftermath of the Katherine Howard affair in 1541/2. Norfolk closed by stating 'I have always shown myself a true man to my Sovereign, and, since these things done, have received more profits of his highness than before', signing himself 'his Highness' poure prisoner, T. Norffolk'.[29] Perhaps by showing how loyal and useful he had been, Norfolk had hoped to induce the king to mercy. Emotion would not have worked with Henry VIII, as he knew, but perhaps a more logical approach could. It would fail.

With both men under arrest, a party including Sir John Gates, Sir Richard Southwell, and Wymond Carew, was sent to the Norfolk residence of Kenninghall via Thetford, to question other family members, including Surrey's pregnant wife, Frances, Norfolk's mistress, Bess Holland, and his daughter and Surrey's sister, Mary, Duchess of Richmond. They left London on Sunday 12 December and arrived at Kenninghall on the evening of Monday 13 December. Mary, Duchess of Richmond, was described as 'sore perplexed, trembling, and like to fall down'.[30] It was decided to break up the household, which suggested that there was little to no chance of a reprieve for the two men. The Norfolk properties and wealth would be forfeit to the crown, restored on the release of the Duke of Norfolk from the Tower in 1553 on the accession of Mary I. Frances de Vere, Countess of Surrey, and her children remained at Kenninghall, while Mary, Duchess of Richmond, and Bess Holland were taken to London.

The countess was around six or seven months pregnant when her husband was arrested, so care was taken for her health. Mary, Duchess of Richmond, proclaimed that 'although constrained by nature to love her father, whom she ever thought a true subject, and her brother whom she noteth to be a rash man' she would tell the truth.[31] She seemed at times to have an axe to grind with her brother, whether it was because she opposed the marriage proposed for her to Thomas Seymour, or because he had tried to persuade her to become Henry VIII's mistress to gain power that way, is unknown. The Duke of Norfolk himself said, when questioned, that he had approached the king for his assistance to arrange a marriage between Mary and Thomas Seymour, so perhaps Surrey was just being over-zealous in promoting his father's wishes.[32] It must not be forgotten that Mary was also daughter-in-law to Henry VIII as she had married the king's illegitimate son, Henry Fitzroy, who had died in 1536. Perhaps this was in her favour, along with the fact that she spoke what she knew. She seemed to believe her father innocent and her brother a rash idiot rather than a treasonous mastermind.

Henry Howard, Earl of Surrey, was tried before a special commission at the Guildhall on 13 January 1547 and was sentenced to death for treason. It was only on the day of his trial that Surrey discovered the full nature of the charges against him. He had largely been kept in the dark up to his point, likely to shock him and stop him forming a coherent defence. Allegedly, the peers initially seemed reluctant to condemn Surrey as he defended himself well against the charges, and Henry VIII had to intervene personally to ensure he was condemned.[33] When the king's wishes were known there were few who would go against him for fear of being executed themselves. It seems likely that this was because Henry VIII knew that he was dying and was determined to prevent his son being overthrown on his death and protect the succession, although Henry VIII did not seem to have any problems executing those who he saw as a threat or who acted against him or his son's interests. Surrey certainly seems to have committed treason under the law by combining his arms with those of Edward the Confessor and talking about the king's death. The peers still seem to have taken time over the verdict, however, suggesting a significant level of doubt over the veracity of the charges.

Surrey was beheaded just a few days before the death of Henry VIII, on 19 January 1547, aged around 30. The old king died nine days later on 28 January, saving the aging Thomas Howard, 3rd Duke of Norfolk from sharing his son's fate. Norfolk had been due to be executed at 9am on 28 January, but Henry VIII died just hours earlier. Surrey was the old king's final victim, though there would be plenty more noble executions under his son and daughters. He was buried first in the Church of All Hallows near the Tower of London, before being moved to the Church of St Michael's at

Framlingham in Suffolk, where many of the Howard family are also buried, including the king's illegitimate son and Surrey's brother-in-law, Henry Fitzroy. Surrey is buried in a tomb with his wife, Frances de Vere, who died in 1577, outliving her husband by thirty years. She would remarry in 1553.

Ultimately, Surrey died as a result of his own pride and idiocy and the king's paranoia over the succession. He had flaunted his royal blood and noble connections, and allegedly attempted to thwart the king's plans for his son's minority. Henry VIII, in his paranoid and ill state could not overlook this, and Surrey was the final person to be executed by a king who killed those high and low who had been loyal to him and loved him. Surrey followed the likes of the Duke of Buckingham, Anne Boleyn, Margaret Pole, and Katherine Howard to the scaffold to have his head struck off.

1. The Tudor succession showing (from left to right): Philip II of Spain and Mary I (1553–1558); Henry VIII (1509–1547); Edward VI (1547–1553); and Elizabeth I (1558–1603).

2. The White Tower, the central building at the Tower of London, a familiar site to all those in this book who were imprisoned within the Tower complex before their executions.

3. A cartoon of the pretender, Perkin Warbeck, reading his confession that he was not in fact Richard, Duke of York, in front of the London crowds. Warbeck would play a critical role in the execution of Edward Plantagenet, 17th Earl of Warwick.

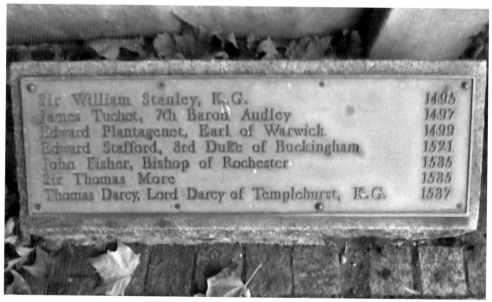

4. One of the memorial stones on Tower Hill, commemorating Edward Plantagenet, 17th Earl of Warwick, executed 1499, and Edward Stafford, 3rd Duke of Buckingham, executed 1521.

5. A silvered brass likeness of King Henry VIII. Henry VIII would execute two of his wives, Anne Boleyn and Katherine Howard, and countless other nobles, including Margaret Pole, Countess of Salisbury, and Edward Stafford, 3rd Duke of Buckingham.

6. Anne Boleyn, second wife of Henry VIII. She is the only one of those discussed in this book not beheaded with an axe, but by a French executioner with a sword. It is widely thought that she was innocent of the charges of adultery against her in 1536.

7. Graffiti at the Tower of London featuring Anne Boleyn's falcon emblem, though uncrowned. It is thought that this was carved by one of the five men who were executed for adultery with Anne, one of whom was her own brother.

8. The execution memorial on Tower Green within the Tower of London, which commemorates, among others, Anne Boleyn and Katherine Howard. The actual site of the executions is now thought to be between the White Tower and the Waterloo Barracks rather than the location of the memorial.

9. Katherine Howard, fifth wife of Henry VIII. She was executed alongside one of her ladies-in-waiting, Jane Boleyn, Lady Rochford, sister-in-law to Katherine's own executed cousin, Anne Boleyn. She was just a teenager when she went to her death.

10. The interior of the Chapel of St Peter ad Vincula at the Tower of London. Anne Boleyn, Katherine Howard, Lady Jane Rochford, Lady Jane Grey, the countess of Salisbury, the Earl of Essex, and the Dukes of Norfolk, Somerset, and Northumberland are buried beneath the altar.

11. The site of the scaffold and memorial on Tower Hill, London. Those executed here include the Earls of Surrey and Essex, and the Dukes of Norfolk, Somerset, and Northumberland. This was the site of public beheadings.

12. Henry Howard, Earl of Surrey, was Henry VIII's final execution in 1547. His father, the 3rd Duke of Norfolk, was due to be executed on the very morning of Henry VIII's death. He was spared by the king's death.

13. Edward Seymour, 1st Duke of Somerset. He was uncle to King Edward VI, and Protector of the Realm. Often known as 'the Good Duke' as opposed to his successor as Protector, the Duke of Northumberland, known as 'the Bad Duke'.

14. A block and axe displayed in the Tower of London. This would have been very similar to that used to execute the men and women detailed in this book, all except Anne Boleyn, who was executed with a French sword.

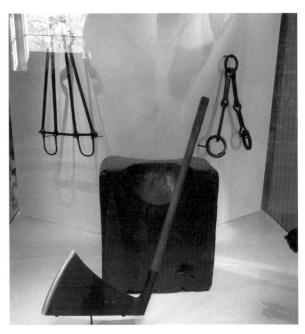

15. A romanticised etching of the execution of Lady Jane Grey in 1554. Although known as the Nine Days Queen, Jane was in fact queen for fourteen days from Edward VI's death until her own overthrow; Edward's death had been kept secret for several days afterwards.

16. Graffiti at the Tower of London featuring the name 'Jane' and the Grey family crest. It is thought that this may have been carved by one of the Dudley brothers, who were imprisoned in the Tower at the same time. Jane was married to Guildford Dudley.

17. Queen Mary I. She was responsible for the executions of Lady Jane Grey and John Dudley, 1st Duke of Northumberland. Northumberland appears to have orchestrated Jane's usurpation of the throne on Edward VI's death and Mary blamed him entirely.

18. Queen Elizabeth I. Both Robert Devereux, 2nd Earl of Essex, and Thomas Howard, 4th Duke of Norfolk, were executed at her hand. Both had been involved in rebellions against the queen and they posed a huge threat to her safety and security.

19. Thomas Howard, 4th Duke of Norfolk. A cousin of Elizabeth I, he became involved in plotting against her, including a suggestion that he would marry Mary Queen of Scots. Elizabeth signed and ripped up the warrant for his death several times before it finally went ahead in 1572.

Henry Courtenay, Earl of Devon 1538
Thomas Cromwell, Earl of Essex, K. G. 1540
Henry Howard, Earl of Surrey 1547
Edward Seymour, Duke of Somerset 1552
Sir Thomas Wyatt 1554
Thomas Howard, 4th Duke of Norfolk 1572
Thomas Wentworth, Earl of Strafford 1641

20. One of the memorial stones on Tower Hill, which commemorates Henry Howard, Earl of Surrey, Edward Seymour, 1st Duke of Somerset, and Thomas Howard, 4th Duke of Norfolk, all of whom were executed on this spot.

21. Robert Devereux, 2nd Earl of Essex. He led a rebellion against Elizabeth I in 1601 to regain his lost power and wealth, but it failed. He was said to be Elizabeth's last favourite and the queen herself would die just two years later.

Chapter 7

Thomas Seymour,
1st Baron Seymour of Sudeley – 1549

S ir Thomas Seymour, brother to Henry VIII's third wife, Jane Seymour, was one of the most scandalous men of the Tudor period. He tried to compromise a princess of the royal blood while married to the dowager queen of England, then attempted to kidnap the young King Edward VI. He was too ambitious for his own good and would end under the executioner's axe with the death warrant signed by his nephew, the king, and endorsed by his brother, the Lord Protector. There were suggestions that Seymour had lost his mind as these were not the actions of a sane man, perhaps driven mad by the death of his wife, Katherine Parr, as a result of childbirth. However, another suggestion was that he was jealous of his brother's power and authority in England and was ambitious to share some of that power himself.

The Seymours were an old family but did not have particularly noble ties until the sixteenth century. They were a courtly family in the sense of their general presence, but not in the way that the Boleyns were in leading a court faction in the 1520s and early 1530s.[1] The Seymours were very much in the background at this point. Thomas Seymour's father, Sir John Seymour, had helped to suppress the Cornish Rebellion in 1497 and had accompanied Henry VIII and the royal court to the Field of the Cloth of Gold summit in 1520. Thomas' brother, Edward, was created Viscount Beauchamp of Hache in 1536 when the king married his sister, Jane, and was then created Earl of Hertford the following year when Jane gave birth to Henry VIII's much anticipated son and heir, the future Edward VI. Thomas, however, did not receive the same distinctions at Edward at this time which likely fuelled his jealousy and the rivalry between the brothers.

The historian, David Loades, traces the family ancestry back to the late seventh century and there is not really a noble connection in the direct paternal ancestry of Thomas Seymour. The family was steady but not particularly distinguished. However, the Seymours were in fact related to the Boleyns through Thomas's maternal great-grandmother, Elizabeth

Cheyney. From Elizabeth's first marriage to Frederick Tylney, there was a daughter, Elizabeth Tylney, who married Thomas Howard, then Earl of Surrey, but later became the 2nd Duke of Norfolk. He was the father of Elizabeth Boleyn, mother of Anne Boleyn, and Edmund Howard, father of Katherine Howard, the second and fifth wives of Henry VIII respectively. When Elizabeth Cheyney's first husband died, she remarried to Sir John Say, and they had a daughter, Anne Say, who married Henry Wentworth. They were the parents of Margery Wentworth, the mother of Jane, Edward, and Thomas Seymour. Thus, Thomas Seymour was a second cousin to both Anne Boleyn and Katherine Howard, and Thomas Howard, 3rd Duke of Norfolk was a first cousin once removed. The maternal side of their family was certainly more noble than the paternal, but most courtly families were interrelated in some way, so it is not that singular. People married to build up their family bloodline, as it seems John Seymour did.

The Seymour name has an interesting history. It has also been seen in documents as 'Semel' or 'St Maur'. It appears that 'St Maur' was the original form in the mid-thirteenth century with William St Maur, but by the end of the fourteenth century it had been corrupted to 'Seymour'. We see it spelled 'Semel' in a letter from the Spanish ambassador, Eustace Chapuys, to Charles V of Spain.[2] This was perhaps a European form of the name Seymour, or a corruption of the correct spelling. There was no standardised spelling in the sixteenth century, so it was not unusual to see things, even names, spelled several different ways.

The Seymours were brought to prominence by Henry VIII's interest in Jane Seymour during the breakdown of his marriage to his second wife, Anne Boleyn. Jane was so different to Anne which helps to explain perhaps why Henry was so attracted to her and chose to take her as his third wife. Thomas and Edward Seymour had both made progress in their careers at court before the king's interest in their sister, but they likely would not have achieved the titles they did without the king's marriage to Jane. She produced the son and heir who would become Edward VI in 1547 on the death of Henry VIII. The Seymours thus were related to royalty, with Thomas Seymour being uncle to Edward VI, and brother-in-law to Henry VIII. Thomas's direct line, however, would die out. He only had a single daughter, Mary, by his wife, Katherine Parr, and she vanishes from the historical record, thought to have died in infancy.

* * *

Thomas Seymour was the third surviving son born to Sir John Seymour and Margery Wentworth, probably at the family seat of Wolf Hall in Wiltshire in 1508 or 1509 and is usually assumed to be older than his sister, Jane, whose birth date is also given around this time. His later years suggest that tutors were not successful in interesting Thomas in intellectual pursuits or reading, and he does not seem to have had much knowledge of Latin, though was fluent in English and probably French, as many courtiers were. Unlike many younger sons of the nobility, he was not intended for the church or an academic career. From what we know of his personality these careers would not have suited him. Thomas was always intended for a life at court and probably around 1525 or 1526 Sir John placed Thomas into the household of Sir Francis Bryan, who was also a kinsman of the Seymours, as a second cousin to Thomas, Edward, and Jane. On 2 October 1536, Thomas Seymour was made a Gentleman of the Privy Chamber, undoubtedly connected to the fact that he was now the king's brother-in-law, his sister having married the king at the end of May that year after Anne Boleyn's execution. Not much seems to be known of Thomas at this time. He had minor employment at court and appears to have been sent on several diplomatic missions to other European courts.

As has been briefly mentioned above, Thomas Seymour did not receive the same level of plaudits and rewards as his brother, Edward, did when their sister, Jane, married the king and gave birth to Prince Edward. It is possible that the jealousy of his brother began here. Both were related to the new prince in the same way though perhaps Edward was seen as more capable and useful. Thomas would receive lands from the king, though not to the extent of Edward, and likely through the mediation of Thomas Cromwell rather than his brother or sister's influence.[3] The siblings do not appear to have been particularly close in the way that, for example, Anne and George Boleyn were. Though this may have been seen as a good thing, given that Anne and George were accused of incest for their closeness.

Henry VIII named Thomas Seymour as one of the assistant councillors in his will, appointed to the regency council to assist Edward VI in his minority, probably because he was an uncle of the new king. Henry VIII also left Seymour £200 (around £55,000 today) in his will. This was nothing compared to what his brother had, but Edward Seymour did oblige Thomas and on 16 February 1547 Thomas Seymour was created 1st Baron Seymour of Sudeley in Gloucestershire and given additional lands worth £500 per year. He was also made Lord High Admiral, given a full place on the Privy Council, and made a Knight of the Garter.[4] For Thomas, however, this still does not seem to have been enough. He believed he was not accorded the respect he deserved as the king's uncle, and he thought that he should be on equal footing with his brother who, against the wishes of Henry VIII's will, was made Lord Protector. Henry VIII had not wanted a protector, but instead a council who ruled together and had equal power and authority.

Thomas Seymour's road to the executioner's axe began with the death of Henry VIII in January 1547 and Seymour's marriage to Henry's widow, Katherine Parr, just a few months later. The two seemed to be planning to marry before Henry VIII had set his sights on Katherine in 1547, but Katherine knew that she did not really have a choice in marrying the king once he had chosen her. The precise date of Katherine and Thomas' wedding is unknown as it was conducted in secret, though it was around May 1547, and was made public in late June 1547. This was considered too early after the king's death for a queen dowager to remarry, and it did harm to Katherine Parr's relationship with Princess Mary, who thought that Katherine had sullied her father's memory by remarrying so quickly. It did not do the same damage to Katherine's relationships with Princess Elizabeth and Edward VI, both of whom continued to have a warm and affectionate relationship with their stepmother.

Widows, especially royal widows, were expected to observe a period of mourning which would have been more than five or six months. And they were expected to gain permission from the new monarch before any remarriage could take place. Katherine Parr and Thomas Seymour broke these rules. This may have highlighted Thomas Seymour's complete disregard for the rules and worried the council, meaning that they kept a closer eye on him and his ambitions. Katherine Parr does seem to have had a good relationship with her stepson, Edward VI, which may have smoothed the way of the newlyweds when news of their marriage broke at court. Edward VI was also fond of his uncle, Thomas, though access to the new king was restricted so Thomas had to bribe his way into favour through John Fowler, a gentleman of the Privy Chamber. Fowler had constant daily access to the king and was told to prepare the ground with the king for Seymour's choice of bride. However, Edward VI first suggested Anne of Cleves as a suitable bride for Seymour, but then decided that Seymour should marry Princess Mary 'to change her opinions'.[5] Mary was a staunch Catholic which Edward disapproved of. The pair would argue many times throughout Edward's reign over Mary's insistence on hearing Mass in her household. Mary was determined to follow in the faith of her mother, Katherine of Aragon, and her Spanish relatives, where Edward VI had been taught by reformist tutors and was a product of the Reformation. Fowler turned the king's mind towards Katherine Parr as a potential bride for Seymour and the king expressed his approval of the match.

The details of Thomas Seymour's courtship of Katherine Parr are unknown, as are details of the wedding. One of the questions over the speed of the courtship and wedding was that, if Katherine feel pregnant, it might be doubted whether the child was that of Seymour or of the late King Henry VIII. It could muddy the waters of the succession, especially if the child was a son. But there was nothing to be done, especially as the young King Edward VI had given his permission. The Lord Protector took out his frustrations by claiming that much of Katherine's jewellery was crown property. She and Seymour argued that it had been gifted to her by the king and so was her personal property.[6] The dispute was never resolved and even when Katherine died in September 1548, Seymour had no intention of giving up something so valuable.

Katherine Parr had taken Princess Elizabeth under her wing after the death of Henry VIII, and Elizabeth was living in Katherine's household at Chelsea. Lady Jane Grey would also join the household, so Seymour would have two heirs to the throne under one roof. He gained the wardship of Jane Grey through promising her father, Henry Grey, 1st Duke of Suffolk, that he would arrange a marriage for her to King Edward VI. Princess Elizabeth was at the forefront of Seymour's attentions, however. She was closer to the throne. If Edward VI and Princess Mary died without issue then Elizabeth and her heirs would inherit the throne. Seymour intended to ingratiate himself with those closest to the throne.

His relationship with Princess Elizabeth was incredibly controversial and Katherine Parr appeared to believe that, if she died in childbirth, Seymour would marry Elizabeth. The relationship between Elizabeth and Seymour was contentious, with some historians in the modern day likening it to sexual abuse or grooming. It is unclear exactly what went on between them. Elizabeth, however, was concerned about losing her place in the succession so refused to commit to anything, though her governess, Kat Ashley, promoted the match.[7] Contemplating marriage with a member of the royal family without the permission of the king amounted to treason, though Somerset seemed initially reluctant to act against his brother. Elizabeth was questioned over the relationship with Seymour when the latter was arrested, but no further action was taken against her.

Seymour resented his brother's influence and power and wanted a share of it. In 1547 he demanded the office of Governor to the King's Person.[8] This was the man responsible for the safety and health of the king, rather than a political role. Somerset had both roles combined under his protectorship, so he was responsible for everything to do with Edward VI.

* * *

Thomas Seymour had hoped to inveigle Henry Grey, 1st Duke of Suffolk, William Parr, 1st Marquess of Northampton, and Henry Manners, 2nd Earl of Rutland, into a revolt against his brother, the Lord Protector. Northampton, Katherine Parr's brother, was already angry at Edward Seymour and may have taken an opportunity to bring him down, when it was presented to him. Northampton had hoped that the Lord Protector would be sympathetic to his plea for a divorce from his adulterous wife. Somerset had divorced his first wife on the grounds of her adultery and Northampton wished to do the same. Somerset refused but Northampton bigamously remarried, and the marquess was banished from court.[9] Thomas Seymour had purchased the wardship of Suffolk's daughter, Lady Jane Grey, because Seymour had promised to arrange a marriage between Jane and Edward VI.

Seymour's plans, whatever they were, were derailed when rumours surfaced regarding his relationship with Princess Elizabeth. Elizabeth had lived with Katherine Parr since her father's death in January 1547, and remained with her when she married Seymour. Seymour was overly familiar with the young princess. It is important to remember that Elizabeth was only aged 13 at the time of Henry VIII's death and when Seymour began to make advances towards her. It is unclear whether Seymour was trying to seduce or molest the princess. Seymour had been known to slap Elizabeth on the buttocks, tickle her, or enter her bedroom unannounced and in a state of undress. Testimony came from Elizabeth's governess, Kat Ashley, who was prone to exaggeration so how much is actually true is unclear.[10] By early to mid-1548 things in the Parr-Seymour household were out of control and Katherine Parr was pregnant with Seymour's child.

Princess Elizabeth was sent away from Katherine Parr's household when Katherine discovered her in a compromising embrace with Thomas Seymour. Seymour was effectively Elizabeth's stepfather as Katherine was her stepmother. Elizabeth wrote to Katherine not long after she left saying she was 'replete with sorrow' to depart her household, but she seemed to have weighed a comment Katherine had made when she left that 'you would warn me of all evils that you should hear of me'.[11] The implication was that Elizabeth needed to be careful of her reputation and wanted to be warned of anything said against her. As sister to the king and an heir to the throne by the 1544 Act of Succession, Elizabeth's reputation could be compromised by too close a relationship with someone of the opposite sex, as would happen when she became queen, and the questions around her relationship with Robert Dudley, 1st Earl of Leicester. There were rumours that Elizabeth's relationship with Dudley was a sexual relationship and even that they had a child together, much the same as the rumours flying around about the relationship between Elizabeth and Seymour. Elizabeth needed to know what rumours were spread about her to be able to tackle them head-on.

Elizabeth wrote to the Lord Protector, Edward Seymour, 1st Duke of Somerset, after Thomas Seymour's arrest, on 28 January 1549. She was questioned at this time about her relationship with Seymour while she was living with Katherine Parr at Chelsea. Elizabeth admitted that her cofferer, Thomas Parry, asked whether 'if the Council did consent that I should have my lord admiral, whether I would consent to it or not'.[12] But only with the consent of the council. Elizabeth also said that Kat Ashley, her governess, had advised that she should not marry without the consent of the Privy Council and the king. Elizabeth needed consent to marry as she was so close to the throne and in the line of succession. Had she married without permission at this time she could have forfeited her position in the line of succession. This is not something Elizabeth would have risked. Those close to Elizabeth at this time seemed to believe that she wanted Seymour and would have him if allowed, but nothing survives from Elizabeth herself expressly saying that she wanted to marry him. The evidence we have comes from others and may not have echoed Elizabeth's own sentiments. She managed to protect and save herself several times before her accession by not saying what she truly thought. This could have been one of Elizabeth's first experiences of having to hold back to save herself, but it would stand her in good stead later in life.

Kat Ashley also reported that rumours abounded that Seymour would come to woo Elizabeth after Katherine Parr's death in September 1548. Somerset certainly believed that Seymour had planned to marry Elizabeth after Katherine's death, and suspected that Kat Ashley, Thomas Parry, and Princess Elizabeth were in on the plan. Elizabeth was questioned at Hatfield and revealed that Parry had brought up the idea of marriage to Seymour.[13] Parry and Ashley, however, both said that they knew the marriage could not go ahead without the approval of the council. Elizabeth herself went on to confirm that she would never marry without the permission of the king and council, knowing that this would jeopardise her place in the succession and her chance of succeeding to the throne. One of the main things that Elizabeth addressed in the letter she wrote to the Lord Protector were the rumours that she was pregnant by Thomas Seymour and imprisoned in the Tower of London as a result, saying that 'these are shameful slanders ... I shall most heartily desire your lordship that I may come to the court ... that I may show myself there as I am'.[14] Elizabeth was determined to tackle the rumours head-on and prove that her reputation was intact by showing she was not pregnant, but Somerset refused her request to travel to the court to disprove the allegations. Elizabeth was still under suspicion herself, and Somerset must have found the whole situation difficult, with his own brother accused of treason and attempting to compromise a royal princess. It put Somerset's position as protector in jeopardy. Elizabeth signed the letter 'Your assured friend to my little power', acknowledging that she had very little power in a male-dominated world and that her fate was entirely at the whim of the king, Protector, and council, though more so at the Protector's door as he had the ear of the king and council. She declared her loyalty to the king, subtly implying that she was not a pawn of Seymour's and would prove it if given the chance.

Thomas Seymour's fall from grace and execution resulted from several blunders and acts of stupidity since the death of Henry VIII including his rushed marriage to the dowager Queen Katherine Parr, his relationship with Princess Elizabeth and attempts to marry her, and his plotting to oust his brother from the Protectorship and take control of Edward VI. As historian, Helen Castor, puts it, he was tipped into a 'restlessly incoherent series of manoeuvres' due to the loss of his royal wife, and the need for him to play second fiddle to his brother in his nephew's government.[15] After Katherine Parr's death in childbirth with their only daughter, Seymour appears to have 'lost his wits'. Seymour's mother, Margery Wentworth, stayed with him to take care of his new-born daughter after his wife's death, and this freed him up to return to plotting and scheming.[16] He no longer had a wife to satisfy or who would keep tabs on him, and his child was being cared for by someone else. There was no one who would stop him.

It is possible, as suggested by Hester Chapman, that Edward VI feared and mistrusted Seymour, rather than loved his uncle. It is possible that Edward was too proud to ask for help against his uncle.[17] Chapman's is an older work, and this opinion is not really seen in more modern works, though it still bears considering. Edward's opinions on his uncle are not really known. His writing in his diary is scant regarding his relationship with Seymour, though we know he tried to bribe the king by increasing his allowance to gain more access to him and some favour.

The nail in Thomas Seymour's coffin was his attempt to kidnap Edward VI. He managed to obtain the key to the privy garden and the king's lodgings. On 16 January 1549, Seymour entered the king's lodgings at Hampton Court Palace through the privy garden, accompanied by two servants as far as the door to the king's chambers, but he was startled by Edward's dog outside the bedchamber and shot the dog. Guards were alerted by the noise and came running.[18] Seymour was questioned but for some inexplicable reason he was allowed to leave. He was arrested the following day, having refused to answer questions. His excuse was that he wanted to check that the king was safely guarded. It seems he aimed to kidnap the king to remove him from his brother, Somerset's, influence, and gain some power for himself, possibly by provoking a civil war within the court. It would have been brother against brother had Seymour's plan come to fruition, and quite possibly there would have been a lot of collateral damage as nobles took sides. There would have been many more deaths if Seymour had not been found out before he could raise rebellion. Seymour had a pistol when he entered the king's chambers, which he used to kill the dog. This was definitely a threat to the king and Seymour could not talk himself out of it. It has been suggested that Seymour 'killed his nephew's affections for him with the same bullet'.[19] Edward VI does not seem to have really turned against Seymour until he was facing a loaded gun in his uncle's hand.

Elizabeth wrote a further letter to Protector Somerset on 6 February 1549, just a week after her last letter, to say that 'for I would not (as I trust you have not) so evil an opinion of me that I would conceal anything that

I knew, for it were to no purpose'.[20] The implication was that there was no point in Elizabeth trying to hide anything because the council would know about it; in other words, how would she hide a pregnancy? And why would she become involved in plotting when she had no reason to? There was little doubt in Elizabeth's mind that the Lord Protector had spies in her household, as he would have done with Princess Mary as well, to keep an eye on the two women next in the line of succession and who could pose a threat to Edward VI. He would know of anything that happened in their households and needed to know in order to protect the king. Elizabeth was rarely alone, surrounded by servants, so others would know of anything that had happened between her and Seymour, as was proven by the testimony of Kat Ashley and Thomas Parry. There were questions raised about how well Ashley and Parry ran Elizabeth's household as a result of this scandal and whether it was proper for them to carry on in their roles.

This refusal of Elizabeth's request to travel to court was probably to the advantage of the Privy Council. Naturally, Somerset was reluctant to act against his brother, but the accusations of a relationship with Princess Elizabeth added fuel to the fire of rumours Seymour had wanted to overthrow the Lord Protector and gain control of the young king himself. Seymour's actions threatened both the king and protector which Somerset would not allow. Elizabeth's governess, Kat Ashley, was arrested and questioned over Seymour's relations with Elizabeth. Ashley reported that she had said after Katherine Parr's death that Seymour 'now is free again. You may have him if you will' but Elizabeth said 'nay'. Ashley continued that 'why not him that was worthy to match a queen should not marry with you?'[21] Kat Ashley certainly seems to have promoted a match between Elizabeth and Seymour, but always with the caveat that the council would need to approve it. However, she does not seem to have doubted that Thomas Seymour could have gained that approval, at least up until his arrest. He was known to be charming and had established contact with the king without the Lord Protector's knowledge, at least initially. He seemed to be able to convince people black was white if he so desired. Ashley's comment regarding Seymour marrying a queen so why not a princess is interesting. Katherine Parr was a commoner who married a king, where Elizabeth was of the blood royal, albeit she had been declared illegitimate after Anne Boleyn's execution and the annulment of her marriage to Henry VIII. Perhaps the taint against Elizabeth put her on equal footing with Katherine Parr in Kat Ashley's eyes.

On 25 February 1549, the lords of the council met to discuss Seymour's fate, where the deposition was read out, accusing him of wanting to take the role of Lord Protector from his own brother. Seymour refused to mount a defence. The bill was read again on 26 and 27 February and it was a unanimous guilty verdict against him. Princess Elizabeth again wrote to Lord Protector Somerset on 7 March 1549, two days after the bill of attainder against Thomas Seymour received royal assent. The bill had been introduced to parliament on 25 February, but it took a week and a half to go through parliament, the lords and then the commons, and then for the king to assent to it, making it law. This meant that there was no going back, and Seymour was condemned and guilty, effectively a dead man walking. He would die. There was no question over that. Elizabeth worked to save those she loved who had been caught up in his treason.

Elizabeth wrote asking the Lord Protector to be kind to her governess, Kat Ashley, who had been questioned in the Tower of London regarding what she knew about Seymour and Elizabeth's relationship. Elizabeth claimed that Ashley had only acted as she did in the matter of the proposed marriage of Seymour and Elizabeth because she believed that Seymour had the consent of the king, protector, and council to approach the princess about a potential marriage.[22] The implication seems to be that they could not believe Seymour would act in the matter without permission. It perhaps shows the deterioration of Seymour's mind after Katherine's death. However, he had married in secret and without permission before, to Katherine Parr, so there was history of him acting impulsively. Whether this was true or whether Elizabeth was trying to protect Kat by metaphorically throwing Seymour under a bus is unclear. It was unlikely Seymour could be saved, especially after breaking into the king's apartments, attempted kidnap, and shooting the king's favourite dog in a panic. It is quite possible that Elizabeth was acting to save Kat, knowing that Seymour was already condemned and would die. She could not help him, but she could help the woman who had effectively raised her and been a mother to her when her own mother could not be there. Elizabeth, however, was also acting in her own interests. She wrote that it 'doth make men think that I am not clear of the deed myself, but that it is pardoned in me because of my youth, because that she I loved so well is in such a place'.[23] Elizabeth worried that people would not think her innocent, but that she was forgiven her crimes due to her youth. Innocence and forgiveness are not the same thing and Elizabeth wanted to make sure that she was seen as innocent in the matter, and not that she was forgiven, which suggested guilt. Perception would become very important to Elizabeth's later image as the 'Virgin Queen' and 'Gloriana' and we can see an awareness of it here.

It is possible that Seymour had hoped to persuade the king to his point of view, rather than just kidnap him. Edward VI had his own views, strong in the case of religion, and perhaps Seymour had hoped to influence Edward's opinions in the case of Somerset and the protectorship.[24] Thomas Seymour had been reprimanded by John Dudley over his behaviour, but he refused to listen. It seems that courtiers had attempted to warn him of what would happen if he continued with his behaviour towards Princess Elizabeth and his unguarded speech against his brother. Had he listened, things could have turned out differently. After his arrest and questioning, the council were not satisfied with his responses, and he remained in the Tower. He was guilty of treason and would die for it.

*   *   *

Thomas Seymour, 1st Baron Seymour of Sudeley, had been increasingly angry and frustrated since the death of Henry VIII in January 1547 over his brother's wealth, power, and influence with the new king. He wanted to share it. He wanted his ambitions to bear fruit. He had spoken first and thought afterwards, with even Katherine Parr seeming to find him difficult to handle at times.[25] Thomas was impulsive, and this got him in trouble. He went after what he wanted but even once achieved, he immediately wanted more. He seemed to lose all sense of reason and clarity after Katherine's death in September 1548. Seymour had claimed he could bring down the government, but it was the government who brought him down instead. His ambition and bravado were his downfall.

Once Seymour was arrested on 17 January 1549, people he had been in contact with were questioned, and tried to disassociate themselves from him. There is always a rush, once someone is arrested for treason, of people who knew the accused trying to distance themselves in order to save themselves. The first reaction is self-preservation. Seymour does not seem to have hidden his views on anything as people were willing to come forward and tell what he had said about the governance of the king and country, bragging about private armies, attempting to win friends through money and favours, and his pleasure that the office of Lord Admiral gave him control of money and ships.[26] William Sharington worked at the Bristol Mint and seemed to have reached some kind of agreement with Thomas Seymour, though the exact nature is unknown. Sharington was arrested on an unrelated matter of debasing the currency in January 1549. His home, Lacock Abbey, was searched on 6 January and papers were found stating that proceeds from the Bristol Mint would be placed at Seymour's disposal for military purposes.[27] Sharington would escape with his life, dying in 1553. It is possible that he did not know Seymour's true purpose. As a result of the search of Sharington's home, Seymour had been summoned to an interview with Somerset which he had declined to attend. This may have prompted questions over the validity of claims against Seymour as he was not willing to defend himself, perhaps suggesting guilt to the council.

The hearsay alone was not enough to condemn him, though it was enough at least to warrant a more thorough investigation into his actions. Seymour was defiant when questioned, claiming he feared no one and that the king would support him. It meant that Seymour's excuses for why he behaved the way he did were questioned, and it was difficult to explain away breaking into the king's apartments with a loaded pistol anyway. What possible explanation could Seymour give for that which was not sinister? His behaviour towards Princess Elizabeth was more serious than a few letters between him and Sharington, and certainly his actions in breaking into the king's apartments eclipsed everything else. That was easily construed as treasonous and the rumours and hearsay supported premeditation, not spur of the moment anger. Edward VI had written a statement against his uncle, which was damning against Seymour. Edward wrote that Seymour had urged him to take control of government himself within two years in order to free himself from the constraints placed upon him by the Protector 'ye are but a very beggarly king now; ye have not to play nor to give to your servants'.[28] Seymour tried to bribe the king by giving him extra pocket money, believing that he would support him when the time came to overthrow the Lord Protector. This was not the case and the king turned against his uncle.

Somerset abstained from voting in parliament against his brother, but Seymour was declared unanimously guilty. Somerset's wife, Anne Stanhope, allegedly pushed Somerset to execute his own brother.[29] There was not really an expectation that Somerset would vote, just as Thomas Boleyn had not been expected to be present at the trials of his daughter and son thirteen years earlier. If there was any chance of a reprieve for Thomas Seymour it was in the Commons, as some members asked why there was not to be a trial.[30] Somerset seems to have considered giving Seymour an open trial, but there were concerns of what might happen. They were also worried that Somerset's family affection might lead to him being lenient. The evidence against Seymour was overwhelming but he was popular and there may have been a concern he would have been acquitted and freed to make more mischief in the future. Any protests were pushed aside, and the bill was passed and became law.

John Dudley, the future 1st Duke of Northumberland, allegedly stopped Somerset seeing his brother, fearful that Seymour would manage to influence him to mercy or forgiveness. Seymour supposedly sent messages to Edward VI and Somerset, but they were never received.[31] Once the bill passed, Seymour was, in the eyes of the law, already dead. Somerset was the first to sign the death warrant of his brother and asked for some of his own servants to be present at the execution to ensure that his brother, and the king's uncle, had a decent burial. Parliament had spoken and left no choice but for Somerset to sign. Once the warrant was signed, Edward VI asked that the execution be carried out without bothering himself or Somerset further.

Sir Thomas Seymour, 1st Baron Seymour of Sudeley, was beheaded on Tower Hill on 20 March 1549, two months after his arrest. On hearing of his death, Princess Elizabeth was quoted as saying 'this day died a man of much wit and very little judgement'.[32] Where this quote came from is unknown, but it has become a Tudor legend and seems apt, given what we know of Seymour's personality. He certainly seemed able to charm the women; Princess Elizabeth was not immune to his charms, and her governess, Kat Ashley, also seemed to be susceptible to Seymour's allure. But his judgement was questionable. Did he really believe he could kidnap and seize control of the king, and no one would quibble or question it, and just let him take over the government of the country? It seems ludicrous. Seymour's brother, Protector Somerset, would fall from power the following year, and the debate still rages over precisely what went wrong for him (see Chapter 8). It is much easier to see how Thomas Seymour ended up in the position that he did. But 'there were many who looked askance at [Seymour's] execution without trial, and Somerset's willingness to behead his own brother was abhorred'.[33] This, in part at least, ensured Somerset's downfall just months after his brother's execution.

The council were determined to ensure that Thomas Seymour's actions would not be repeated by others after his execution. That no one would be able to threaten the king or gain access to him with a weapon ever again. Rather like the poor reputation that Anne Boleyn had after her execution, Thomas Seymour suffered in a similar manner. It was not enough that he had been executed, 'the council now took pains to ensure that the assault on his reputation continued with a viciousness that matched the manner of his dispatch'.[34] It was rumoured at the time that he had written letters to both Princesses Mary and Elizabeth while in the Tower before his death; this was reported by Bishop Hugh Latimer who wrote that Seymour had written 'one to my lady Mary's grace, and another to my lady Elizabeth's grace, tending to this end, that they should conspire against my lord Protector's grace: surely so seditiously as could be … they were found in a shoe of his: they were sewed between the soles of a velvet shoe'.[35] He relied on a servant to deliver them but was discovered and the letters used as further evidence against him, never reaching the intended recipients. The Starz television drama, *Becoming Elizabeth* (2022), has Seymour's servant revealing the existence of the letter in the moments before Seymour's execution on the scaffold, and then gloating over the body. If letters did exist and were discovered there is no evidence that this happened on the scaffold, as it would have been reported.

Sermons were preached against Thomas Seymour, including the one above by Hugh Latimer, so that his ideas and accusations would not be acted upon by others who might feel disgruntled with the new Protestant regime or the protector, though Somerset largely seemed to be popular among the general populace of England, if not wholly within the court. There was still a lot of controversy around religion at this time, with this period often called the 'mid-Tudor crisis' because of the changes between Henry VIII, Edward VI, Mary I and Elizabeth I across just twelve years. People were unsure how they should be worshipping, and it was obvious almost from the beginning of his reign that Edward VI's government were taking a more radical reformist and Protestant stance than Henry VIII. On Henry VIII's death in January 1547, England was largely Catholic in doctrine, though without the figurehead of the Pope, or the monasteries. Seymour had been a popular figure so it made sense that the government would want to destroy that popularity, and with it his ideas about the division of power and the ambition of those who wielded it.

Thomas Seymour supposedly wrote a poem in the Tower of London before his execution, though as with most execution-based poems and letters, the provenance is questionable. He lamented that he had forgotten God in order to love a king and pursue the path of ambition. This almost seems to be against the grain of Seymour as a person. There is little evidence of him showing any interest in faith or religion, though perhaps what he really lamented was the position he found himself in, and his imminent death. It is this sense of religion which makes the poem of questionable authenticity, though perhaps facing execution made him reconsider his priorities. It is possible Seymour felt that he had allowed his pride and ambition to get in the way of good sense, intelligence, and devotion to his faith and he was about to pay the price for that:

> Forgetting God
> To love a king
> Hath been my rod
> Or else nothing,
>
> In this frail life,
> Being a blast
> Of care and strife
> Till it be past.
>
> Yet God did call
> Me in my pride,
> Lest I should fall
> And from Him slide.
>
> For whom loves He
> And not correct,
> That they may be
> Of His elect?
>
> Then, Death, haste thee.
> Thou shalt me gain
> Immortally
> With Him to reign;
>
> Who send the king
> Like years as Noye

> In governing
> His realm in joy;
>
> And after this
> Frail life, such grace
> As in His bliss
> I may have place.[36]

Seymour had loved his king and tried to use his king to get what he wanted. It was this ambition that brought him down in the end. He wanted what his brother had. He had lived for passion and excitement in a 'frail life' which could be over sooner than anyone expected. He had made a rod to beat himself with, and it was his own folly that had led him here. Had Seymour accepted his position, inferior in power to his brother, he may not have been found guilty of treason as he likely would not have attempted to kidnap the king. There is a note of sadness and regret which comes through which, if Seymour did write the poem, could have been either an apology over his pride and ambition or a regret that his life was ending before he could reach the lofty heights of his brother.

The undertone of the poem suggests that God was calling Seymour to him now so that he did not slide further from the faith and into his own pride if he was allowed to live longer. The poem is phrased in such a way as to imply that death was the solution to Seymour's problems rather than a punishment as such, indicated by phrases like 'shalt gain me immortality with him to reign' and 'as in bliss I may have place'. The focus is very much on how good the afterlife will be for him and how much there was to gain from it. The emphasis is not on his sentence or on what he was accused of.

The French ambassador believed that it was John Dudley, later 1st Duke of Northumberland, who pushed Somerset into condemning his brother to death.[37] Somerset's condemnation of his brother can be seen as the beginning of his own end. It seems like a foreshadowing of Somerset's own fall, examined in Chapter 8, and his replacement as Lord Protector by John Dudley, 1st Duke of Northumberland. Seymour's actions helped to damn his brother and saw the fall of the Seymour family until the rise of the Stuarts to the English throne and the resurrection of the Somerset dukedom after the English Civil War. Seymour's direct line became extinct with the death of his infant daughter.

It was predicted by some that the fall of one brother would be the overthrow of the other.[38] Thomas Seymour was executed in March 1549 and Edward Seymour, 1st Duke of Somerset, would be ousted from power in October of that year, and executed in 1552. Thomas Seymour's fate would influence that of his brother because his actions reflected badly on Somerset, and it would be used by his enemies against him in his own downfall. Thomas Seymour, 1st Baron Seymour of Sudeley, was the beginning of the downfall of the Tudor Seymours, but he would not be the last to suffer.

Chapter 8

Edward Seymour, 1st Duke of Somerset – 1552

E dward Seymour, 1st Duke of Somerset, was an ambitious courtier under Henry VIII and Lord Protector of the Realm under Edward VI, until a brutal coup by John Dudley, then Earl of Warwick, and later 1st Duke of Northumberland, overthrew him. Unusually for those taken to the Tower of London under the Tudors, Somerset was originally released from his imprisonment and allowed to return to court before another coup had him back in the Tower, and this time beneath the executioner's axe. He benefitted greatly from his sister, Jane's, triumph in marrying Henry VIII in 1536 and providing him with the son and heir he so desperately wanted the following year. It meant that Somerset was uncle to the king of England from 1547, though Somerset benefitted more from the connection than Thomas Seymour, his brother, which angered Thomas.

As discussed in the previous chapter on Edward's younger brother, Thomas, 1st Baron Seymour of Sudeley, the Seymours were an old family but did not have particularly noble ties until Jane, Edward, and Thomas's generation. They were a courtly family in the sense of their general presence and steady loyalty to the crown, but not in the way that the Boleyns were in leading a court faction in the late 1520s and 1530s.[1] However, had Edward Seymour had a tight-knit circle of supporters around him in 1549 and again in 1552 he may have had more support against the successful attempts to oust him from power and then take his life. He may not have been toppled quite so easily. However, it must be remembered that Anne Boleyn had a faction around her, but losing the favour of the monarch could be fatal when combined with enemies whispering in the monarch's ear against you.

Edward's father, Sir John Seymour, served both Henry VII and Henry VIII. Edward was created Viscount Beauchamp of Hache in 1536 when the king married his sister, Jane, and was created Earl of Hertford the following year when Jane gave birth to Henry VIII's much anticipated son and heir. He would create himself Duke of Somerset in 1547 when Edward VI succeeded to the throne, and he became the uncle to the monarch. He would not grant his brother, Thomas, the same distinction.

Both brothers had the same ancestry; no real noble connection in the direct male line, but a connection to the Howard dukes of Norfolk and thus the Boleyns through Edward's great-grandmother, Elizabeth Cheyney (see Chapter 7 on Thomas Seymour for full descent). What is different between the two brothers is that Edward Seymour's line survives today in the current Duke of Somerset, but Thomas's line died out with his daughter, Mary Seymour, who vanished from the historical record and is not thought to have survived infancy. Edward married twice, first to Catherine Filiol, though that marriage was dissolved, and their children were excluded from inheriting due to their mother's adulterous relationships with other men. Their paternity was questioned. Edward remarried to Anne Stanhope, and it would be their children who would inherit the Somerset dukedom, though not directly after Edward's own execution. His eldest son would bear the title Earl of Hertford.

The male line of Edward Seymour and Anne Stanhope died out with the death of Algernon Seymour, 7th Duke of Somerset, in 1750, and today the Dukedom of Somerset is in the hands of Edward's descendants by his first wife, Catherine Filiol. So, the dukedom is still in the hands of Edward's offspring, but from a line that began with questionable paternity rather than the unquestionably legitimate line. After the death of Algernon Seymour, it was decided to track back to the nearest male heir rather than go down the female line. It was never certain that Somerset's children from his first wife were illegitimate, and they always supported Somerset in his times of need. Queen Elizabeth II and her heirs are also descended from Edward Seymour, 1st Duke of Somerset, through his marriage to Anne Stanhope. Somerset's son, Edward Seymour, 1st Earl of Hertford, married Katherine Grey, the great-granddaughter of Henry VII through Mary Tudor, Duchess of Suffolk, and sister to the ill-fated Lady Jane Grey. Both were imprisoned in the Tower by Elizabeth I as they had married in secret and without royal approval. However, they still managed to produce two sons, the eldest from whom the Queen Mother, Elizabeth Bowes-Lyon, was descended.

From what we know of Somerset, he was ambitious and ruthless and likely would have made a good career for himself at court, but he more than likely would not have been able to seize the protectorship in 1547 had he not been uncle to the new king. Somerset owed a lot of his exalted position as Lord Protector to his sister and luck that it was she, and not another lady at court, who caught the king's eye.

* * *

Edward Seymour was born as the second son to Sir John Seymour and Margery Wentworth in 1500. He had an elder brother, John, named for their father, though not much is known about him. It seems likely he died in infancy or early childhood, and certainly before 1520, judging on how Edward's court career progressed. Many of the honours he received from this date would traditionally have gone to the eldest brother. Another brother, Henry, was born around 1504 and Thomas followed around 1508. A first sister, Jane, was born in around 1509, then Margery, Elizabeth, and Dorothy, although dates are uncertain as to when they were born. Jane's birth date is estimated based on how old she was said to have been when she died. Some accounts list Elizabeth as the elder sister, but Henry VIII was said to have joked with John Seymour at the beginning of his reign about his penchant for producing sons.[2] This suggests that the first daughter must not have been born until the middle or end of 1509 as Henry VIII only came to the throne in April 1509. Perhaps the king's comment was made when John Seymour told the king that his wife was again with child, and the king was himself hoping that his new wife, Katherine of Aragon, would soon conceive and produce a son. The fact this did not happen paved the way for Edward's sister to catch the king's eye many years later and for his own court career.

We do not have much information on Edward Seymour before his sister came to the king's attention. It is only when we read of him receiving honours and positions that we can place him at the court or in noble households. Edward was named as a page to Mary Tudor, Henry VIII's younger sister, when she travelled to France to marry the ageing king, Louis XII, in October 1514, so he and his father were obviously well-known enough around the court for him to be granted this honour. In August 1523, Edward seems to have accompanied Charles Brandon, 1st Duke of Suffolk, to France on campaign and must have distinguished himself as he was knighted by the duke before returning to England. He was made an Esquire of the Household in 1524, then became Master of the Horse for Henry VIII's illegitimate son, Henry Fitzroy, after he was created Duke of Richmond and Somerset in 1525. In July 1527, Edward was named on the roll of people accompanying

Cardinal Thomas Wolsey to France; a mission which ultimately failed but was intended to set up a kind of interim church while the Pope was imprisoned in the Castel de San Angelo, and grant King Henry VIII an annulment from his first wife, Katherine of Aragon, so that he could marry Anne Boleyn.

Edward Seymour was also likely present at his family's ancestral home of Wolf Hall in Wiltshire in September 1535 when Henry VIII and Anne Boleyn visited on their final royal progress together. Some historians suggest that it was at this time that Henry first became acquainted with, and fell for, Edward's sister, Jane. Yet, Jane had been at court for many years already, having first been in the household of Katherine of Aragon before transferring to serve Anne Boleyn when she became queen in 1533. Jane had been in receipt of New Year's gifts from the king in previous years, as many of the queen's ladies were, so Henry would have already been acquainted with her. However, this may have been the time when Henry VIII first began to take a romantic or courtly love interest in Jane and saw her as more than merely another lady serving his wife. There is no real evidence to suggest that Jane did in fact accompany the royal couple to Wolf Hall, but there is also nothing to imply that she was not present either. Quite simply, we cannot be sure whether Jane was in fact there, but it seems probable Jane was present at her family home at Wolf Hall serving Anne Boleyn in September 1535.

A dispensation was granted on 19 May 1536, the very day on which Henry VIII's second wife, Anne Boleyn, was executed (see Chapter 3), for Henry to marry Jane Seymour. They were fifth cousins, though any common grandparent or even great-grandparent between Jane Seymour and either of Henry VIII's first two wives, Katherine of Aragon and Anne Boleyn, could have meant that a dispensation was required for the marriage. Jane Seymour and Anne Boleyn shared a great-grandparent in Elizabeth Cheyney, as previously discussed, though there is some debate over just how close the degree of consanguinity needed to be for a dispensation to be required. It is likely that Edward Seymour had helped to coach his sister, Jane, on how to attract the king, and then hold him off, much in the same way that Anne Boleyn had done a decade before. He had been at court during the royal courtship and would have seen how Anne behaved in those early stages. The difference was that Henry VIII's marriage to Anne Boleyn was weaker and easier to end than his marriage to Katherine of Aragon had been. The Seymours created their own faction, with Edward and Jane at the heart, to oust Anne and replace her with Jane.

Edward Seymour's marital life caused some controversy at the time. His first wife was Catherine Filiol, whom he married sometime around 1518. They had two sons together, John born 1527 and Edward born 1529. Both would be excluded in 1540 from receiving any inheritance on their father's death, as there had been questions raised over Catherine Filiol's extra-marital affairs, and Edward was not certain that he was actually the father of his sons. He favoured the children born to his second wife, Anne Stanhope, whom he married around 1535. However, the sons born to his first wife would support their father throughout his problems in the late 1540s and early 1550s and would in fact be imprisoned with him in the Tower of London.

It is interesting to compare the works of the Catholic polemicist, Nicholas Sander, and the Protestant author of the *Book of Martyrs*, John Foxe, in their opinions of Edward Seymour, though both must be taken with a grain of salt, each promoting their own religious views. Foxe described Somerset as 'a man not so highly advanced for his consanguinity, as also for his noble virtues; and especially for his favour to God's word, worthy of his vocation and calling'.[3] Foxe also credits Somerset with abolishing the Act of Six Articles, which under Henry VIII had restored many Catholic tenets of faith to England. In complete contrast to Foxe, Nicholas Sander wrote that Somerset 'had nothing more at heart than to pollute and defile still more that wretched and disfigured form of religion which Henry had commanded to be observed'.[4] Henry VIII had not fully made the English Church Protestant. At the time of his death, it was still largely Catholic though without the figurehead of the Pope. This is the 'disfigured form' that Sander refers to. What is clear from both Sander and Foxe is that Somerset promoted the reformed religion and would work to complete the Reformation that Henry VIII had halted, with the encouragement of Edward VI.

On the death of Henry VIII and the accession of Edward VI in January 1547, there was a power vacuum of sorts. Henry VIII had been such a strong and forceful personality that many courtiers and councillors had obeyed his wishes almost without thinking. With the old king dead, there was now a child on the throne of England and the government had to reshape itself to that new situation. Thomas Seymour was added to the council and the council then elected Somerset as Lord Protector and Governor of the King's Person. The decision appears to have been unanimous, though Thomas Seymour objected that he should have equal status as his brother, both being equally the king's uncles. The decision appears to have been that the council should be headed by a single identifiable person, and that person should be Somerset as the king's uncle. In a council meeting on 1 February 1547, Edward VI formally endorsed the decisions made on his behalf, though it seems likely he had little or no input into them.[5] Sir William Paget claimed that Henry VIII had intended to make certain peerage promotions and other honours, but his declining health had prevented him from doing so. As a result, Edward Seymour became Duke of Somerset, Katherine Parr's brother, William Parr, was created 1st Marquess of Northampton, John Dudley was made 1st Earl of Warwick (later 1st Duke of Northumberland), and Thomas Wriothesley was created 1st Earl of Southampton. Somerset had reached the pinnacle of power with these titles and positions. He would have far to fall.

* * *

Edward Seymour's downfall can be seen to begin when he announced that he would be Lord Protector during the minority of Edward VI, although it was his brother, Thomas's, execution in 1549 that solidified it. In his will, Henry VIII had advocated a Regency Council to rule during his son's minority, and not one man set above the others. Somerset pursued a number of policies which those in government found controversial. These included his support of the common people in the 1549 rebellions and more generally. Historian, Leanda de Lisle, argues that Somerset was destroyed by ambition.[6] This certainly seems accurate given his determination to overrule Henry VIII's will and become Lord Protector, rather than be part of a Regency Council who had equal power. Although the council had chosen Somerset as Protector, it seems that he had been gathering supporters and lobbying in the run-up to Henry VIII's death. The final parliament of 1547 was effectively bullied into granting Somerset the authority to rule in Edward VI's name until such time as the king himself removed him by a handwritten document sealed with the Great Seal of England. Somerset had control of the Great Seal so it would have been very difficult to remove Somerset even if the king began to favour someone else.[7] Somerset wanted to be the one making decisions as uncle to the king, and believed it was his right as the king's closest familial relation. He believed that no one could protect and aid Edward as he could.

At the time of Henry VIII's death in January 1547 and the proclamation of Edward VI as king of England, Somerset (or the Earl of Hertford as he then was) travelled to escort Edward to London and tell him of his father's death. Edward VI was told the news alongside his sister, Elizabeth, at Enfield, before being taken on to London. There was often a delay between the death of one monarch and releasing the news of the death and proclaiming the next king, as there was in 1547. This was largely a question of putting procedures in place rather than anything sinister. When Somerset initially fell from power in 1549, a more ominous motive was suggested: that Somerset had wanted to seize the king's treasure for his own use and that he 'robbed and embezzled from the king's majesty the treasure and jewels left by his majesty's father of noble memory King Henry the 8th not appointing commissioners for the view of the same until 2 months after the decease of the said king'.[8] The delay in arranging the viewing of valuables was used against Somerset, though it does not seem to have been an unusual practise, given how much there was to arrange and secure on the accession of a new monarch.

The only possibly questionable action Somerset took in the wake of Henry VIII's death with regards to wealth was to seize the jewels of the dowager queen, Katherine Parr. This triggered a bitter feud between Katherine and Somerset's wife, Anne Stanhope, which escalated when Edward's brother, Thomas Seymour, married Katherine just months after the king's death. Somerset allowed his wife to wear some of the queen dowager's jewels at Edward VI's coronation, which did not go down well in the eyes of some of the court. The wife of the Protector was not of equal status to the dowager queen and so should not wear royal jewels. This probably alienated parts of the royal court, along with his attempts to solidify his power and position. Councillors became concerned that Somerset would attempt to rule the king indefinitely and would not be willing to give up power once the king reached his majority.[9] Somerset was certainly ambitious and power-hungry, but had he worked more with the council and allowed the king some power himself during his protectorship, there is no reason to believe that Edward VI would not have continued to favour his uncle even once he obtained his majority and full powers.

There were problems in Scotland at the time of Henry VIII's death in 1547. Scotland was under the minority rule of Mary Queen of Scots, with her father, James V, having died after the Scottish defeat at the Battle of Solway Moss in 1542. Somerset established a series of garrisons after a further Scots defeat at the Battle of Pinkie Cleugh in September 1547. The garrisons were intended to intimidate the Scots into complying with

English demands, though it merely seems to have angered them further.[10] Henry VIII had hoped to marry his son, Edward VI, to Mary Queen of Scots, and this was agreed to in the Treaty of Greenwich in 1543. However, Somerset's policy against the Scots meant that those in power in Scotland headed by Mary's mother, Mary of Guise, turned to favour a French alliance, that traditional auld alliance, and in 1548 Mary was sent to France to be raised in the French court and was betrothed to the future Francis II, an agreement cemented by the Treaty of Haddington. Somerset's garrison policy was unpopular, and the English had lost the benefits of a marriage to the young Scots queen as well.

In addition to failure in Scotland, there was widespread discontent in rural areas of England, in particular with the enclosure of common land by the nobility and gentry. This meant that the common people had less land to graze their animals on, with the consequence that they had a more restricted food source. This led to additional hardships for the people. Somerset was said to be against enclosure, but many of the council were for it, so there were divisions at the heart of government itself. There were other social, economic, and religious grievances which pushed the situation to a head in 1549. The new Book of Common Prayer was introduced which promoted Protestant values rather than the religion favoured by Henry VIII and many people disagreed with further reformist measures.

The rebellions of 1549 in the west centred around Exeter and the one led by Robert Kett in Norfolk in particular contributed to Somerset's downfall because it was thought that he was too sympathetic to the labourers.[11] His protectorate fell apart, as he had pushed policies which had failed, and the council would no longer support him. Kett was rebelling against social issues like enclosure and poor economic conditions in July and August 1549. The Western Rebellion was ongoing at the same time, protesting against the introduction of the new Book of Common Prayer, but it is often the Kett Rebellion which is better known, and the two are often confused or amalgamated into a single rebellion. Kett sent a list of demands to Somerset, supported by around 15,000 protestors who had gathered on Mousehold Heath outside Norwich. Norwich was the largest city outside London at the time and the rebels took the city at the end of July 1549, which was a huge blow to the king and government. The populace wanted to undo many of the socio-economic changes that had been made by the Tudors, but the currency was so debased that this was not feasible.

It has been argued that this was one of the most significant rebellions of the Tudor century and that 'Tudor rule of England had rarely been so threatened'.[12] It was certainly one of the largest in terms of the numbers of people involved. The largest Tudor rebellion was the Pilgrimage of Grace under Henry VIII, which protested largely against the royal supremacy and the dissolution of the monasteries, rather than the socio-economic grievances aired by the Kett rebels in 1549. The Pilgrimage of Grace at one point had upwards of 40,000 people involved, where the Kett Rebellion had around 15,000 rebels.

On 18 July 1549, martial law was declared and the bodyguard around Edward VI was increased. On 1 July, a summons had been sent out to nobles and gentlemen to attend the king at Windsor with as many horsemen and footmen as could be arranged.[13] It was feared that the rebels would attempt to seize the king to force the government to acquiesce to their demands. As King Edward VI was underage, power in England really lay with the Protector. Lord Protector Somerset seemed to be sympathetic to the rebels, but other Privy Councillors were much less so. Perhaps it was Somerset's sympathy with the common people that earned him the nickname 'the Good Duke' where his successor as Protector, John Dudley, 1st Duke of Northumberland, was known as 'the Bad Duke' in contrast. Northumberland would also be the one who would take an army into Norfolk and quash Kett's Rebellion, executing many rebels. Perhaps when he overthrew Somerset, the people remembered. Somerset offered concessions to the rebels and claimed that if they laid down their arms and agreed to send a couple of men to London with a list of their grievances that he would listen, and he even invited them to participate further in the political process.[14] This is quite astonishing, and not something that had been seen before. Henry VIII had offered some concessions in the Pilgrimage of Grace in 1536, but he had never intended to keep the promises made. The sense we get from Edward Seymour is that he did intend to keep his promises and let the people become more involved in the running of the country, giving them a stake in their own future. Somerset could be seen to have quite the moral compass; he wanted power for himself, but to use it to help the people. Northumberland would not follow in Somerset's footsteps.

Somerset sent John Dudley, 1st Earl of Warwick to quash the rebellion with 6,000 foot soldiers and 1,500 cavalry. Kett's soldiers would not allow him to meet Warwick to talk, fearful that he would be arrested or even killed on sight, and that would lead to the failure of their cause which they believed was just. Dudley opened fire in Norwich itself when he gained access to the city, and a group of rebels were immediately captured and hanged as a deterrent to the rest. Kett moved with his rebel army to Dussindale, where a battle took place, though Kett and other rebel leaders fled leaving around 2,000 rebels lying dead on the field. Kett had hidden in a barn around eight miles from the battlefield but was discovered and arrested, taken back to Norwich and then London. He was tried and hanged in chains from Norwich Castle, having been returned there from London. The aim of this was likely to make an example of Kett in the place where he had so much power. Somerset's sympathy for the rebels would not be forgotten by either government or people, and it would be used against him in a government coup.

This rebellion and the economic issues it raised, combined with the debasement of the coinage and the cost of maintaining Boulogne against French attack, meant that Somerset's position was increasingly unstable. This was coupled with the fact that France had declared war on England and the proposed marriage of Edward VI to Mary Queen of Scots had failed.. Given this mix of problems which did not just affect the general populace, but the ongoing political and diplomatic situation, 'it is hardly surprising that the Council turned against Somerset'.[15] Not everything that happened could be attributed to Somerset, but when things happen, they are often blamed on the person in power, even if they could not stop it happening or change the outcome. At least some of the problems Somerset was facing in 1549, however, were partly down to him, such as the debasement of the coinage and the war with France. The debasement of the coinage was begun by Henry VIII in 1544, but it was a policy continued by Somerset to fund the wars against France and Scotland. This Great Debasement combined with foreign wars had knock-on effects on the political situation in England.

Somerset's promotion of the reformed faith is interesting. It was in deep contrast to his sister, Jane Seymour, who appeared to favour conservatism and, during the Pilgrimage of Grace in 1536, had asked King Henry VIII to restore and maintain the monasteries. The king refused, but her willingness to raise the subject with a volatile king shows her devotion to her belief that they should be saved. Jane's brother, Edward, by contrast, was determined to promote reform in the church and to see the monasteries dissolved. John Foxe, author of the *Book of Martyrs* wrote that the 'monstrous hydra with six heads (the Six Articles, I mean), which devoured up so many men before, was abolished and taken away' and 'the holy Scriptures he restored to the mother tongue. Masses he restricted and abolished'.[16] Foxe saw Somerset as cleansing the corruption of the Catholic church by introducing reformist measures. However, as Somerset's protectorship collapsed, it was thought that he was damaging more than protecting the new Protestant way in England. Northumberland may well have used this as a reason to justify his uncle's execution to Edward VI. Edward was known to be a staunch Protestant, as evidenced by his determination in 1553 that his Catholic half-sister, Mary, would not succeed to the throne.

It could be argued that it was because of John Dudley, 1st Earl of Warwick, later 1st Duke of Northumberland, that Somerset was overthrown and then executed. Somerset had no option but to surrender when it became obvious that Northumberland had galvanised the council against him, and he had very few supporters who would back his continuation in the role of Lord Protector. He had lost all credibility and feared he would be overthrown, largely due to his actions during the Kett Rebellion, and the execution of his brother, Thomas Seymour, 1st Baron Seymour of Sudeley, earlier that same year. These two events, one coming so quickly on the heels of the other, undermined Somerset and his intentions and he knew that forces were gathering against him. He panicked, not wanting to lose his power and position and, quite possibly, his life. Nicholas Sander claimed that Northumberland 'promised certain persons – so it is said – whom he knew to be Catholics, to restore the Catholic religion, and to banish heresy, if they would help him to remove the protector'.[17] This does not seem to be suggested in any other sources. Sander was known to be a polemicist against those who supported reform, like Anne Boleyn. He was also the source of rumours that Anne had a sixth finger. This was one of Sander's methods to undermine the Reformation, by turning people against those who supported it, and making them seem untrustworthy.

Somerset made a huge misstep when he fled with King Edward VI from Hampton Court Palace to Windsor Castle, though his position was already floundering. This could be construed as kidnap and made his position much worse. On 6 October 1549, Somerset called for the support of the people and ordered the defence of Hampton Court, but this did not yield anything, so around 9pm that night Somerset fled with the king to the more easily defensible Windsor Castle. Somerset was willing to use armed force if necessary to defend Windsor against attack and messages went backwards and forwards for a few days between Windsor and the council in London. Both sides issued proclamations in the king's name, and it seemed as though the government was collapsing in upon itself with bitter infighting. This was the most dangerous moment of Edward's reign when the government seemed to be disintegrating and there was no obvious resolution. The bulk of the councillors had convened at the Tower of London and let it be known that they intended to force Somerset to step down as Lord Protector. This forced Somerset to act, though he told the king that it was the council who had rebelled.[18] Exactly when the council had come to the decision that Somerset had to go is not clear as there is no real evidence of animosity prior to the Kett Rebellion.[19] Edward VI had trusted his uncle and these events must have shaken him, scared him even. The king was still only 12 years old in 1549; sometimes in the midst of the court politics and bitter infighting of the time, it is easy to forget he was just a boy.

Edward VI seems to have been pulled along by family loyalty to his uncle and perhaps was reassured by the fact that Thomas Cranmer, Archbishop of Canterbury, and Sir William Paget were also at Windsor with him, though there was a lack of food, provisions, and heating as their arrival at the castle was spontaneous and unplanned. The king seems to have been strangely quiet around these events. Cranmer and Paget communicated with the council in London trying to reach a peaceful settlement. Had they not been at Windsor, the situation may have ended more bloodily than it eventually did. On 8 October 1549, Edward VI himself wrote to the council asking for a peaceful agreement to end the stand-off. By 11 October 1549 it was all over. It was only five days from the flight to Windsor Castle to the Duke of Somerset's total and complete surrender and arrest.

* * *

Edward VI had written to the council from Windsor Castle, vigorously defending his uncle Somerset. However, the letter has to be taken with a pinch of salt as to the king's true feelings as it is entirely possible, and indeed likely, that Somerset had a hand in drafting the letter so that he came off in the best possible way. Somerset knew that he needed the support of the king and the council to continue as Lord Protector but knew that the council had to listen to the king as he got older and knew his own mind. The letter was sent to the council in London on 8 October 1549:

'And finally what opinion you have conceived of our dearest uncle, the Lord Protector. For answer whereunto, we let you to wit that, as far as our age can understand, the rather moved by the visages that we see of our said uncle and councillor, and others our servants present here with us, we do lament our present estate being in such an imminent danger as, unless God put it into the hearts of you there to be careful to bring those uproars into quiet, as we see our said uncle and councillor to be here, we shall have cause to think you forget your duties towards us ... howsoever you charge our said uncle with wilfulness in your said letter, we and our council here find him so tractable, as (if you fall not into the same fault wherewith you burthen him) we trust that both you and he may continue in such sort and surety without suspicions, by a friendly determination and agreement among yourselves ... Each man hath his faults, he his, and you yours; and, if we shall hereafter as rigorously weigh yours, as we hear that you intend with cruelty to purge his, which of you shall be able to stand before us?'[20]

The letter puts a lot back onto the council, which suggests Somerset's hand is there behind Edward VI's writing. Somerset had grudges with members of the council and they with him, so it is logical for him to try and put some blame back on them. The overuse of the term 'uncle and councillor' throughout the letter is emphasising Somerset's familial connection to the king while also highlighting his usefulness and purpose. The implication in the letter is that Somerset will not be overthrown, but that the king expects the council to work with the Protector to govern the realm. The council took steps to ensure that they were not seen as the bad guys and published articles in London accusing Somerset of mismanagement, misconduct, and scaring the king by claiming the council were trying to kill him.[21] Whatever the truth of the matter, within three days of the king's letter to the council, Somerset would surrender and be imprisoned in the Tower of London.

Somerset was soon released from the Tower and restored to the council, though not as Lord Protector. He would never have that level of power again. Northumberland became Lord President of the council on Somerset's downfall. Northumberland believed there should not be another protector as Edward VI was aged twelve at this point and old enough to start attending council meetings and taking part in some of the business of the realm. Northumberland would oversee the council and guide the king. When

Somerset was released and restored to the council, it was agreed that Northumberland's son and heir, John Dudley, 2nd Earl of Warwick, would marry Somerset's daughter, Anne Seymour. The wedding took place on 3 June 1550, and John became Earl of Warwick the following year when his father was elevated to the dukedom of Northumberland. Northumberland did not really have a choice but to restore Somerset; Somerset was incredibly popular with the people and even en route to the Tower of London after his initial arrest in 1549 the people cheered him. This can help to explain why someone who posed such a threat was restored. He was popular, as well as being a blood relative of the king. A protector has to be careful not to do anything that might mean the king would turn against him when he came of age.

The Duke of Northumberland remained the leading figure in the English government until the end of Edward VI's reign and would play a pivotal role in the attempted 'coup' to put Lady Jane Grey on the throne on Edward's death in 1553. Although Jane was named the heir by Edward VI, Mary I certainly considered it a coup. Northumberland attempted to resolve the issues of Somerset's protectorship and rapidly instigated talks with the French to end the war, which centred on Boulogne and how much the French were willing to pay. The Treaty of Boulogne, signed in March 1550, returned the city to the French for 400,000 crowns, less than a quarter of what had been agreed four years earlier. Northumberland had little choice but to end the war to focus on other things.[22] Northumberland ending the war so quickly after Somerset's overthrow highlighted Somerset's failure in the international sphere, though it did not restore the betrothal of Mary Queen of Scots to Edward VI. Mary would marry the French dauphin, the future Francis II, in 1558 after having been raised in the French court since she was a child. Somerset had failed on the international stage as well as in the domestic sphere.

Twelve initial charges had been drawn up against Somerset. But Northumberland realised how much Somerset was loved by the people so knew that if he were executed, Northumberland himself would lose any love that the people had for him, and it would make it harder for him to rule as Lord President of the council. Edward VI asked the lords of the council to spare his uncle's life. He had already lost one uncle, who was rumoured to have been involved in some kind of relationship with his sister and even to have compromised her. Edward VI was surely reluctant to execute more of his family, already having been orphaned as well. Northumberland was said to have replied 'My lords, we must return good for evil. And as it is the King's will that that Duke should be pardoned, and it is the first matter he hath asked of us, we ought to accede to His Grace's wish'.[23] There is little evidence that Edward VI tried to intervene to save his uncle Thomas, so it seems significant that he intervened to try to save Edward.

The chronicler, Martin Hume, recounted a story whereby the Duchess of Somerset, Anne Stanhope, had come to see King Edward VI to plead for her husband's life, asking for a pardon for him. Edward VI was taken aback and asked where Somerset was. The duchess replied that he was in the Tower of London and that 'if he did not pardon him, members of the Council would kill him'. The Archbishop of Canterbury, Thomas Cranmer, was then summoned and said that 'if the Duke had not been imprisoned great harm would have been done'.[24] Edward VI could not believe at this point that his uncle had wanted to harm him, and it was on his orders that Somerset was released and restored. Somerset had governed Edward's country to what he believed was the best of his ability, and promoted the Protestant Reformation, so perhaps the king saw it as only fitting, rewarding, and right to attempt to save his life.

By October 1551, Northumberland had enough support on the Privy Council to destroy Somerset completely, having already removed him as Lord Protector in 1549. Northumberland believed that Somerset was the leader of opposition to his policies and wanted him out of the way. It has been suggested that Somerset had intended to bring the Duke of Northumberland down, but Northumberland struck first, having been made aware of Somerset's plans.[25] How true this is, with Somerset trying to overthrow Northumberland having already been arrested and deposed himself is unclear. Would Somerset have acted against the person who had overthrown him once and had the power to get him executed? Was he that ambitious for power? It is possible. On 16 October 1551, Somerset was rearrested by Sir Anthony Wingfield and taken to the Tower of London, where he was housed in the Lieutenant's Tower.[26] Others were also arrested to substantiate the charges against him, as had happened in 1536 with Anne Boleyn. Edward VI was told that Somerset had plotted to kill Northumberland and William Parr, 1st Marquess of Northampton, brother to the late Queen Katherine Parr.

Somerset was tried on 1 December 1551 on charges of plotting to seize and rule the young king, Edward VI. It was alleged that he had attempted to seize the Great Seal and capture the Tower of London. He was actually acquitted of high treason but found guilty on a felony charge.[27] The punishment for committing a felony was still death. Somerset knelt and thanked the court, asking for mercy for his wife and children. Northumberland claimed that he would plead with the king for Somerset's life, though whether Somerset really believed he would, is unknown. Somerset was then returned to the Tower to wait seven weeks for his execution to be carried out. Perhaps the execution was postponed in the hope that public feeling would die down.[28] Edward VI did seem to struggle to sign the final documents to authorise his uncle's death, and Northumberland made sure that none of Somerset's allies gained access to the king to change his mind. This was the same tactic used when Henry VIII cut someone out of his life, which often ended in execution: like Anne Boleyn, Thomas Wolsey, and Thomas More. Once Henry had decided to get rid of someone, he did not want to see them again and his advisers tried their hardest to keep those who might speak up for the accused away from him. It appears that Edward VI's advisers acted in a similar way.

In the third week of January 1552, it seems that Edward VI considered Somerset's pending execution at a council meeting. The minutes appear to have been doctored but it looks like Edward commanded his uncle's execution.[29] Whatever pressure or manipulation Northumberland had been applying to the king looks like it worked, or whether he reached the decision himself after consideration is unknown. Northumberland is certainly accused more often than not of manipulating the young king over the execution of Somerset, the *Devise for the Succession*, and the nomination of Lady Jane Grey as his successor.

Edward Seymour, 1st Duke of Somerset, and one-time Lord Protector to King Edward VI, was executed by beheading on Tower Hill at sunrise on 22 January 1552. Not for him the mercy of a private execution on Tower Green within the Tower of London. Edward VI had allegedly appealed for mercy and for his life; Northumberland said that he wished the sentence could be commuted but that it was too dangerous, as the crown and reformation could not be safe until Somerset was dead.[30] No doubt the one thing that would persuade Edward VI of the need for his uncle's death was if he believed he was saving the Protestant Reformation. Edward's belief in his faith was certain, as evidenced by his *Devise for the Succession* in 1553, which left the throne to the Protestant Lady Jane Grey rather than the Catholic Mary.

Religion was the main reason for the change in succession. When Somerset was executed, Edward VI recorded it blandly in his diary in a single sentence: 'The duke of Somerset had his head cut off upon Tower Hill between eight and nine o'clock in the morning'.[31] There was no emotion or thoughts about it, just that single line. The martyrologist, John Foxe, wrote that Somerset was found guilty of being a 'felon, briber, and extortioner'.[32] He was found guilty of a felony, but the accusations of bribing and extortion were rumours spread to smear Somerset's name.

No one had come to Somerset's assistance, and his estates were split up and redistributed. His son, Edward Seymour, 1st Earl of Hertford, did not regain his title until the accession of Elizabeth I and would go on to marry Katherine Grey, younger sister of Lady Jane Grey. Both would be sent to the Tower of London for their secret marriage. Unlike with Somerset, however, the title was granted to Hertford directly, rather than being a subsidiary of his father's dukedom. The dukedom of Somerset would eventually be re-granted to Hertford's grandson, William Seymour, 2nd Duke of Somerset, in 1660 by King Charles II, recognising his role in the royalist cause during the English Civil War.

Edward Seymour, 1st Duke of Somerset, was taken down by his own ambitions, and the machinations of others who were jealous of him and his wealth and power. Whether he really acted against the Duke of Northumberland is unknown, though it is possible given how ambitious he was. Perhaps he could not stand to just be a rank-and-file councillor after having been the most powerful man in England. Acting against his nephew, however, seems incredibly unlikely. Had his nephew been killed or overthrown, Somerset would have lost everything. Those charges against him at least were concocted to bring him down. He was never found guilty of high treason officially, just a felony, so perhaps the evidence was not entirely compelling.

Chapter 9

John Dudley, 1st Duke of Northumberland – 1553; & Queen Jane Grey – 1554

Lady Jane Grey, also known as the Nine Days Queen, even though her reign technically lasted for thirteen days, had royal blood. She was one of those closest to the English throne on the death of Henry VIII in 1547. The line of succession by the Act of Succession 1544, was Edward VI, only son of Henry VIII, and his heirs, then Princess Mary (later Mary I) and her heirs, then Princess Elizabeth (later Elizabeth I) and her heirs. Once the direct line of Henry VIII had expired, the crown would pass to the descendants of Henry VIII's younger sister, Mary. Lady Jane Grey was the eldest granddaughter of Mary Tudor through Mary's eldest daughter, Frances. Mary Tudor's sons and grandsons predeceased the king. Only the future Edward VI stood between Henry VIII and a female line of succession.

Mary Tudor was the youngest child of Henry VII and Elizabeth of York who made it to adulthood. By the general laws of succession in England, the elder daughter, Margaret, should have been in line before Mary. Henry VIII changed the succession in 1544 to place the line of his younger sister ahead of that of his elder sister. Margaret had married into the Scottish royal family, whereas Mary had married an English duke after the death of her first husband, Louis XII of France in 1515. The English did not want a Scottish 'foreigner' ruling in England, even though there were others in line ahead of the Scots line. Henry VIII took steps to tackle this by changing the line of succession in parliament. However, ultimately the line of Margaret Tudor would triumph with the accession of James I (James VI of Scotland) in 1603 on the death of Elizabeth I.

Mary Tudor had two daughters and two sons by her second husband, Charles Brandon, 1st Duke of Suffolk. Her sons both died young, aged 6 and 11, predeceasing Henry VIII. Their elder daughter was Frances, who married Henry Grey, 3rd Marquess of Dorset, and later 1st Duke of Suffolk by right of his wife, after the death of his father-in-law. Their younger daughter, Eleanor, married Henry Clifford, 2nd Earl of Cumberland. Jane Grey was the elder daughter of Frances and Henry Grey, and had two younger sisters, Katherine, and Mary, who would suffer under Elizabeth I for marrying without the queen's permission as they had royal blood and were in the line of succession. Jane Grey did not appear to want to be queen but was pushed into it because of her royal blood by her parents and in-laws. It demonstrates the ultimate push from nobility to the greatest power and then the furthest fall. Anne Boleyn and Katherine Howard had been queen consorts who were executed, but Jane Grey was the first person who had ruled England in her own right to latterly be executed, although she was never crowned or anointed. She came from royal blood and can potentially be seen as the forerunner to the executions of Mary Queen of Scots in February 1587 and Charles I in January 1649, both of whom were crowned and anointed regnant monarchs executed on the orders of the English parliament. Other regnant monarchs like Edward II, Richard II and Henry VI had been murdered but never condemned by parliament in the way that Jane was.

In contrast to Jane Grey, John Dudley, 1st Duke of Northumberland, was not from royal blood, and his father, Edmund Dudley, had been executed by Henry VIII in 1510. Edmund Dudley had been made a Privy Councillor by Henry VII. He was an administrator and financial agent but not descended from nobility. Henry VIII blamed Edmund Dudley and Richard Empson for many of Henry VII's unpopular policies, particularly regarding finance; they were both accused of treason and executed. John Dudley would only become a duke under Edward VI when he ousted Edward Seymour, 1st Duke of Somerset, from the protectorship during Edward's minority. He had previously been created Earl of Warwick in 1547 on the death of Henry VIII and accession of Edward VI when he was made part of Edward VI's Regency Council. He appears to have been more of a military leader than a politician or courtier, although he did become a favourite of Henry VIII in the king's later years, hence possibly his inclusion on the Regency Council.

John Dudley had married Jane Guildford around 1525 and together they had thirteen children, including Robert Dudley, 1st Earl of Leicester (and a favourite of Elizabeth I), and Guildford Dudley, who married Lady Jane Grey and was executed due to his role in her nine-day reign. Two successive sons would become Earls of Warwick after their father; John and Ambrose, and Northumberland's daughter, Katherine, would become Countess of Huntingdon. He seemed to be determined to be seen as nobility and to marry his children into the highest echelons of society.

Lady Jane Grey and John Dudley, 1st Duke of Northumberland, had very different backgrounds and levels of experience but both would end their lives under the executioner's axe. Northumberland deservingly in the eyes of Mary I for attempting to deprive her of her birth right, but Jane potentially as an innocent used as a pawn by those more powerful and ambitious than she was.

*   *   *

It is thought that Lady Jane Grey was born possibly at the family seat of Bradgate Park in Leicestershire in autumn 1537, or possibly in London. The exact date is unknown, like so many women of the time. She was the eldest daughter of Henry Grey, later 1st Duke of Suffolk, and his wife, Frances Brandon. Frances was niece to Henry VIII through his younger sister, Mary, Duchess of Suffolk, and Dowager Queen of France. Jane was followed in 1540 by a sister, Katherine, and another sister, Mary, was born in 1545. The marriage of Henry Grey and Frances Brandon did not produce any living sons meaning that, when Edward VI died, it was an all-female succession, though the throne was initially intended to pass to a son of Jane's, rather than Jane herself, as evidenced in the *Devise for the Succession*. This was changed when it became clear that Edward VI would not live long enough for Jane to produce a son. Jane was said to have been named for Henry VIII's third wife, Jane Seymour, who was also the child's godmother.[1] This must mean that Lady Jane Grey was born prior to Jane Seymour's death on 24 October 1537 in order for Jane Seymour to be her godmother.

Roger Ascham, who also tutored the future Elizabeth I in Latin between 1548 and 1550, met Jane at her childhood home at Bradgate, as he recounted in his work *The Schoolmaster*, published posthumously in 1570 during Elizabeth's reign. Ascham entered Jane's chamber to find her reading Plato rather than out hunting with her family. Ascham related that he asked Jane why she was so dedicated to her studies to which she replied that 'one of the great benefits that ever God gave me is that he sent me so sharp and severe parents and so gentle a schoolmaster'.[2] Her schoolmaster was John Aylmer who later became Bishop of London. Jane went on to say that her parents expected her to do everything so perfectly and if she failed she was 'sharply taunted, so cruelly threatened, yea, presently sometimes, with pinches, nips, and bobs, and other ways which I will not name for the honour I bear them' and then she went to Aylmer who encouraged her learning and treated her gently, so it gave her pleasure.[3] Jane seems to have taken solace in her learning to escape from something she did not want to dwell on. It was this pleasure in learning that was then further nurtured by Katherine Parr from 1547 to 1548. Jane would also take comfort in her studies while imprisoned in the Tower of London in 1553 and 1554 before her execution. Learning seemed to be a great solace to Jane in hardship. Ascham ended this section by saying that he remembered this talk well because it was worthy of recalling, and because it was the last time that he saw Lady Jane, yet he still remembered her so many years later.

On the death of Henry VIII in January 1547 and the remarriage of his sixth wife, Katherine Parr, to Thomas Seymour, 1st Baron Seymour of Sudeley, Jane Grey was sent to live with the pair at Chelsea, along with Princess Elizabeth. It is unknown exactly when Katherine and Thomas married, though it appears to have been around May 1547, just four months after the death of Henry VIII. Thomas Seymour realised that Jane could be valuable to him, and allow him to thwart his brother, the Lord Protector. There was a suggestion that Edward Seymour wanted to marry Lady Jane Grey to his own son, Edward.[4] There was an ongoing and public rivalry between the two brothers and gaining Jane's warship meant that Thomas would have a say in who she married. No doubt he relished the chance to put paid to his brother's plans.

As discussed in Chapter 7, Thomas Seymour appears to have taken advantage of the young Princess Elizabeth and she was sent away to live at Cheshunt to protect her reputation. He seems to have made no such move on Jane, who remained with Katherine and Seymour and was only removed from the care of Thomas Seymour after Katherine Parr's death in September 1548. It was not considered appropriate for a young woman or girl to live with a widowed man with no woman in the house to act as chaperone, as her father, Henry Grey, 1st Duke of Suffolk, wrote in a letter to Thomas Seymour:

'Considering the state of my daughter and her tender years, wherein she shall hardly rule herself as yet without a guide … all such good behaviour as she hereforeto hath learned by the queen's and your most wholesome instructions should either be quenched in her or at the least most diminished'.[5]

Jane would act as chief mourner at Katherine Parr's funeral at Sudeley Castle after which she was summoned home by her parents. In addition to worry over Jane's position in the household of a widowed man, there were rumours of Seymour's actions in plotting against the king, and the Grey family did not want to be involved in any kind of treason; possibly a little ironic considering their later actions in 1553 with regards to the succession. But in 1548, there was no reason to suppose that Edward VI would not marry and produce heirs of his own body. There was no reason to believe that Princess Mary would ever come to the throne at this time.

Jane wrote to Thomas Seymour after she left his house and returned to her parents, thanking him for his kindness towards her and declaring 'you have become towards me a loving and kind father so I shall be always most ready to obey your motions and good instructions' and she signed off 'your humble servant during my life'.[6] This suggests that Jane was happier during her time with Katherine Parr and Thomas Seymour than she had been up to that point, and perhaps after as well. This may have been the happiest part of her life, with a mother figure who cared for her and promoted her education and religious beliefs. There is also no reason not to believe that Thomas Seymour was a father figure to her. There was no hint of the impropriety with Jane that dogged Thomas Seymour's relationship with Edward VI's half-sister, Princess Elizabeth. Evidence we have suggests that Jane's life with her parents was not entirely happy as they were strict and sometimes unkind to her, as has been discussed earlier.

It was said that Thomas Seymour had planned to marry Jane Grey to Edward VI as the two were of an age with each other, and Jane shared Edward's staunchly Protestant beliefs. That was allegedly why Seymour had wanted Jane Grey's wardship in the first place. It was fairly common for wardships to be used for personal advantage, such as that of Margaret Beaufort, mother of Henry VII. Her wardship was granted to Edmund Tudor, 1st Earl of Richmond, and brother to Henry VI. He ended up marrying her himself as she was a great heiress, and he was unmarried. Jane's parents likely knew of Seymour's plans and had actually worked to get closer to him with this marriage in mind, knowing that the pair shared their strong Protestant religious views and together could have children to stop either Princesses Mary or Elizabeth from succeeding to the throne. However, the marriage plan never came to fruition as Seymour was arrested and executed for treason, and then Edward VI died in 1553 before he reached the age of sixteen.

Katherine Parr's household supported reformers, including her chaplain, John Parkhurst, and her almoner, Miles Coverdale. Parkhurst was a friend of Jane's tutor, John Aylmer, and Coverdale had been responsible for the first translation of the Bible into English.[7] Being around these men and such a passionate and dedicated reformer as Katherine Parr herself must have inspired Jane further in her religious beliefs and devotions. It was no longer dangerous, as it had been under Henry VIII, to shelter and promote reformers. Under Edward VI, in fact, it was encouraged, and Jane must have found it a vibrant learning environment, which she seems to have taken full advantage of. She certainly would not be willing to change her beliefs at the end of her life, facing execution.

* * *

Lady Jane Grey would in the end marry Guildford Dudley, the youngest son of John Dudley, 1st Duke of Northumberland, on 25 May 1553 at Durham House in London. She would not be queen as Thomas Seymour had hoped and planned. By this time, it was known that the king was ill, and probably suspected, at least by those in the inner circle at court, that he would not live long. He certainly would not live long enough to get married and father an heir, which left the succession as the most important issue to be resolved. Edward VI did not want his sister Mary to succeed him, as in their father's will, as she was a Catholic. It has been suggested that this marriage was Northumberland's play to bring Jane into his family, having already conceived the idea to change the succession and make Lady Jane the heir to Edward VI, rather than Princesses Mary or Elizabeth. The princesses were still illegitimate in law, despite their father reinstating them to the succession, which posed a moral issue to Edward VI, on top of Mary's religious beliefs, so contrary to his own.

Rather than Seymour's idea to have Jane Grey marry the king, Northumberland intended to make her queen in her own right, and have his son, Guildford, as king. Jane and Guildford's betrothal was agreed at the end of April 1553, with the consent and approval of the king and council. The pair married on 25 May 1553 in a joint ceremony with Guildford's sister, Katherine Dudley (who married Henry Hastings, later 3rd Earl of Huntingdon), and Jane's sister, Katherine Grey (who married Henry Herbert, later 2nd Earl of Pembroke).[8] Katherine Grey's marriage was later annulled after Lady Jane's failed reign and subsequent execution, as it was never consummated. Herbert's father did not want his family to be associated with the traitorous Greys and would instead marry his son to Lady Catherine Talbot, daughter of George Talbot, 6th Earl of Shrewsbury.

It was Edward VI's *Devise for the Succession* which changed the course of Lady Jane Grey's life. When Edward VI was dying in 1553, he wrote this article which aimed to resolve the succession once and for all. It was intended that it would replace the 1544 Act of Succession and the stipulations in Henry VIII's will in 1547. The *Devise* excluded Princesses Mary and Elizabeth from the succession to the throne on the grounds of their illegitimacy. Henry VIII's marriages to their mothers, Katherine of Aragon, and Anne Boleyn respectively, had been annulled in 1533 and 1536. Although the princesses were restored to the succession in 1544, they were never made legitimate, so Edward VI thought them unworthy to inherit the throne. Edward VI was the undisputed, lawful heir of Henry VIII without a stain of illegitimacy. His mother, Jane Seymour, married the king when his previous two wives were already dead, so there was no question of him being illegitimate in that way, like there was for Princess Elizabeth. However, the real reason for cutting the princesses out of the succession was that Mary was a Catholic and Edward was a staunch Protestant. He could not stomach the thought of his sister restoring Roman Catholicism and Papal obedience to England and so, in order to disinherit her, he also had to disinherit Elizabeth who was likewise illegitimate. Of course, with the benefit of hindsight, we know that this would not work as both Mary I and Elizabeth I would rule England in their own rights.

The text of the *Devise for the Succession* is interesting because it was altered several times while it was being written as matters progressed. The throne was initially to be left to 'the L Franceses heires masles' then to 'the L Janes heires masles' then to the male heirs of Jane's sisters, Katherine, and Mary.[9] However, when it became obvious to Edward VI that he was dying and that there would not be any male heirs born before his death, he made an insertion to the *Devise* to say 'the L Jane and her heires masles'.[10] This was absolutely critical as, with the insertion of two words 'and her', Edward VI left the throne to his cousin, Jane Grey, who was married to Guildford Dudley, son to the Duke of Northumberland. Jane's mother, Frances, was overlooked in the line of succession, only being mentioned for any sons she may bear. She was aged 36 in July 1553 so her having a son was not entirely out of the question, after all, Katherine Parr was aged 35 when she conceived for the first time in 1547. But it was more likely that male issue would come from one of Frances's daughters, hence probably the change to make Jane the heir herself. If Edward had to leave his throne to a female, he chose someone who undoubtedly shared his Protestant faith, and would have the support of the powerful Duke of Northumberland. Princesses Mary and Elizabeth did not even get a mention in the *Devise*, almost like they had been erased from Edward's thoughts as if they did not matter.

The accession of Lady Jane Grey to the English throne in July 1553 was 'highly questionable'.[11] The *Devise for the Succession* drafted by Edward VI overturned Henry VIII's will and the parliamentary statute which upheld it. The *Devise* was never ratified by parliament or put into law so, legally, Mary I remained the rightful heir to her half-brother, Edward VI. There was a question over whether it was even possible for Edward to change the succession in this way and have it stand up legally. The people of London were not impressed when Jane was declared queen rather than Mary. They had expected the declaration of Mary as queen of England. The people knew that Mary was the rightful heir in law and was seen by many as the only legitimate daughter of Henry VIII, as opposed to Elizabeth who many across Catholic Europe and in England considered a bastard. Jane had little support from the common people, where Mary had 40,000 people who gathered to fight in her name at her stronghold of Framlingham Castle in East Anglia and ensure her succession to the throne.[12] When she rode into London after Jane Grey's overthrow she was acclaimed by the people as the rightful queen.

It has often been assumed that it was the Duke of Northumberland who influenced Edward VI over the succession of Lady Jane Grey, but there is actually no real evidence to suggest that it was not wholly the king's own idea. The betrothal of Jane Grey and Guildford Dudley does not seem to have occurred until after Edward VI fell ill and he had already outlined his plans for the succession and the decision for the betrothal also seems to have been the king's. Accounts suggest that Jane's parents were not very happy with the idea of an upstart duke's son for their daughter when it was hoped once that she might marry the king.[13] Edward VI died on 6 July 1553 and Lady Jane Grey was declared queen on 10 July. Jane is known as the Nine Days Queen but was effectively queen for thirteen days from the day of Edward's death, even though her reign was not declared immediately. She only ruled for nine days until her overthrow when the council declared for Mary I.

John Dudley, 1st Duke of Northumberland, was executed immediately when Mary I came to the throne. Mary believed that he had been the one behind the *Devise for the Succession* and pushing for Jane Grey to be declared queen on the death of Edward VI. It was he who had pushed the other council members to declare for Jane. It was also he who had set out after Mary herself, pursuing her into Suffolk to capture or kill her, reaching as far as Bury St Edmunds before retreating to Cambridge where he eventually declared Mary queen of England. While Northumberland had been pursuing Mary into East Anglia, the council in London had left the Tower, realised that Mary had too much support, she was not going to give up, and declared Mary the rightful queen on 19 July 1553. Northumberland followed suit the following day when he received a message from the council. Mary I showed Northumberland no mercy. He only declared her queen when there was no hope left for Jane. Northumberland was arrested on 24 July 1553 by Henry FitzAlan, 12th Earl of Arundel, and taken back to London, where he was paraded through the streets to the Tower of London as a traitor. He was joined by his brother, Andrew Dudley, and his sons, Robert Dudley, later 1st Earl of Leicester, John Dudley, 2nd Earl of Warwick, Ambrose Dudley, later 3rd Earl of Warwick, and Henry Dudley.[14] His wife, Jane, Duchess of Northumberland, his youngest son, Guildford Dudley, and his daughter-in-law, Lady Jane Grey, had never left the Tower; it was transformed from their palace to their prison.

On the eve of his execution, Northumberland converted to Catholicism after trying to change the succession specifically to prevent the Catholic Mary from taking the throne. Perhaps he hoped for a last-minute reprieve from the queen, but this did not come. Mary would not leave Northumberland alive to potentially plot against her in the future. He had tried to deprive her of her birth right, and quite possibly would have succeeded had he managed to capture her. Possibly Northumberland had felt betrayed by his Protestant allies who had defected to Mary the minute he left London, but his conversion meant that he was seen as a traitor by Catholics and an apostate and hypocrite by Protestants, hated by both sides.[15] He took Holy Communion in the Chapel of St Peter ad Vincula within the Tower of London, and he proclaimed his belief that the Catholic Mass was the true way, in spite of promoting the reformed religion for many years and exhorting Mary I to convert to the reformed faith.[16] He now gave in to Mary and begged the forgiveness of all those who had gathered to witness his revocation of the reformed faith. No one, except his children, seemed to care when he died. There had been a suggestion that Northumberland's last-minute conversion to Catholicism before his death convinced some others to turn back to Catholicism as well, although exact numbers are unknown.[17] It also is not known how many of these conversions were sincere, or how many believed they needed to do it to survive, knowing how fanatical Mary I was regarding her own religion. Her religion was that of her mother, Katherine of Aragon, who was persecuted by her father and who broke with Rome in the 1530s; Mary I would do what she believed she needed to do to restore it to England. She would ultimately fail and would gain the epithet of 'Bloody Mary' for her attempt.

John Dudley, 1st Duke of Northumberland's 'scheming, plotting, ruthless ambition, and ultimate betrayal of the Protestant faith' all combined to lead to his execution on Tower Hill on 22 August 1553.[18] Northumberland died first, then a couple of his followers, Sir John Gates and Sir Thomas Palmer. Perhaps he hoped for a last-minute reprieve because of his conversion to Catholicism the previous day, but in this he would be disappointed. His head was taken off with a single blow.

Mary I did not initially intend to have Lady Jane Grey and her husband, Guildford Dudley, executed. It was only after Wyatt's Rebellion in January 1554 that she finally signed the death warrants for the pair, having been pressured by her council and the Spanish. The Spanish declared that Philip II of Spain, who was to marry Mary I, would not travel to England while Jane Grey still lived. The Wyatt Rebellion was led by Sir Thomas Wyatt the Younger (son of the poet, Sir Thomas Wyatt the Elder, who had once wooed Anne Boleyn). He and his followers marched from Kent to London, and they looked likely to succeed at one point, having almost reached the royal palace where the queen was residing, intending to seize her. Mary I was advised to flee London, but she held her nerve and gave a speech at the Guildhall which rallied Londoners to block Wyatt's entry to the city. Wyatt eventually surrendered and was imprisoned in the Tower of London. It was suggested that, had Wyatt succeeded, he intended either to restore Jane Grey to the throne, or put Princess Elizabeth on the throne and marry her to Edward Courtenay, 1st Earl of Devon. Courtenay was the great-grandson of Edward IV so had Yorkist royal blood. He had been imprisoned in the Tower of London in 1538. His father, the Marquess of Exeter, was executed in December 1538 after the discovery of the Exeter Conspiracy. Courtenay was only released from the Tower on the accession of Mary I in 1553. His involvement in the conspiracy against Mary I when she had been kind to him was an insult to the queen. As a result of her suspected involvement in the rebellion, Princess Elizabeth was also imprisoned in the Tower of London, and Mary finally signed the death warrants of Jane Grey and Guildford Dudley.

Even when Lady Jane Grey and Guildford Dudley were tried for treason in November 1553, it was Mary I's intention to pardon them and allow them to live. However, the trial was likely necessary so that the people of England could see that Jane was beaten and that Mary was triumphant. It was said that the queen's conscience would not allow her to have Jane put to death, despite the fact that it may have been safer to have her killed.[19] Lady Jane Grey and Lord Guildford Dudley were tried on 13 November 1553, along with Guildford's brothers, Henry and Ambrose Dudley, and Thomas Cranmer, Archbishop of Canterbury. They were taken from the Tower of London to the Guildhall. The procession through the streets was led by a man carrying an axe; a reminder that they were being tried for a capital crime, for which the punishment was death if found guilty. Jane carried a prayer book, and another hung at her waist, a sign of defiance in her defence of her faith.[20] Transcripts of the trial do not survive, but they were all found guilty of treason and Jane was sentenced to be burned alive, the automatic penalty for any woman found guilty of treason. As the procession returned to the Tower, the axe was turned towards the condemned as a symbol of their guilt.

Mary I sent Jane Grey her chaplain, John Feckenham, the abbot of Westminster, a couple of days before the execution, to try and persuade Jane to convert from the staunch Protestantism she promoted and embodied, to Roman Catholicism. Feckenham failed and Jane wrote down what they discussed in order to bolster Protestant support. She was determined to die as a martyr to her faith. Feckenham and Jane debated over the sacraments; Feckenham espoused the traditional Catholic seven, but Jane affirmed that there were only two: baptism and the Lord's Supper. Jane questioned by what Scripture Feckenham found seven sacraments, to which he failed to give an answer. The pair then discussed the idea of transubstantiation which Catholics believed meant that the bread and wine given in the Mass actually became the body and blood of Christ. Protestants, like Jane, believed 'that at the supper I neither receive flesh nor blood, but bread and wine, which bread, when it is broken, and which wine, when it is drunken, putteth me in remembrance how that for my sins the body of Christ was broken, and his blood shed on the cross'.[21] Protestants effectively believed that the bread and wine were symbolic of the body and blood but did not become it. Catholics believed that the bread and wine literally became the body and blood of Christ during the Mass. This is a key disagreement between Catholics and Protestants (though 'Protestant' itself was not a word widely in use in the sixteenth century). The word 'Protestant' came from the word 'protest' as those who followed the new faith protested against Catholic traditions.

* * *

The day before the executions of Lady Jane Grey and Guildford Dudley, Guildford requested to see Jane one final time. Mary I agreed to the meeting if it would be of consolation to the young couple, but Jane refused, saying it would 'only increase their misery and pain' and it would be better to put it off until they could 'meet shortly elsewhere and live bound by indissoluble ties'.[22] There is not really much evidence of the relationship between the two during their short marriage, but it does not seem to have been close. Many perceptions show Jane as hating Guildford, though it appears more like indifference. She did refuse to make him king during her short tenure as queen, saying she would make him a duke instead. He was not the one with royal blood and a claim to the throne. Perhaps Jane understood that making Guildford king might alienate the people from her rule even further, given that the Duke of Northumberland was known generally as the 'Bad Duke', compared to the executed Duke of Somerset who was known as the 'Good Duke'. There is no real evidence Jane Grey showed the slightest interest in Guildford during their imprisonment either. The word 'Jane' is carved into the wall of the chambers shared by the Dudley brothers during their imprisonment in the Tower, but there is no evidence it was carved in love, or even that it was Guildford Dudley who carved it. It may have merely been a way to alleviate the boredom of imprisonment.

That same night, the night before her execution, Jane Grey wrote in a Greek Testament to be gifted to her sister, Katherine. In it she wrote 'And if you with a good mind read it, and with an earnest desire follow it, it shall bring you to an immortal and everlasting life. It will teach you to live and learn you to die … trust not that the tenderness of your age, shall lengthen your life'.[23] Jane clearly believed that her faith would sustain her to the moment of her death, and so it proved. Katherine was thought to be more flighty and more concerned with material things rather than her soul, at least that seems to be what Jane implies when writing to her. Jane exhorted Katherine to spend more time reading the word of God and living by the precepts of the scriptures. She added an ominous warning from her own life, that youth does not necessarily mean that you have a long life ahead of you; that you should always be prepared for death which may wait just around the corner. Katherine herself would discover the vagaries of monarchs when she found herself imprisoned in the Tower of London in the reign of her cousin, Elizabeth I, for a marriage not approved by the queen.

As well as writing to her sister the night before her execution, Jane also wrote a message in her prayer book for her father. It can be argued that it was because of him that Jane was now being executed, as he had participated in Wyatt's Rebellion which had pushed the queen to sign her death warrant. She wrote that 'though it hath pleased God to take away two of you children, yet think not that you have lost them, but trust that we, by leaving this mortal life have won an immortal life'.[24] There seems to be no overt blame attached to her father for the situation she found herself in. Perhaps she was feeling it inside but did not want to end her earthly life with blame and negativity, focusing on the fact that her trials would soon be over. She likely also knew that the prayer book would be preserved, and her messages read down the years.

Guildford Dudley was executed first, taken at 10am on 12 February 1554 to Tower Hill to be beheaded. Unlike Jane, he was not granted a private execution within the walls of the Tower of London but was executed in public. Jane Grey stood at her chamber window and watched him leave, then waited for the cart bringing his body back to the Tower to return. He was beheaded with a single stroke from an axe after saying his prayers. He had been accompanied to his execution by Sir Anthony Browne and John Throckmorton who he asked to pray for him as well.[25] His brothers remained imprisoned in the Tower, though they also had been found guilty and condemned to death. The brothers, Robert, Ambrose, and Henry were released in late 1554. The eldest brother, John, died in October 1554 shortly after being released from the Tower. Guildford was buried in the Chapel of

St Peter ad Vincula within the Tower complex. His wife, Lady Jane Grey, would join him within hours.

Jane herself was to be executed on the privacy of Tower Green, next to the White Tower, within the Tower of London itself, much like Queens Anne Boleyn and Katherine Howard before her. It has been suggested that Jane's scaffold was on the exact same spot as that of Anne Boleyn eighteen years earlier. From where she was imprisoned in the home of Nathaniel Partridge, the Gentleman Gaoler, she would have been able to see and hear her scaffold being built. She had been sentenced to be either burned or beheaded at the queen's pleasure, but the queen chose a sentence of beheading, the kinder death. Burning was the traditional punishment for a woman convicted of treason, but beheadings seem to have been more common, perhaps as a nod to mercy.

On 12 February 1554, when Jane Grey left Partridge's house for the final time to walk to the scaffold, she was leaning on the arm of Sir John Brydges, the Lieutenant of the Tower, accompanied by two ladies: Mrs Ellen and Elizabeth Tylney, who were both sobbing. Mrs Ellen had been with Jane since her childhood and had been her nurse, so this must have been very distressing for her. Jane herself seemed remarkably calm and collected, dry-eyed, and wearing the same black dress she had worn to her trial in November 1553. She had an open prayer book in her free hand, determined to die as a Protestant martyr. It is sometimes easy to forget in the face of her dignity and maturity in an unbearable situation that she was just 16 or 17 years old. Once on the scaffold, Jane turned to address the audience who had gathered to watch her die:

'Good people, I am come hither to die, and by a law I am condemned to the same. The fact, indeed, against the Queen's highness was unlawful, and the consenting thereunto by me: but touching the procurement and desire thereof by me or on my behalf, I do wash my hands thereof in innocency, before God, and the face of you, good Christian people, this day. I pray you all, good Christian people, to bear witness that I die a true Christian woman, and that I look to be saved by none other mean, but only by the mercy of God in the merits of the blood of his only son Jesus Christ: and I confess, when I did know the word of God I neglected the same, loved myself and the world, and therefore this plague or punishment is happily and worthily happened unto me for my sins: and yet I thank God of his goodness that he hath thus given me a time and respect to repent. And now, good people, while I am alive, I pray you to assist me with your prayers.'[26]

In her final speech, Jane acknowledged that acting to take the throne from the hands of Mary I was unlawful, but she stated outright that it was not her choice nor her will, but something forced on her by others. She was a pawn for ambitious men in power. By stating she died a 'true Christian woman' Jane referred to her Protestant religion as the true religion, and not Mary's Catholicism. Jane reinforced the idea in her final words that she died a Protestant and not in the religion of the new queen, as Northumberland did, recanting his Protestantism when faced with death. She claimed that death is right for her to atone for her sins and seemed to be grateful for the extra time she got after the end of her reign; she had an extra seven months, even though it was spent imprisoned in the Tower of London. She appeared to use her time to continue her studies.

In keeping with the Protestant faith she espoused, Jane then recited the 51st Psalm, the Miserere, in English. John Feckenham, who had accompanied her to the scaffold at Jane's own request, repeated it after her in Latin. She then handed her gloves and handkerchief to Elizabeth Tylney and her prayer book to John Brydges' brother, Thomas, to pass on to the Lieutenant as her final gift. She did not seem to resent him or blame him for her imprisonment and realised he acted under orders but wanted to thank him for his care of her. Jane began to untie her outer gown but shrank away when the executioner stepped up to assist and take it from her. Traditionally, outer garments of the accused were a part of the executioner's payment. The executioner knelt for forgiveness as was customary, and Jane was then handed a handkerchief to tie around her eyes as a blindfold. She knelt down in the straw around the block and blindfolded herself. However, she could not then find the block to lay her head on. Someone assisted her to find it and place herself on it then a single blow severed her head from her body.

François de Noailles, a French diplomat, arrived in London on 12 February 1554 and reported seeing Jane's body lying on the scaffold after her death, commenting on the huge amount of blood which came from such a small body.[27] There was a delay in moving the body, hence Noailles saw the amount of blood that came from it, probably due to uncertainty or reluctance to make any kind of decision over what should be done with it, rather than any kind of disrespect. Mary I did not seem to have any kind of grudge against Jane Grey or Guildford Dudley, and in fact seemed inclined to forgive, until it became obvious that others would use Jane to their own advantage. It seems likely that Mary would have wanted her cousin to have a proper and decent burial as befitted a princess of the royal blood.

There has been some doubt over the years as to the details of her burial. Tradition persisted that Jane was returned to her childhood home of Bradgate Park for burial. However, there is no reason to doubt that the remains of Lady Jane Grey were buried in the Chapel of St Peter ad Vincula within the Tower of London between those of the other executed queens, Anne Boleyn and Katherine Howard, and close to the body of her husband, executed just hours earlier. Jane's execution, which seems 'coldy horrifying' to us today, essentially a 'judicial murder', made no real public stir at the time and public opinion, which would assist Princess Elizabeth so much, was not used to help Jane.[28] Perhaps the lack of sympathy towards Jane, as the 16-year-old went to her death, was because she was linked too closely to the unpopular Dudleys, and a part of the coup that tried to take the throne from Mary I. Mary was popular as the daughter of Henry VIII and Katherine of Aragon, legitimate in the eyes of the Catholic church and the Pope, and was seen by most of England as the rightful heir to Edward VI as per Henry VIII's will.

In the prayer book which Jane Grey handed to Thomas Brydges on the scaffold, and he passed to his brother, Edward Brydges, the Lieutenant of the Tower who had been responsible for her imprisonment, Jane had written the following:

'If my faults deserve punishment, my youth at least and my imprudence were worth of excuse. God and posterity will show me favour ... Live still to die, that by death you may purchase eternal life, and remember how the end of Methuselah, who, as we read in the scriptures, was the longest liver that was of a man, died at the last: for as the Preacher says, there is a time to be born and a time to die; and the day of death is better than the day of our birth'.[29]

Jane said that she was young, and the implication is that she was not wholly responsible for her actions, doing as her parents, father-in-law, and husband told her to do; her fault was in being unwise and a little naïve. She believed that God would forgive her, and that history would remember her favourably.

Her belief in her reformed religion as a Protestant was absolute, as shown in her quoting of the scriptures, and her implied belief that it was not good works that got you into heaven. She believed that, despite her unwise actions, she would be treated favourably by God and received into Heaven on her death. But in saying that, she also believed that it was her time to die, and she seemed to glory in that, and the fact that soon she would be past her pain.

Monsignor Giovanni Franceso Commendone was sent by Pope Julius III to report on the situation in England and he informed the Pope that 'the girl, born to a misery beyond tears, had faced death with far greater gallantry than it might be expected from her sex and the natural weakness of her age'.[30] In spite of her tragic story, what Jane appears to have left behind is a sense of her strength as a young woman sticking to her convictions and making the most of the circumstances that she found herself in, determined to leave a mark on the world and make a difference. The execution of Lady Jane Grey is perhaps one of the most shocking and upsetting of the Tudor period, because the evidence suggests that she really did not want to accept the crown in July 1553 but was forced to do so by her parents and in-laws. Then, when it was thought that she might be spared by Mary I's mercy, her own father was a part of the rebellion that doomed her. She had so much hope and promise as a noblewoman and a queen, but her royal blood and the ambitions of those around her were against her. Like so many others of high and even royal blood she tragically ended her life under the executioner's axe.

Chapter 10

Thomas Howard, 4th Duke of Norfolk – 1572

Thomas Howard, 4th Duke of Norfolk, was part of one of the premier families in England under the Tudors. The Howard family were deeply involved across the whole period in cases of treason. Norfolk was also the first peer of the realm to be executed for treason during the reign of Elizabeth I. She had lasted fourteen years without executing a peer, but Norfolk unquestionably acted against her and left her with no choice, unless she consistently wanted to be under threat from him. As we have seen in previous chapters, two of his cousins, Anne Boleyn and Katherine Howard, became queens of England as the second and fifth wives of Henry VIII respectively. However, the family was tainted by treason as both women were executed by the king for adultery and treason. This was over fifty years after John Howard, 1st Duke of Norfolk, was killed fighting for Richard III at the Battle of Bosworth Field in 1485. His son, Thomas Howard, later 2nd Duke of Norfolk, was imprisoned in the Tower of London as a result of fighting for Richard but was later released. He regained the Norfolk dukedom in 1514 after the Battle of Flodden Field the previous year as a reward for his services to the crown and his role in defeating the Scots.

Thomas Howard, 4th Duke of Norfolk, was the son of Henry Howard, Earl of Surrey, who was the last man to be executed by Henry VIII just days before the king's own death in 1547 (see Chapter 6). The paternal grandfather of the 4th Duke of Norfolk was Thomas Howard, 3rd Duke of Norfolk, the fourth duke's namesake, who himself narrowly avoided being executed by Henry VIII only because the king himself died. The 3rd duke had been imprisoned alongside his son, the earl of Surrey, accused of hiding his son's treason (misprision). The 3rd duke survived his son's folly and death, and lived into the reign of Mary I, dying in 1554, though he spent the entirety of Edward VI's reign (1547–1553) in the Tower of London, and was only released on Mary's accession in July 1553 after the aborted reign of Lady Jane Grey. Jane was imprisoned as the 3rd duke of Norfolk was released.

Norfolk's mother was Frances de Vere, the daughter of John de Vere, 15th Earl of Oxford, from a long line of nobility, although John de Vere was the second cousin of the 14th earl, and the great-grandson of the 11th earl. The earldom had not passed down from father to son and Frances's father would not have expected to inherit. After her husband, Henry Howard, Earl of Surrey, was executed in 1547, Frances remarried to Thomas Steyning and had two other children, Henry and Mary, who were Norfolk's half-siblings. Not much appears to be known about these half-siblings, or Norfolk's stepfather.

As well as Thomas Howard, later 4th Duke of Norfolk, Henry Howard had four other children who were Thomas' siblings: a second son, Henry Howard, later 1st Earl of Northampton, and three daughters, Jane, Katherine, and Margaret. Jane Howard became Countess of Westmorland through her marriage to Charles Neville, 6th Earl of Westmorland. Westmorland would be involved in the Northern Rising of 1569, perhaps another connection which drew Norfolk into the rebellion. Charles escaped execution but fled to Flanders in the aftermath and would not see his wife again. Katherine Howard married Henry Berkeley, 7th Baron Berkeley, and Margaret Howard married Henry Scrope, 9th Baron Scrope of Bolton. Margaret had been born posthumously, after her father's execution in 1547. Henry Howard the younger died unmarried. The 4th duke's siblings married into other noble families and strengthened the Howards' connections. The Howard family was dogged by treason, but even the current dukes of Norfolk are descended from the 4th duke's father, Henry Howard, Earl of Surrey, and are now known as the Fitzalan-Howards. They managed to survive as the Tudor Howards struggled to do and retained the family title, the dukedom of Norfolk, which was still relatively new under the Tudors. The title came to the Howards from Thomas Mowbray, 1st Duke of Norfolk. His great-grandson, the 4th duke, had died without male issue and the title descended to his daughter's husband, Richard, the younger of the Princes in the Tower. When the title reverted to the crown in 1483 after the Princes in the Tower were rumoured to be dead, it was re-granted to John Howard, 1st Duke of Norfolk, in 1483. This is the line which still survives to this day.

The Howard family seems to be one constantly dogged by the threat of treason, and this Thomas Howard would be no exception. From the surviving evidence it seems almost certain that Norfolk was guilty of treason, involved in a plot against the queen and had planned to marry against her wishes to someone who had claimed the English throne in the past, and was also plotting against the queen even from her imprisonment in various locations across England. Norfolk created his own end by his folly, combined with the lure of a crown in the form of Mary Queen of Scots.

* * *

Thomas Howard, later 4th Duke of Norfolk, was born on 10 March 1536 at the Howard family seat of Kenninghall in Norfolk, to Henry Howard, Earl of Surrey, and his wife Frances de Vere, daughter of John de Vere, 15th Earl of Oxford. He was the eldest child of five, and had one younger brother, Henry Howard, 1st Earl of Northampton, and three sisters: Jane, Katherine, and Margaret. There were four years between Thomas and Henry. The exact birthdates of the sisters are unknown, and it is even debated whether Jane was older or younger than Thomas.

When his father, the Earl of Surrey, was executed in 1547, Thomas and his siblings were removed from their mother's care and placed into the custody of Sir John Williams at Rycote. This was quite usual when a noble father died, particularly when the parent was executed. It was a way of making sure that the children were raised not to approve of the actions of the parent and cause problems later on, by placing them with someone unquestionably loyal to the crown. In 1548, the siblings were placed into the care of their aunt, Mary Howard Fitzroy, Duchess of Richmond and Somerset, at Reigate Castle.[1] Mary was the widow of Henry VIII's illegitimate son, Henry Fitzroy, who died in 1536, aged 17. She never remarried. As a close relative, Mary may have been considered the right person to raise the children. Thomas's tutor when under the care of his aunt was John Foxe, later the author of the *Book of Martyrs*. However, Foxe was forced into exile when Mary I acceded to the throne in 1553. He was a staunch Protestant while Mary espoused Roman Catholicism, to the point where she burned those who did not share her beliefs. Foxe was present when Norfolk was executed in 1572.[2] Perhaps it was of comfort to the duke to have his old tutor there. Foxe had returned to England under Elizabeth I though he had waited a while after her accession to see what her stance on religion would be. He did not want to return and then be forced to flee again. Elizabeth had kept her true feelings on religion fairly well-concealed over the preceding years. His *Book of Martyrs* was first published in 1563 by publisher John Day in London, who specialised in printing Protestant literature.

After the death of Edward VI and the accession of Mary I to the throne, Thomas's grandfather, Thomas Howard, 3rd Duke of Norfolk, was released from the Tower of London, where he had been since 1547. The 3rd duke assigned the further education of his grandson and heir to John White, the Roman Catholic bishop of Lincoln and then Winchester.[3] So it appears that the 4th duke was educated by both Catholic and Protestant tutors. It seems little wonder that no one is entirely sure what his religious inclinations were in later life.

Thomas Howard was created a Knight of the Bath on 29 September 1553 as part of the ceremonies surrounding the coronation of Mary I. He assisted his grandfather, Thomas Howard, 3rd Duke of Norfolk, in his role as Earl Marshal at the coronation and Lord High Steward at the following celebratory banquet. In the first parliament of Mary I in October 1553, the attainder against Thomas Howard because of his father's execution was declared void, meaning that he could inherit the dukedom when the 3rd duke died, and he was recognised as the rightful Earl of Surrey and heir to the Norfolk dukedom. That same parliament declared Mary I legitimate and the marriage of Henry VIII and Katherine of Aragon legal and valid, emphasising Elizabeth I's illegitimacy. If Katherine of Aragon's marriage was valid, then that of Anne Boleyn had to be invalid as the two crossed over. When Mary I married Philip II of Spain in 1554, Thomas became his first gentleman of the bedchamber.[4] Thomas Howard inherited the Norfolk dukedom on 25 August 1554 when the 3rd duke died around aged 80. He had only had his freedom for just over a year after over six years in the Tower of London. The 3rd duke was buried in the Church of St Michael at Framlingham, close to Framlingham Castle, a Howard residence.

During the early years of Elizabeth I's reign from 1558, Thomas Howard seemed to be favoured by the new queen, perhaps as a relative of the young queen on her mother's side (Thomas Howard, 4th Duke of Norfolk, was a first cousin once removed of Anne Boleyn and thus a second cousin to Elizabeth I). Elizabeth seemed to enjoy having her maternal relatives around her, even if it was rare she spoke of her disgraced mother. Her cousin, Catherine Knollys (née Carey) was one of the queen's closest ladies-in-waiting right up to her death in 1569, aged 45. Catherine was the daughter of Anne Boleyn's sister, Mary Boleyn, and her first husband William Carey, though it has also been suggested that she may have been an illegitimate daughter of Henry VIII. Catherine's daughter, Lettice Knollys, certainly bore a marked resemblance to Elizabeth I.

As Earl Marshal, Thomas Howard, 4th Duke of Norfolk, supervised Mary I's funeral in December 1558, and then Elizabeth I's coronation a month later on 15 January 1559. Norfolk was created a Knight of the Garter on 24 April 1559, admitted to Gray's Inn on 28 December 1561, and given the freedom of the City of London in January 1562. Gray's Inn is still today one of the Inns of Court which focuses on the law and training barristers. The freedom of the city meant that Norfolk could trade in the city freely and was often granted privileges in the governance of the city. The status still exists today, though largely as a tradition without any real privileges. Norfolk attended both Cambridge and Oxford Universities in 1564 and 1568 respectively. He was obviously well-educated as befitted his noble status and the expectations for his future. He was being trained to take up a place at the centre of English governance and court life.

Thomas Howard married three times across his lifetime. The first was to Mary FitzAlan, daughter of Henry FitzAlan, 12th or 19th Earl of Arundel, in 1555 (he appears to be numbered both ways as an earl, though it is unclear as to why. The numbering reverts to the higher figure with his son). They had a single son, Philip Howard, 20th Earl of Arundel. Mary died after two years of marriage in 1557, and Thomas remarried to Margaret Audley, daughter of Thomas Audley, 1st Baron Audley of Walden. They had four children together: Thomas Howard, 1st Earl of Suffolk, Lord William Howard, Elizabeth Howard who died in childhood, and Margaret Howard who married Robert Sackville, 2nd Earl of Dorset. When Margaret died in 1563, Thomas married for a third time to Elizabeth Leyburne, daughter of Sir James Leyburne and widow of Thomas Dacre, 4th Baron Dacre of Gillesland. Norfolk's three sons by his first two wives, Philip, Thomas and William, married the Dacre sisters who were the daughters of Elizabeth Leyburne by her first husband, Thomas Dacre. Thus, Norfolk's sons married their stepsisters: Philip married Anne, Thomas married Margaret, and William married Elizabeth Dacre. This was not entirely unusual in the Tudor period, in order to keep the family wealth and titles in the family. A dispensation would have been required from the Archbishop of Canterbury for the marriages to go ahead. Elizabeth Leyburne died in 1567. As will be seen, Thomas Howard attempted to marry a fourth time, to Mary Queen of Scots. The Howards were prolific in the marrying and birthing of children. It is little wonder that the Howard line can still be traced down to the present day.

The 4th duke of Norfolk seemed to have a life many in the Tudor period could only dream of. But he would become entangled in two rebellions he could not extract himself from and end up beheaded like his father before him. The Howards were ambitious, and it undid many of them in the end.

* * *

Thomas Howard's fall from grace began with his involvement with Mary Queen of Scots. Mary fled to England in 1568 from her native Scotland, having been forced to abdicate her throne by the Protestant lords in favour of her son, James VI of Scotland (later James I of England). Mary had never really managed to be successful at ruling in Scotland. Although Queen of Scots from the age of six months, she was sent to France as a girl where she married the future Francis II and ruled as queen of France from 1559 until Francis' death the following year in 1560. When Mary I died in England in 1558, Mary Queen of Scots had declared herself queen of England, possibly with the support of the French royal family, and began quartering the royal arms with her own. Mary's mother, Mary of Guise, had been ruling as regent in her place in Scotland. After Francis' death Mary returned to Scotland but was out of touch with the common people and the religion of the country. Scotland was a Protestant country, but Mary Queen of Scots was a staunch Catholic, having been raised at the Catholic French court. Also, having been raised away from the country she was ruling, Mary did not have any close friends and allies to support her on her return. She did not have the network that many monarchs of the time had around them and this weakened her and made it easier for the Protestant lords to overthrow her.

When Mary Queen of Scots fled to England in 1568, she had hoped that her cousin, Elizabeth I, would raise an army to help her regain the Scottish throne. But Elizabeth did no such thing. Although Mary abdicated, she never really accepted it. She saw it as forced so not legal. Mary was instead put under what was effectively house arrest in various locations across England while the English government decided what to do with her. These included Bolton Castle, Tutbury Castle, Sheffield Castle, and Sheffield Manor Lodge, the latter two of which was where Mary would spend the majority of her nineteen years imprisoned in England. Mary would remain in English captivity until her execution in 1587 in the great hall at Fotheringhay Castle after the failed Babington Plot. She became involved in several rebellions aimed at obtaining her own freedom, overthrowing Elizabeth I from the English throne, and taking it herself jointly with the throne of Scotland, or at least ruling the latter in conjunction with her son.

Within a year of Mary fleeing to England, rumours spread that Mary aimed to marry Thomas Howard, 4th Duke of Norfolk, which would mean the union of the Scottish throne to the premier duke in England also with a claim to the English throne. This was the light to the touchpaper of rebellion in England and was the beginning of the end of dukes in England under the Tudors. Norfolk was the only duke in England at this time. There had been two dukes executed under Mary I, leaving Norfolk as the only surviving duke. They were John Dudley, 1st Duke of Northumberland, who was executed for supposedly masterminding the nine-day reign of Lady Jane Grey in 1553, and Henry Grey, 1st Duke of Suffolk, the father of the ill-fated Lady Jane Grey, who was executed in 1554. The historian, Susan Doran, expresses the opinion that the scheme to marry Mary Queen of Scots to the Duke of Norfolk was harmless in and of itself, but that it did trigger a major Catholic revolt in the north of England, so would begin to cause problems for Elizabeth I.[5] It is interesting to note that the first rebellion under Elizabeth I was within a year of Mary Queen of Scots arriving in England, and it involved the top peer in the realm. Norfolk initially denied the scheme, and it would not have been possible in any case until Mary was divorced from her third husband, James Hepburn, 4th Earl of Bothwell. Bothwell would die in 1578 after a long imprisonment in Denmark. There have been constant debates over the validity of his marriage to the Scots queen, and whether it really came about as a result of kidnap and rape.

Elizabeth I appears to have suggested a marriage between Mary Queen of Scots and Thomas Howard, 4th Duke of Norfolk, in the early 1560s when Mary was newly widowed and ruling in Scotland.[6] However, these plans came to nothing and when the scheme again arose, it was when Mary was captive in England and the plans were made behind Elizabeth I's back, which put everyone involved in greater danger. Norfolk, as a subject of Elizabeth, was probably in the greatest danger, even more so because he had denied the plans just months before Elizabeth knew about them for sure. Norfolk had said that he did not like the rumours swirling about a match between himself and Mary and that he did not desire it but, just a few months later, it was demonstrated that he had in fact been lying.[7] Norfolk was told to abandon any thoughts of such a match, otherwise he would be accounted hugely disloyal to his queen and country.

Norfolk argued that the marriage scheme with Mary Queen of Scots would ensure a stable succession in England after Elizabeth I, but the fact that it had been conducted in secret without her knowledge alarmed the queen.[8] The succession was also a sore point with Elizabeth I, and one she often refused to talk about, saying that she would not marry as she was married to her country. She also understood the position of being the heir and how the person in that position could be used by others, with or without their knowledge, as she was in the Wyatt Rebellion under Mary I in 1554, for which she ended up imprisoned in the Tower of London. Elizabeth knew that Mary Queen of Scots posed a threat to her reign, especially given that Mary had declared herself as rightful heir to the English crown on the death of Mary I in 1558, when she was married to Francis II of France. She had also produced a son who was ruling in Scotland, England's closest neighbour. It would have been easy enough for James VI of Scotland to launch an invasion of England across the shared border. Mary Queen of Scots would also be the figurehead for Catholics in England who disliked the Elizabethan Religious Settlement and church reforms Elizabeth made which undid many Catholic tenets restored by Mary I. Mary Queen of Scots played on her Catholicism to gain support and set herself up in opposition to Elizabeth I. Norfolk became a victim of Mary Queen of Scots through her charisma and position almost as a damsel in distress in need of rescue, combined with his own folly.

Norfolk was arrested in October 1569, and he remained imprisoned for nine months, although at this point there was no concrete evidence against him. There was also the distinct possibility that Elizabeth was reluctant to act against any of her Howard/Boleyn relatives as she kept her mother's family around her for her whole life. She relied on Henry Carey, 1st Baron Hunsdon (son of her aunt, Mary Boleyn), appointing him Captain of the Gentleman Pensioners, and effectively making him her personal bodyguard for several years in the 1560s. Norfolk was released in 1570 after the conclusion of the Northern Rising. He almost immediately became involved in further plotting, which would lead to his arrest and execution in 1572 after the failed Ridolfi Plot.

In June 1570, Norfolk gave a solemn undertaking not to interfere any more in the marriage of Mary Queen of Scots. After making this promise, Elizabeth I believed that it was safe to release Norfolk from the Tower, which happened in August 1570 when he confessed to his involvement in the Northern Rising of 1569 and the scheme to marry Mary Queen of Scots and begged for mercy. Elizabeth I mistakenly trusted in Norfolk's word. He was then confined to his London home in Charterhouse Square in the charge of Sir Henry Neville. After Norfolk's final arrest, Francis Walsingham, Elizabeth I's spymaster, wrote to William Cecil on 8 October 1571 regarding the relationship between Mary Queen of Scots and the

4th duke of Norfolk, describing Norfolk as 'a most dangerous subject, and that he should be so earnest in seeking the Queen of Scots' liberty, who was to the Queen so dangerous an enemy'.[9] Walsingham obviously saw both Norfolk and Mary as a serious threat to Elizabeth I and her reign, recognising that combined they proved far more of a danger than individually. Hence his subsequent involvement in the Ridolfi Plot was a huge worry for the Elizabethan government, as it threw Norfolk and Mary back together alongside a potential threat from foreign support and even invasion. The government knew after the Northern Rising that Norfolk needed to be watched and they were proven correct.

Within a year of his release from the Tower of London in 1570, Norfolk was again involved in plotting against the queen. It was a Florentine banker, Roberto di Ridolfi, who devised a plot to assist Catholic noblemen in England, with Norfolk foremost among them, to rise against Elizabeth I, rescue Mary Queen of Scots, and proclaim her queen of England in Elizabeth's place. It was said that Norfolk told Ridolfi that he was a Catholic, but he also patronised the Protestant chronicler, John Foxe, author of the *Book of Martyrs*, possibly as Foxe was one of Norfolk's former tutors from his childhood.[10] There has even been a suggestion that Norfolk was made by Ridolfi to sign a declaration stating that he was a Catholic.[11] Norfolk could have changed, or claimed to have changed, his convictions to suit his purpose, of course. Norfolk was to lead the Catholics in England, assisted by a Spanish invasion from the Netherlands. Other plotters included the Spanish ambassador Guerau de Spes, who would give Spanish support, and John Leslie, Bishop of Ross. Perhaps they were encouraged by the publication of the *Regnans in Excelsis* bull of excommunication against Elizabeth I by Pope Pius V in 1570. The scheme seems unfeasible today given geographical complexities and the political scene and was completely unrealistic in conception.[12] There has been a suggestion that Ridolfi was actually in the pay of William Cecil and was acting as an *agent provocateur* in the plot to attempt to entrap Mary Queen of Scots. Mary would escape this plot with her life largely through the intervention of Elizabeth I, though Norfolk would not. Elizabeth sacrificed Norfolk in order to save Mary, though whether they could have gotten a treason conviction at this point is uncertain as her involvement was little more than knowledge of the plan.[13] This was still misprision of treason which could have provided a potentially better excuse to keep Mary imprisoned, but even this would have been difficult with the queen protecting her.

In March 1571, Roberto di Ridolfi left England for Rome, taking with him letters from Mary Queen of Scots and Thomas Howard, 4th Duke of Norfolk. He stopped in Brussels to see Fernando Alvarez de Toledo, 3rd Duke of Alba, who would lead the Spanish invasion from the Netherlands if the plot came to fruition. Alba was not convinced by Ridolfi's plans, but when Ridolfi reached Rome, Pope Pius V was enthusiastic about the scheme and gave a letter to Ridolfi imploring the Catholic Spanish king, Philip II, to co-operate with the plot. Pope Pius V had issued the bull of excommunication, *Regnans in Excelsis*, against Elizabeth I on 25 February 1570 after the Northern Rising. This was intended to deprive Elizabeth of her throne, but a foreign invasion was needed to realise it. Perhaps Pius V saw this plot as the physical embodiment of his Papal bull. Although the Northern Rising had ultimately failed, here was another plot which could be used. The co-operation of Philip II of Spain was crucial, as his men were needed to form the army to invade England and none of his soldiers would invade without the critical support of their king.

Ridolfi told Philip that seldom did an opportunity land in the lap of a Christian prince to do God's work with so little cost to himself.[14] Ridolfi's persuasive efforts were successful and Philip, though cautious at first, became more enthusiastic, believing Ridolfi's claims that the English ports were undefended, and that it would be easy for them to obtain victory. Ridolfi advised Philip that Elizabeth I was already distraught and suspicious, and that Mary Queen of Scots would be forever grateful, preserving peace between France and Spain and would even send her son, James VI of Scotland, to Spain to be raised a Catholic under Philip's watchful eye. James was at that point being raised as a Protestant in Scotland under his regent who, by the end of 1571, was John Erskine, 6th Earl of Mar. Mary did not approve of James's religious inclinations and wanted him to be raised in her own Catholic faith but being imprisoned in England she had no say over it.

Norfolk's house was searched in summer 1571 and coded letters were discovered, some under a mat in his bedroom and others hidden in the roof tiles of his Charterhouse home. On 29 August 1571, Norfolk's own secretaries, Robert Higford and William Barker, handed a package to a Shrewsbury draper called Thomas Browne, telling him it was silver, and instructed him to deliver it to Laurence Bannister, one of the duke's officials in the north of England. Thomas Browne opened the package, suspicious that it was too heavy to merely contain silver and discovered between £500 and £600 in gold (amounts differ depending on the source, but this is around £120,000 to £140,000 in today's money), along with several letters in cipher. The ciphered letters made him particularly suspicious as why write in cipher if the letters were innocent? Browne could have done as instructed and hoped that his involvement would either not be discovered, or would be overlooked, or he could contact someone at court. Thus, Browne alerted William Cecil and the council in London. It was the safer option for him. Norfolk's properties were searched for the cipher which was found and proved his involvement in a plot to marry Mary Queen of Scots and usurp Elizabeth from the throne of England.

Norfolk had been caught in the act of sending letters and money to supporters of Mary Queen of Scots. It also appears that he had continued to court Mary Queen of Scots while in the Tower of London during the Northern Rising, sending her gifts at Christmas 1569 and midsummer 1570, and she sent him letters affirming her love and devotion.[15] A Dr Thomas Wilson wrote to William Cecil, Lord Burghley, on 1 October 1571 that he had been occupied during the day in trying to find those who conveyed letters to and from the duke of Norfolk while in the Tower. One of these appears to have been the wife of the Tower minister and another 'a woman of the Tower Hill practising with the jailor's maid'. Wilson also wrote that they stated 'some particulars to prove these matters' and in the postscript said that he would supply by word of mouth what was not written, so we do not seem to have any further information.[16] In early September 1571 an English spy in Flanders, John Lee, heard rumours that Norfolk was involved in a plot and advised that he should be arrested, which he duly was on 7 September.[17] He was questioned and decided to admit involvement in the plot but downplay his own role in proceedings.

Norfolk likely did not realise the extent of the evidence that Cecil and Walsingham had against him, and that he could easily be charged with treason for which the punishment was death. When originally questioned he did not know that his secretaries had confessed or that letters had been found in a search of his house, so he denied everything. On 11 October 1571, Norfolk got a message to the Earl of Bedford, the Lord Admiral, the Lord Chamberlain, and Lord Burghley 'beseeching them to make declaration to the Queen of his sorrow and penitence for his offences. Never acted by plain writing or by cipher to the prejudice of Her Majesty'.[18] Given that ciphered letters were found in his house and that his secretaries had been questioned and confessed to what they knew, his pleas were seen as lies and probably as evidence of his involvement rather than his innocence. Norfolk's servants agreed to speak against him at trial to save themselves, and so his fate was sealed. He was sent back to the Tower of London after questioning to await his trial on charges of treason.

*   *   *

Thomas Howard, 4th Duke of Norfolk, was tried for treason in Westminster Hall on 16 January 1572. George Talbot, 6th Earl of Shrewsbury, presided as Lord High Steward, and he was tried by a jury of his peers, as was usual for noble cases of high treason. There was actually little need for a trial. The evidence that the council had gathered was enough that Norfolk could have been condemned through Act of Attainder.[19] There were three main charges, to which he pleaded not guilty:

> That Thomas, Duke of Norfolk, as a false traitor ... not having the fear of God in his heart or weighing his true allegiance but seduced by the instigation of the Devil ... [intended] to cut off and destroy Queen Elizabeth ...
> That [he intended] to make and raise sedition in the kingdom of England and spread a miserable civil war ... and to endeavour a change and alteration in the sincere worship of God.
> That [he knew that] Mary Queen of Scots had laid claim and pretended a title and interest to the present possession and dignity of the imperial crown of England ... [and] traitorously sought and endeavoured to be joined in marriage with Mary and had writ diverse letters to her and sent [her] several pledges and tokens ...
> That [he] procured Roberto Ridolfi, a foreign merchant, to send to the Bishop of Rome and to the Duke of Alva to obtain ... certain sums of money towards the raising ... of an army to invade this kingdom.[20]

The charges effectively were that Norfolk intended to force a change to religion in England against the established government and monarch, to marry Mary Queen of Scots and overthrow Elizabeth I, rule England alongside Mary, and had intended to ferment rebellion with the Pope and Duke of Alba, implicitly with the Spanish as well, to make the plan come to pass. Fermenting rebellion was treason, especially acting with a foreign power to do so, never mind the intent to overthrow the monarch which was the more dire charge. Both the 1534 Treason Act under Henry VIII and the 1547 Treason Act under Edward VI were repealed by the 1554 Treason Act enacted under Mary I. The 1554 Treason Act abolished all forms of treason created since 1351, except the 1351 Treason Act itself. Therefore, Norfolk was judged by the 1351 Treason Act which said that it was treason for a person to 'compass or imagine the Death of our Lord the King', or if a person did 'levy War against our Lord the King in his Realm, or be adherent to the King's Enemies in his Realm, giving to them Aid and Comfort in the Realm, or elsewhere'.[21] The charges against Norfolk suggested that he had plotted with foreign powers to overthrow the queen, and although the 1351 Treason Act specified 'king', by the reign of Elizabeth I it was understood to mean 'monarch'. In 1351 a queen regnant was unheard of in England so they did not make provision for it. It is interesting that Mary I decided to roll back what had happened since Henry VIII annulled his marriage to her mother, Katherine of Aragon. But it meant that Norfolk was judged by an act that was over 200 years old and did not even make provision for a woman to rule a country. The 1554 Treason Act was eventually repealed in two parts, in 1863 and 1967.

Norfolk was refused any legal representation, as was usual in treason trials at the time, lamenting 'I am brought to fight without a weapon'.[22] Testimony was read out from Norfolk's servants, though they were themselves not in court so Norfolk could not cross-examine them. There were suggestions that some of the testimony was falsified, which could explain why the servants were not in court to be able to deny it. The peers took an hour and a quarter to find Norfolk guilty on thirteen counts of treason and he was sentenced to death.

Thomas Howard's execution was delayed several times before it eventually happened. Elizabeth dithered over signing the warrant, as she would later do with Mary Queen of Scots in 1587. Norfolk had expected to be executed shortly after the sentence was passed and wrote a quick note to Elizabeth I on 21 January 1572, five days after sentence was passed against him, signing it 'with the woeful hand of a dead man'.[23] Having been condemned he was already legally dead. This was also, coincidentally, the day originally set for his execution. He also wrote to his children as just 'Thomas Howard' as the dukedom, lands, and honours had been stripped from him when he was condemned. He wrote his will asking to be buried at Framlingham with his Howard ancestors, including his parents, Henry Howard, Earl of Surrey, and Frances de Vere. Incidentally, you can visit the Church of St Michael at Framlingham in Suffolk today and see the tombs of Henry Howard and Frances de Vere, as well as Henry Fitzroy, Duke of Richmond and Somerset, the illegitimate son of Henry VIII, and Thomas Howard, 3rd Duke of Norfolk. However, Thomas Howard, 4th Duke of Norfolk, was actually buried, like so many executed before him, in the Chapel of St Peter ad Vincula within the Tower of London, near his cousins Anne Boleyn and Katherine Howard, former queens of England.

On 9 February 1572 Elizabeth I signed the death warrant, but she later sent for William Cecil, whom she had created 1st Baron Burghley on 25 February 1571 for his service and dedication to her and to England and rescinded the order. The spectators who gathered the following day to see the execution of a duke had instead to watch the execution of a couple of commoners, which no doubt was a disappointment to them. The same thing happened again a fortnight later. The council could not understand why the queen hesitated when it was proven that Norfolk had committed treason. Elizabeth I did not want to come across as unmerciful, particularly not towards her own family. She also did not want to lose the love of the people; she played on this throughout her reign, having seen how the people celebrated when her half-sister, Mary I died, even though they had celebrated just five years earlier when she had won the throne from Lady Jane Grey. Elizabeth I signed the death warrant for the third and final time on 31 May 1572. On 1 June, Elizabeth I actually visited the Tower of London to check the preparations made for Norfolk's execution, though she did not visit the condemned man.[24] Elizabeth getting so involved suggested a very personal connection, and perhaps a reluctance or guilt over what was to happen. The warrant was put into effect quickly so that the queen could not change her mind.

Thomas Howard, 4th Duke of Norfolk, and cousin to the reigning queen, Elizabeth I, was executed in public on Tower Hill on 2 June 1572, over four months after he was condemned to death. Norfolk had been sentenced to be hung, drawn, and quartered, as was the traditional sentence for treason, but the queen had commuted the sentence to beheading as an act of mercy for a noble kinsman. Norfolk had ordered a special set of clothes for his execution; a white fustian shirt worn underneath a black satin doublet.[25] He was taken from the Tower of London at 8am and led to Tower Hill for execution. No mercy of a private execution for Norfolk within the Tower of London, despite being the queen's cousin. The scaffold had to be strengthened and raised as it had been so long since it had been used.[26] Norfolk's was the first noble execution of Elizabeth's reign, and Elizabeth would continue to be reluctant to sign death warrants. Norfolk was accompanied by Alexander Nowell, Dean of St Paul's, who offered him spiritual comfort at the end.

William Camden, Clarenceux King of Arms, was one of those who heard Norfolk's speech on the scaffold, which is reproduced in full here:

> I acknowledge that my peers have justly judged me worthy of my death, neither is it my meaning to excuse myself. That I have treated with the Queen of Scots I freely confess and that in matters of great consequence, without consulting my sovereign; which I ought to have done; for which I was cast into the Tower. I was afterwards set free, upon my humble submission, and giving my faith that I would have no more to do with her. Yet I confess I did the contrary, and this troubleth my conscience. But at the Communion Table (as is commonly reported) I neither promised nor swore it. Ridolpho I never talked with but one and that not to the prejudice of the queen. For many men know I had dealing with him for money matters upon bills and bonds. I found him to be a man who envied the tranquility of England, and of a prompt and ready wit for wicked design. Two letters from the Bishop of Rome I saw, to which I attended to not; nor yet to the Rebellion in the North. I have not been addicted to Popery since the time that I had any taste of religion, but I have always been averse from Popish Doctrines and embraced the true religion of Jesus Christ, and have put my whole truth in the blood of Jesus Christ my redeemer and blessed saviour. Yet can I not deny but I have had among my servants and familiars some that have been addicted to the Popish religion. If I have thereby offended God, the Church or the Protestants, I beseech God and them to forgive me.[27]

Norfolk admitted straight away to his dealings with Mary Queen of Scots and his error in not approaching Elizabeth I with the scheme and gaining her permission. However, he probably knew that she would reject the marriage out of hand, as she seemed to resent Mary and her popularity, and knew that marrying Mary Queen of Scots to the duke of Norfolk would increase the threat from her as heir, or supplanter. Norfolk also confessed on the scaffold to breaking his promise to have no more to do with Mary Queen of Scots after his first release from the Tower of London in 1570. He effectively rejected any claims that he was involved with the Ridolfi Plot in 1571, despite coded letters being found in his house and evidence from others that he was in contact with Ridolfi. Perhaps he hoped for a last-minute reprieve, but this was not to happen. Norfolk admitted to some correspondence but claims that it was innocent rather than scheming. He ended his speech by discussing his approach to religion and asked forgiveness for any offence caused. Norfolk appears at different points in his life to have embraced both Protestantism and Catholicism. It is perhaps not unusual that Norfolk had some Catholic servants, given that his grandfather, the 3rd duke, was a notable Catholic and he likely inherited some of his servants, and then their descendants could have continued to serve the 4th duke.

Norfolk granted forgiveness to the executioner as was traditional and commended his spirit to the Lord. He refused a handkerchief to cover his eyes saying that he did not fear death. It took a single stroke to sever his head from his body. No botched execution here. It was quick and clean, mercifully. The head was held up by the executioner 'to the sorrowing and weeping people'.[28] Norfolk appeared to have been popular with the people and they mourned his passing. William Camden, who witnessed the execution and reported his final speech, went on to say that the Pope took Norfolk's death 'heavily' and the Spanish were 'troubled at it'.[29] They had expected the Ridolfi Plot to succeed, for Norfolk to marry Mary Queen of Scots, and for the Catholics to triumph in overthrowing Elizabeth I and putting Mary and Norfolk on the English throne to rule and restore Papal supremacy. They expected Catholicism to win, believing that God was on their side and would not allow the heretics victory. After his execution, Norfolk's remains were taken to the Chapel of St Peter ad Vincula within the Tower of London and he was buried not too far from the remains of Elizabeth I's mother, Anne Boleyn, under the altar. His wishes to be buried at St Michael's Church in Framlingham with his father, Henry Howard, Earl of Surrey, were ignored. He was, instead, buried with others who had been executed by the Tudors. Norfolk's mother, Frances de Vere, would die six years after her son and be buried at Framlingham.

Norfolk's would-be fourth wife, Mary Queen of Scots, would survive another decade and a half before being executed in the great hall at Fotheringhay Castle, on 8 February 1587, having become involved in one plot too many (the Throckmorton, Parry, and Babington Plots would follow that of Ridolfi), and agreeing in writing to the assassination of Elizabeth I. Like Norfolk, she condemned herself through her foolishness and folly. Mary had denied all knowledge of the Ridolfi Plot which led to Norfolk's execution but, like Norfolk, a letter written and signed in her own hand made her complicit as, in the letter, she agreed to an invasion of England. Mary Queen of Scots would remain a threat to Elizabeth I and the English throne, even without the possibility of Norfolk as her fourth husband, until her own execution. Elizabeth I did not like to be seen as unmerciful and she dithered over signing the death warrants of both Thomas Howard, 4th Duke of Norfolk, in 1572, and Mary Queen of Scots in 1587.

Historian, Robert Hutchinson, described Norfolk as being 'trapped in a web partially of his own foolish making' as 'there is little doubt Ridolfi was a government *agent provocateur* who formed the bait for a trap and the duke's lack of foresight, or common sense, allowed him to be ensnared'.[30] Norfolk seemed to lose his sense of what was right and sensible, falling into the trap of believing Mary Queen of Scots to be a damsel in distress who needed to be rescued, and willing to engage in plotting to fulfil that dream. It resulted in his own execution and contributed to the later execution of Mary Queen of Scots.

Chapter 11

Robert Devereux, 2nd Earl of Essex – 1601

Robert Devereux, 2nd Earl of Essex, was the last notable execution of Elizabeth I's reign, though it was probably one of the hardest for her to contemplate, aside from that of Mary Queen of Scots in 1587. Essex had been one of Elizabeth's favourites, taking over in a way from his stepfather, Robert Dudley, 1st Earl of Leicester, who died in 1588. However, Essex would never hold Elizabeth's heart in the way that Leicester had. It has been said that Elizabeth would have married Leicester if she could. It is easy to believe that Elizabeth I sought comfort in her old age from Leicester's stepson, the Earl of Essex. Essex was executed not because he was bad, but because he was dangerous; his death was justified 'because of the peril which was implicit in his life', as we will see.[1] He was selfish and full of folly. Perhaps even idiocy.

Robert Devereux was the son of Walter Devereux, 1st Earl of Essex, and Lettice Knollys. Walter Devereux had been entrusted at one point with the custody of Mary Queen of Scots and had fought in Ireland for Elizabeth I. Lettice Knollys was the granddaughter of Mary Boleyn through her daughter, Catherine Carey, and Francis Knollys, and was thus the great-niece of Queen Anne Boleyn. It has been debated whether Catherine Carey was in fact the daughter of Henry VIII through his affair with Mary Boleyn, but this has never been proven and Henry VIII never recognised her as such as he did with Henry Fitzroy. If the rumours of Catherine's paternity were true, this would make Robert Devereux the great-grandson of Henry VIII. Even without this connection, Essex was still, however, a cousin to the queen through her Boleyn relatives. It has been suggested that this is in fact why Essex managed to get away with so much, and the favour that Elizabeth showed him before his eventual arrest and execution.[2] Elizabeth I had proven that she was reluctant to punish or execute family on her mother's side – her cousin, Thomas Howard, 4th Duke of Norfolk, was only executed in 1572 as a compromise with parliament so that she did not have to execute Mary Queen of Scots.

Robert Devereux was in fact descended from Edward III through a daughter of Thomas of Woodstock, 1st Duke of Gloucester, Edward's youngest son. This daughter, Anne Plantagenet, married William Bourchier, 1st Count of Eu, and their son, Henry Bourchier, 2nd Count of Eu, married Isabel Plantagenet, herself a great-granddaughter of Edward III through Edmund of Langley, 1st Duke of York. Henry Bourchier would also be created 1st Earl of Essex, hence how Robert's father, Walter Devereux, gained the Essex earldom. Isabel was sister to Richard Plantagenet, 3rd Duke of York, and thus was aunt to Edward IV and Richard III. Robert Devereux thus had illustrious and royal connections, though fairly distant in terms of succession to the throne.

Essex himself married Frances Walsingham, the daughter of Elizabeth I's spymaster, Francis Walsingham, in 1590. Frances was the widow of Sir Philip Sidney, who died in 1586 fighting in the Netherlands. Sidney sustained an injury while fighting at the Battle of Zutphen and died of gangrene as a result. Robert and Frances had five children together, three of whom survived infancy. Their son, Robert Devereux, 3rd Earl of Essex, regained the Essex earldom in 1604 after the death of Elizabeth I, three years after his father's execution. He was married, aged 14, to Frances Howard, but the marriage was annulled, and he then married Elizabeth Paulet, a cousin of the Marquess of Winchester. He would fight for the Parliamentarians in the English Civil War. There is little information regarding Robert's daughter, Dorothy Devereux, but his other daughter, Frances Devereux, became Duchess of Somerset through her marriage to William Seymour, 2nd Duke of Somerset. The attainder against Edward Seymour, 1st Duke of Somerset, was reversed in 1660, 108 years after his death, allowing Essex's daughter to become a duchess.

Historian, Robert Stedall, describes Essex as 'little more than a spoilt prig, wholly unsuited to high command, suffering from fits of depression and lacking in judgement and stability under pressure'.[3] It appears to be something that most historians agree about Essex; that he was spoilt and would fail at court. These qualities would assist in Essex's downfall as he either did not seem to understand the danger that he was in, or he lost all sense of proportion and believed that the queen would forgive him.

* * *

Robert Devereux, 2nd Earl of Essex, was born on 10 November 1565 to Walter Devereux, 1st Earl of Essex, and Lettice Knollys, and was thus a descendant of the Boleyn and Howard families. Essex would only know Elizabeth I as his monarch across his whole lifetime. She had already been queen for seven years when he was born, and she was a cousin through his mother's side. Devereux's father died in 1576 and he inherited the Essex earldom aged only 11. William Cecil, Lord Burghley, became his legal guardian, and he grew up alongside Burghley's son, Robert Cecil. This was a relationship that would hugely influence his life. Essex's mother, Lettice Knollys, would go on to marry Elizabeth I's favourite, Robert Dudley, 1st Earl of Leicester, in 1578 which angered the queen. Lettice would not be welcome back at court again. Elizabeth I did not like favourites splitting their attentions between her and their wives, and she was particularly angry when her absolute favourite and possible love of her life, married one of her ladies-in-waiting.

Robert Devereux's great-grandfather, also named Walter like his grandson, was a close ally of John Dudley, 1st Duke of Northumberland, supporting him in the accession of Lady Jane Grey in 1553 on the death of Edward VI. Walter spent a period in the Tower of London as a result. However, this did not seem to stop the rise of the Devereux family.

Robert was not the eldest child of his parents. His elder sister, Penelope, was born in January 1563 and Elizabeth I stood as godmother. Penelope would go on to marry Robert Rich, 3rd Baron Rich, and later 1st Earl of Warwick. The pair would divorce in 1605 on the grounds of Penelope's adultery. A second daughter, Dorothy, arrived in September 1564. She would marry Henry Percy, 9th Earl of Northumberland, though he would be suspected of involvement in the Gunpowder Plot and would spend time in the Tower of London. In November 1565 Robert himself was born, followed by Francis who died as an infant, then Walter, who was killed in 1591 at the Siege of Rouen.

With the death of their father in September 1576, Essex was sent to live in the household of William Cecil, 1st Baron Burghley. He had been made a ward of the crown, as was usual with young nobles whose parents died before they reached their majority. Essex was split from his siblings, with his sisters and younger brother sent to live instead with Henry Hastings, 3rd Earl of Huntingdon, and his wife, Katherine Dudley, Countess of Huntingdon. Essex had been left with significant debts by his father, with

Walter's attempts to seize lands in Ireland leaving his heir around £18,000 in debt, much of it owed to the crown. The responsibility for overseeing the estates during the new earl's minority, and for working to reduce said debt, lay with one Richard Broughton, a lawyer who had served Robert's father.[4] In May 1577, Essex began his studies at Trinity College, Cambridge. Essex does not seem to have helped to reduce the debt of his family estates. While at Cambridge he appears to have spent lavishly, which can help to explain his later desperation when Elizabeth I removed some of his financial safety nets and privileges.

Essex seems to have come under pressure from his mother, Lettice, now Countess of Leicester, to go to court. He arrived there in September 1585 but attracted little notice, as the focus of the court was on the war in the Netherlands.[5] Essex was granted permission to accompany his stepfather, Robert Dudley, 1st Earl of Leicester, to war in the Netherlands, as Leicester had just been appointed to command the army. Essex was still a royal ward at this point, so would have required royal permission. Essex was appointed colonel-general of the cavalry, though much of the routine administration and planning was done by Sir William Russell as Essex was undergoing an apprenticeship of sorts. But it was a prestigious appointment. It was at Utrecht that Essex made his debut in the joust. In September 1586, Essex participated in Leicester's capture of Doesburg and the siege at Zutphen, which resulted in the death of Sir Philip Sidney. Essex and a small body of horsemen allegedly charged a much larger Spanish force and triumphed. On his return from war in October 1586, he caught the queen's eye. He was no longer a royal ward and had been dubbed a knight-banneret on the battlefield by Leicester as a reward for his bravery in the Netherlands.

Elizabeth I granted the Earl of Essex some financial privileges, including the lease of York House on the Strand in London, which was traditionally the courtesy residence of the Lord Chancellor, who at the time was Sir Christopher Hatton. However, he had no need of it, already having his own London residence. On 12 January 1589, Elizabeth I also granted Essex his stepfather's former lease of customs on sweet wines, which was very lucrative.[6] However, Essex seemed to consistently live beyond his means and thought he could resolve his debts through exploration and plunder.

Essex served during the Dutch Revolt, the invasion threat by the Spanish Armada in 1588, and the raid on Cadiz in 1596. He was also involved in espionage and discovered that the queen's physician, Dr Roderigo Lopez, had plotted to poison Elizabeth I in 1594.[7] However, Essex felt he did not get the reward he deserved for saving the queen. Essex's actions against Lopez may have been partly selfish, as Lopez had previously served Essex, but the earl turned against him, allegedly because Lopez had revealed in conversation what diseases he had treated Essex for. Lopez was found to have sent messages to Philip II of Spain from 1591, though the plot to poison the queen was not hatched until 1593. Lopez was hung, drawn and quartered at Tyburn on 7 June 1594.[8] Essex seems to have discovered the letters and revealed the plot. The queen's favourite and Essex's stepfather, Robert Dudley, 1st Earl of Leicester, had died in 1588 just after the defeat of the Spanish Armada and the queen mourned him deeply. Essex took over Leicester's old position of Master of the Horse, perhaps due to his link to Leicester. Essex thus became an influential figure at court and a favourite of Elizabeth I.

As has already been alluded to, Essex suffered periods of the queen's disfavour sporadically throughout his court career. When an expedition was sent against Spain in 1589, led by Francis Drake, Essex was determined to join it, but he knew that Elizabeth I would veto his going and want him to stay by her side, so he slipped away and succeeded in joining the expedition against the queen's wishes. Elizabeth was angry with him on his return but forgave him quickly. She did not seem to like to be without Essex for long. Perhaps he brightened Elizabeth's days as he was said to be flamboyant and cheeky.

Essex again angered Elizabeth when, in 1590, he secretly married Frances Walsingham, the daughter of Elizabeth's spymaster, Sir Francis Walsingham. Within a few months of the wedding, Essex was again restored to favour. Elizabeth could not seem to stay angry at Essex for very long. The relationship seriously began to deteriorate from around 1598. In late June or early July that year, Elizabeth and Essex quarrelled, and Essex turned his back on the queen which earned him a sharp rebuke and she was said to have struck him on the ear. Essex reacted by turning and drawing his sabre, which was a serious offence, but Charles Howard, 1st Earl of Nottingham, intervened and diffused the situation.[9] This was an affront to Elizabeth's dignity and sense of majesty which she would not have been quick to forgive.

To understand Essex's downfall and involvement in treasonous activities, we need to understand the man himself. As historian, Laura Brennan, puts it, this uprising was 'motivated by one spoilt young man's ego and his immature reaction to losing his position as Elizabeth's favourite'.[10] He had no real political ability or skills and relied on his charm to move upwards. He also seems to have been emotionally immature and unable to deal with rejection, particularly from such an important person who had the power to ruin him.

* * *

Robert Cecil and Robert Devereux had known each other since childhood. Essex had been raised in the Cecil household after his father's death. Cecil succeeded to many of his father, William Cecil, 1st Baron Burghley's, political offices. He was a hunchback, known by Elizabeth I as her 'pigmy' or 'little elf', and he was close to the queen, though others of Elizabeth's favourites appeared to have little time for him.[11] Cecil was relied on by Elizabeth greatly after she lost Burghley. Burghley had groomed his son to follow in his footsteps. Unlike Leicester, Burghley, and even Robert Cecil, Elizabeth I did not give the Earl of Essex a nickname. This was seen by some as a lack of intimacy between them.[12] Perhaps Elizabeth was trying to fill the hole left by those she loved dying around her, leaving her to carry on. Robert Dudley, 1st Earl of Leicester, had been known as her 'Eyes', William Cecil, 1st Baron Burghley as her 'Spirit', and Sir Francis Walsingham as her 'Moor'. Essex quite possibly felt left out.

However, Robert Cecil did stick up for Essex, claiming that he had never intended to usurp the throne. Essex had planned to rely on popular support to move those around the queen who he believed were poisoning her mind, removing her 'from infamy in as smooth and orderly a fashion as possible'.[13] Part of the concern was over the succession. Elizabeth I had not named a successor, though it was assumed by most that it would be James VI of Scotland, son of Mary Queen of Scots. Though, Essex implied that Robert Cecil would prefer it to be the Infanta Isabella Eugenia of Spain, daughter of Philip II, especially with Cecil at the forefront of peace negotiations with Spain in 1600. Cecil was, however, openly supporting the accession of James VI, not the Infanta Isabella, and he would continue to serve James in government after Elizabeth's death. Essex was scaremongering, jealous of the fact that Cecil was effectively in charge of the government of England, and he tried to thwart every one of Cecil's plans and proposals.[14] Essex assumed that everyone would recognise that Cecil was grasping and dishonest, and he believed obsessively in his own popularity, which he thought would win through.

Essex's downfall began with his sojourn in Ireland to tackle rebellions against Elizabeth I's rule there. In 1599, as Governor General of Ireland, Essex was sent to Ireland to suppress rebels there, but he did not have sufficient resources to mount an attack and defeat them, so sought a truce as his only viable option. Francis Bacon wrote in his treatise after Essex's rebellion in 1601 that Essex while in Ireland had intended to 'pleasure and gratifie the Rebell with a dishonourable peace, and to contract with him for his owne greatnesse'.[15] The implication was that Essex acted against the orders of his queen, and that he intended to promote his own interests rather than those of the queen and country. He had attempted to promote Henry Wriothesley, 3rd Earl of Southampton, to be his Master of Horse while in Ireland, but Southampton had been in disfavour with the queen since his secret marriage to one of her ladies, Elizabeth Vernon, in 1598. Elizabeth wrote to Essex in a letter of July 19, 1599, just after his arrival in Ireland, having found out what he intended for Southampton: 'all the commanders cannot be ignorant that we not only not allowed of your desire for him, but did expressly forbid it'. She went on to say that Essex had disobeyed her in appointing Southampton 'wherein our own pleasure to the contrary is made notorious'.[16] Essex could not have failed to pick up Elizabeth's tone and her fury at him going against her orders in the matter of Southampton, but this would not be the first time that Essex disobeyed the queen's orders in Ireland. It would demonstrate to Elizabeth that Essex could not be trusted in command or, more generally, to control his capricious instincts.

In a letter Elizabeth I herself wrote to the Earl of Essex when he was in Ireland on September 14, 1599, she lets her frustration and disappointment in his actions ring through, saying that he had 'possessed us with expectation that you would proceed as we directed you', but that Essex had not done so, and had in fact acted against her wishes, giving her no time to countermand him.[17] Essex had negotiated a truce with the Irish rebels rather than using his army as Elizabeth had told him to. It left Elizabeth and the English government looking weak and unable, or unwilling, to fight against the rebel Irish. Essex did not act as the queen had directed him, and in fact had completely disregarded her instructions. He was in deep trouble and would never find his way back into the queen's good graces again.

Elizabeth I was furious at what she saw as disobedience to her instructions, and she forbade Essex from leaving Ireland at that time. She wanted him to stay and sort the mess out that he had created, with some additional oversight of his actions. However, Essex arrived unannounced at Nonsuch Palace in Surrey where Elizabeth was residing and burst into her bedchamber suddenly and unexpectedly on 28 September 1599. He was determined to explain himself to her in person and was concerned that others may be speaking against him in his absence. Essex saw the queen deshabille without any gown, wig, or make-up, which meant that Elizabeth's image as the ever youthful and majestic Gloriana was shattered. Elizabeth would not forgive him this blatant disregard for her.

He was interrogated by the Privy Council the following morning and placed under house arrest the same day. He had disobeyed the queen's explicit instructions in Ireland, left his post without permission, and then burst into the queen's private chamber without leave. Essex was tried and acquitted but he lost his wealth and influence, as well as the queen's favour, and he was unwilling to accept this very public fall from grace. Essex believed his charm and popularity would win out, but he had not taken into account the Tudor temper and Elizabeth's ability to hold a grudge. He determined to regain all that he had lost, but it would in fact spell his death at the blade of an executioner's axe.

As argued in a previous work, 'Essex let his paranoia take over once he was isolated from the court and what were probably steadying influences on him'.[18] He seemed to lose sense of what was right and wrong, and plotted to regain favour. What made him think that a rebellion would help him to gain favour with the queen and council, given what he must have heard about rebellions involving Mary Queen of Scots and the Duke of Norfolk, is difficult to grasp. It demonstrates just how much Essex had lost touch with reality, and how he had failed to read and understand his queen and her innate understanding of monarchy and image, specifically her own image and power, which Essex had greatly underestimated.

The final nail in Essex's coffin was his rebellion in 1601. With that, things began to move quite quickly. Elizabeth I had refused to renew Essex's customs licence on sweet wines, which was where most of his income came from. He knew he would be ruined as long as Elizabeth remained on the throne. He turned to treason, amassed followers, and even appealed to Elizabeth's assumed but unofficial successor, James VI of Scotland, for aid.[19] Essex gathered support at his home at Essex House in the Strand. On 6 February 1601, he sent representatives down to The Globe Theatre and asked the Lord Chamberlain's men to perform Shakespeare's play *The Tragedy of Richard II*.

Shakespeare was associated at this time with the Lord Chamberlain's Men, but they declined to perform at first, saying that it would not be popular. However, they agreed when offered forty shillings more than their usual wage to perform.[20] Essex had also requested that the scene which shows the deposition of Richard II be included, which was often excluded at the time because of the connotations of including it; the suggestion that it could be right to depose an anointed monarch. The controversial scenes usually took place off stage. The Tudors had seized the crown on the battlefield in 1485 and there were others with a better claim to the throne, so any insinuation that it could be right to depose them was stamped down on, even over one hundred years after Bosworth.

The actors themselves were not aware that this performance was part of a plot to depose Elizabeth I. The play was performed on 7 February 1601, but if Essex had hoped that the performance would stir the people of London to rise up in revolt, he was disappointed. The staging of *The Tragedy of Richard II* was controversial. In English history, Richard II was usurped by Henry IV in 1399 and he died sometime around February 1400, having been thought to have been starved to death so that there were no marks of violence on the body. To save himself and his throne, Henry believed that he had no choice but to kill Richard. Whether the Earl of Essex believed that he needed to kill the queen is unknown. He certainly wanted his power and wealth back, as otherwise he could not continue living the life to which he had become accustomed. It seems likely that Robert Cecil and other councillors believed that Elizabeth would not be safe while Essex lived as he was too volatile and unpredictable, much as Francis Walsingham and William Cecil believed that Elizabeth would not be safe while Mary Queen of Scots lived, twenty years earlier. Mary, however, had posed a more international threat than Essex did, and her death had much wider consequences to consider. Robert Cecil seems to have initially attempted to save and defend Essex, but his rebellion was too much.

The staging of the play was intended by Essex to mark the beginning of a rebellion and he expected the people of London to rise for him. The people did not want another rebellion. At this point there were rising prices and increased poverty. The population of England had more important things on their minds than the petty squabbles of the nobility. Essex did not understand this and focused on the possibility of deposition. In Richard II's final speech in Shakespeare's play, having been deposed by his cousin, Henry IV, and as he is dying, he declares:

> 'Thy fierce hand
> Hath with the king's blood stain'd the king's own land.
> Mount, mount, my soul! Thy seat is up on high,
> Whilst my gross flesh sinks downward, here to die'.[21]

Richard II knew that he would die before it happened and who was ultimately responsible for it. There could not be two kings in England, as Edward IV would learn in 1470. There was always a chance of a restoration. The insinuation was that, by killing Richard, Henry had stained England in a way that he would find it difficult to recover from. Within a couple of decades England would sink into the civil war known today as the Wars of the Roses with cousin fighting cousin, and it would only finally end when the Tudors came to the throne. However, if Essex was expecting this kind of chaos as a result of his own rebellion then he would be sorely disappointed. Essex did not have a serious claim to the throne, or a real cause that he was fighting for. He was lost, paranoid, and selfish. That was not a cause that people would rise for.

On 8 February, the day after the performance of Shakespeare's *Richard II* at The Globe, Essex and his closest followers, including his stepfather, Sir Christopher Blount (the third husband of his mother, Lettice Knollys), and close friend Henry Wriothesley, 3rd Earl of Southampton, attempted to enter the City of London to try and obtain an audience with Elizabeth I. The Lord Keeper, Sir Thomas Egerton, and three other members of the council had arrived at Essex House that morning to question the earl, but Essex's followers kept them hostage. The rebels were repelled by a blockade at Queenhithe in Ludgate. Essex had not attempted to raise any affinity from his own estates, so was dependent completely on support from London itself, which disappointed him. Estimates suggest he only had around 300 supporters to take London.[22] Other estimates suggest only 200 supporters,[23] or even as low as 140.[24] He never had a real chance of success, though he was desperate, which made him reckless. Essex claimed that Robert Cecil and Sir Walter Raleigh wanted to kill him and that his uprising was to prevent that happening. No one really believed this it seems or, if they did, it was not enough of a reason to rebel against the queen. Essex intended with this rebellion to overthrow those he saw as 'parasites' which, aside from Cecil and Raleigh, included Charles Howard, 1st Earl of Nottingham, Thomas Grey, 15th Baron Grey of Wilton, and Thomas Sackville, Lord Buckhurst, later 1st Earl of Dorset.[25] Essex hoped his popularity would encourage the people to support him. Word came from the court that Essex had been declared a traitor, and thus anyone in London who may have been debating joining him had their minds made up for them. They did not want to die.

The rebels returned to Essex House where the four Privy Councillors, who had been held hostage since 10 o'clock that morning when they had arrived to question Essex, had been released without Essex's consent. They were Thomas Egerton, 1st Viscount Brackley and Lord High Chancellor, Edward Somerset, 1st Earl of Worcester, William Knollys, and Chief Justice John Popham. One of the conspirators, Ferdinando Gorges, had gotten cold feet and knew that having imprisoned Privy Councillors would not do their cause any favours, so released them. Those rebels who had remained at Essex House had backed out of the rebellion when Robert Cecil had declared Essex a traitor. They did not want to get into any more trouble than they were already in. Essex and his fellow conspirators were besieged at Essex House, but eventually surrendered.

In the aftermath of the rebellion, Francis Bacon wrote a treatise on the earl of Essex and his attempt at revolt, with the collusion of the Privy Council called *A Declaration of the Practises & Treasons attempted and committed by Robert late Earle of Essex and his Complices, against her Maiestie and her Kingdoms, and of the proceedings as well at the Arraignments & Conuictions of the said late Earle, and his adherents*. As such, this is essentially a piece of government propaganda and cannot be taken at face value, but it is interesting to see how the government wanted the English people to view Essex's actions. The account claims that Essex's supporters were to deploy themselves throughout Whitehall Palace ready to clear Essex's way to the queen when he arrived. This implies that Essex still had some friends at court willing to act for him, or at least friends who could gain access to the court. But, of course, Essex never made it to Whitehall. Sir John Davies wrote down which men would be positioned where in the palace; some at the Gate, some in the Hall, guard chamber, and Presence Chamber, and others to accompany Essex to the Queen.[26] Essex was forced into impulsive and premature action when he was summoned to appear before the council with word of their plans having reached the court, which could perhaps explain why the rebels did not appear to be well-organised and the revolt was put down so quickly.

Essex had lost and lost spectacularly. Not only would he never regain his wealth, power, and position, but he would never regain his freedom and his life would be forfeit for his actions. Historian, Anne Somerset, claimed that 'he took to railing against the queen in a frenzied manner that suggested to some of his acquaintances that he was no longer altogether sane'.[27] Essex had thrown his toys out of the pram when he could not get his own way and he would pay the ultimate price.

* * *

Robert Devereux, 2nd Earl of Essex's rebellion against Elizabeth I was the final nail in his coffin. The historian, Lisa Hilton, explains that Elizabeth I had no choice but to execute Essex, as she could not spare him without looking weak; his actions struck at the core of her 'personal power'.[28] As well as her power, Essex's actions struck at the heart of the queen's sense of majesty. Image and perception were crucial to Elizabeth's image as Gloriana and Essex's actions damaged the gloss. As a female monarch, Elizabeth I was still seen by many to be not as strong as a king, despite her actions across her reign in uncovering and surviving rebellions, building a strong navy and defeating the Spanish, and promoting religious unity without resorting to the burnings of her half-sister, Bloody Mary's, reign. She had to act in many ways as a man, rather than a woman, in order to protect her own power and position, and to secure England for the future. Essex's friend and accomplice in his rebellion, Henry Wriothesley, 3rd Earl of Southampton, wrote to his wife after they had been arrested that 'God's will must be done and what is allotted to us by destiny cannot be avoided'.[29] Perhaps Essex had thought that it was his destiny to be a favourite of the queen and could not believe that it was at an end. He was determined to regain what had been lost. He would fail.

What is now known as the Essex ring was reputed to have been given by Elizabeth I to Robert Devereux, 2nd Earl of Essex, on the understanding that she would grant clemency to him if he returned it to her when he was in need.[30] When under sentence of death after his trial, Essex attempted to return the ring to the queen at this time in an effort to gain mercy for his reckless actions. However, the ring never reached Elizabeth I, falling instead into the hands of Essex's enemies, who did not want him to live. They saw Essex as too dangerous to their own power and interests, at least in part because he seemed to be able to charm people, including the queen herself. After Essex's execution, the ring was given to his widow, Frances Walsingham, and it passed through the family for three centuries until 1911 when it was sold.[31] The ring features an image of Elizabeth I wearing an auburn wig. Some historians, however, consider the story of the ring being used as a token of need to be a myth, as it did not appear until after Essex's death. However, the rumour persists and is often cited as being fact despite there being no contemporary evidence for it.

The historian, David Hume, related the story of the so-called Essex ring. He wrote *The History of England* published in 1754, over 150 years after Essex's execution. When Essex returned from the raid on Cadiz in 1596, Essex returned to the queen, lamenting that he must be so often from her side and worried that his enemies would turn her against him in his absence. In order to allay his jealousy and worries, it was said that Elizabeth I presented him with a ring and 'desired him to keep that pledge of her affection, and assured him that, into whatever disgrace he should fall, whatever prejudices she might be induced to entertain against him, yet, if he sent her that ring, she would immediately upon the sight of it recall her former tenderness, would afford him a patient hearing, and would lend a favourable ear to his apology'.[32] Whether Elizabeth would have remembered, or wanted to remember, this in her fury with Essex is uncertain, though what does seem certain is that Elizabeth I never received a ring from Essex in his hour of need, even if the legend of the ring is true. Given that Essex had rebelled against the queen, it is understandable that those around her would not want Essex returned to favour.

On 19 February 1601, just eleven days after his attempted assault on the City of London, Essex was tried on charges of treason, for attempting to usurp the throne and assassinate the queen. Essex appeared to be angry at these insinuations, claiming that his objective had not been the overthrow of the queen herself, but the deposition of leading members of the council. He intended to become the preeminent member of the council to smooth the way for the accession of James VI of Scotland on Elizabeth's death.[33] Elizabeth would have considered this out of order. She reacted angrily against anyone who thought to try and force the succession. Robert Cecil would claim in the trial to Essex's face that 'I stand for loyalty; you stand for treachery. You would depose the queen; you would be King of England'.[34] There does not seem to have been any sense that Essex wanted to be king of England and there were others who had a much greater claim than he did, so he must have known, even with his mind seemingly failing him, that this would not have held. Kingship came with responsibilities which Essex could not have handled. He was too reckless and impulsive to make considered decisions and Essex as king would have been a disaster. The unanimous guilty verdict was a foregone conclusion and Essex was sentenced to death. He seemed to take it well and claimed that he welcomed death. However, when Cecil and Nottingham visited him in the Tower after the trial, Essex failed to take any responsibility for his actions, blaming anyone but himself for the mess he found himself in.

The actors of the Lord Chamberlain's Men who had performed *The Tragedy of Richard II* at Essex's request on 7 February were questioned but were exonerated of any involvement in the plot. They did not know that their performance was intended as a catalyst for rebellion. But surely, they must have wondered with the amount they were paid why Essex was so determined to have the play performed? Perhaps he told them it was at the queen's request, or that as a respected courtier he must have permission to request it. Henry Wriothesley, 3rd Earl of Southampton, was also condemned to death, though both he and Essex had pleaded not guilty to the treason charges brought against them. Robert Cecil urged the queen to show clemency and, as such, Southampton's sentence was reduced to life imprisonment. He would only serve around two years, being released from prison on the death of Elizabeth I and the accession of James I in 1603. Essex had been courting James as heir to Elizabeth before his rebellion, so possibly there was a sense of James owing Essex something. Essex had hoped that James would offer him support in his rebellion in payment.

At 1am on 25 February 1601, the Lieutenant of the Tower, Richard Berkeley, informed Essex that he was to be executed that very morning. Essex had requested that he be allowed to die within the confines of the Tower of London, rather than the more public location of Tower Hill; a request that the queen granted. He was the last to receive that honour if honour it be. Essex spent the remainder of that morning in prayer with Chaplain Ashton. Elizabeth I had revoked the first death warrant, but another was prepared and executed quickly, in case the queen changed her mind, as she had with Thomas Howard, 4th Duke of Norfolk in 1572, and then again with Mary Queen of Scots in 1587. Elizabeth had form in dithering over death warrants.

Robert Devereux, 2nd Earl of Essex was beheaded on 25 February 1601 with an axe in the privacy of Tower Green. The beheading was botched, and it took three strokes to separate his head from his body though at least it was conducted in private. Essex had left his room between 7 and 8 o'clock that morning, accompanied by three servants and wearing all black but with a scarlet waistcoat. He was beheaded by Thomas Derrick while reciting the 51st psalm, the very same psalm that Lady Jane Grey had recited on the scaffold at her execution nearly fifty years earlier. There were around one hundred spectators present including aldermen from the City of London and several knights including Sir Walter Raleigh, Lord Thomas Howard, and George Clifford, 3rd Earl of Cumberland. Raleigh, as Captain of the Guard, allegedly watched the execution from a window in the Tower armoury.

In part due to his execution, although also his exploits adventuring with Drake and in battle in the Netherlands, Essex developed a reputation for heroism and bravery, and even made a performance out of his own death. His body was buried in the Tower chapel of St Peter ad Vincula, near the remains of other nobles executed for treason including Anne Boleyn, Katherine Howard, Edward and Thomas Seymour, and Lady Jane Grey. As a result of the rebellion, Essex's stepfather, Sir Christopher Blount, was also executed on Tower Hill along with fellow conspirator Sir Charles Danvers. Conspirators of lower rank like Gelly Meyrick and Henry Cuffe were hung and disembowelled at Tyburn for their involvement. But these were the only executions as a result of Essex's rebellion. Others were punished with fines, but these do not seem to have been paid.

The historian, Lacey Baldwin Smith, has suggested that Essex was trapped into treason, 'a victim of society and the paranoia it spawned'.[35] However, this implies that the treason was not Essex's fault. The fact is that Essex would not have been executed for treason had he not risen in revolt against Elizabeth I in the streets of London. Elizabeth was very forgiving to those she loved, and there was no doubt that she loved Essex, even just as a reminder of her favourite, Robert Dudley, 1st Earl of Leicester, who died in 1588. There was paranoia in England at this time as the country was still at war with Spain, even twelve years after the defeat of the Armada, and the memory was still alive of the conspiracies which had surrounded the doomed Mary Queen of Scots.

During the reign of James I, in 1635, a ballad was published about the fate of the Earl of Essex thirty-four years earlier. Exactly when it was written is unknown, but the fact that it was in print so long after Essex's death is interesting. Evidently his life, rebellion, and ultimate fate still excited comment. Written as twelve verses set to music, it laments Essex's fate and seems to portray Essex as a chivalric figure, showing forgiveness for his actions and wishing people a better life than his. Perhaps it was intended as a lesson to people on how to be and what not to do. One verse speaks of Elizabeth I and her council, whom Essex seemed to have an ongoing feud with, but the ballad speaks of them in kind terms, quite against what Essex said at his trial and in the run-up to his rebellion:

> Farewell Elizabeth my gracious Queene,
> God blesse thee and thy Councell all:
> Farewell you Knights of Chivalry,
> farewell my Souldiers stout and tall,
> Farewell the Co [...] great and small,
> into the hands of men I light,
> My life shall make amends for all,
> for Essex bids the world good-night.[36]

Calling Elizabeth I 'gracious' is a traditional sentiment for those accused of treason, though whether Essex would have believed this after she condemned his actions in Ireland, failed to renew his monopoly on sweet wine imports, and then had him condemned to death is highly questionable, especially given his mental state at the time of his execution. But these types of ballads and poems were not intended to reflect the true story; more often than not they were a romanticised version of story to either put the people in them on a pedestal, or as a morality tale. 'God blesse thee and thy Councell all' also seems unlikely as something that Essex would have wished. The following verse says 'Comfort your selves, mourne not for me, although your fall be now begun' which echoes what Essex saw as his own importance. The suggestion is that Essex's family could not survive and grow without him. However, his son would regain the Essex earldom after his father's death; he would not have any children, but his sister would become the Duchess of Somerset and mother a dynasty. The final lines of the ballad are 'Spreading my armes to God on high, Lord Iesus receiue my soule this night'. Essex was executed, but seemed to accept it in the end, not making a scene on the scaffold and suffering a botched beheading.

Elizabeth understood threats to her throne; how could she not after so long and the agony of deciding to execute an anointed queen in 1587? She faced censure for executing Essex, however, and many could not understand why he had to die. They believed that the queen could have pardoned him had she wished to. People blamed Robert Cecil, later 1st Earl of Salisbury, who was said to have a rivalry with Essex and conspired to bring him down, but there is little evidence to support this theory. Essex could have lived away from the court in seclusion and would, in all probability, have outlived Elizabeth herself, who died just two years later, but he could and would not accept the loss of wealth and power, and the possibility of bankruptcy. He was essentially selfish, and it doomed him. Essex was certainly paranoid, of losing his wealth, power, and way of life. He had been at the centre of the English court, a favourite of the queen, and could not accept that this was over. He needed the sun of Elizabeth I at the centre of his world and without it he was lost, thereby he dived into rebellion and lost his head as a result.

Epilogue

'All trials are theatrical but perhaps none more so than that for treason'.[1]

A nd no trial more deadly, either.

It has been thoroughly enjoyable writing this book and researching cases of treason that I had investigated before and those that were more unfamiliar to me. Looking at cases from across the century or more of Tudor rule has given me a sense of how treason developed and how the definition expanded.

What has been particularly interesting to explore in this work is the idea that the Tudors wiped out their nobility in order to preserve their own power. The Tudors seized the throne on the battlefield when Henry VII killed Richard III at the Battle of Bosworth Field in 1485 and, as a result, they were not entirely secure in their own power. They were very aware of the fact that many of the old nobility also had connections to the royal family, and even a claim to the throne. These included Edward Plantagenet, 17th Earl of Warwick, who was executed in 1499, Edward Stafford, 3rd Duke of Buckingham, who was executed in 1521, and Margaret Pole, Countess of Salisbury, who was executed in 1541. It was these royal scions who were the first noble executions of the Tudor century.

By the end of the Tudor period there were no dukes at all remaining in England, as the last, the 4th Duke of Norfolk, had been executed in 1572. Another duke would not be created until 1623 when George Villiers was created 1st Duke of Buckingham by James I. Therefore, England was without a duke for fifty-one years. This is interesting to consider, because dukes were the highest nobility and tended to be at the height of government, supporting the monarch, suppressing rebellions, fighting in battles, and wielding political power. However, the Tudor monarchs came to rely on commoners. Henry VIII depended heavily on Thomas Wolsey, who was the son of an Ipswich butcher who became a Cardinal, and Thomas Cromwell, who was the son of a Putney blacksmith and became the 1st Earl of Essex. Elizabeth I relied on Francis Walsingham, her spymaster, and William Cecil, who became 1st Baron Burghley. They did not rely on the 'old' nobility who resented the rise of these 'new men'. It set a precedent for monarchs who followed.

Treason underwent many changes under the Tudors, beginning with Henry VIII and the English Reformation. He introduced a new Treason Act in 1534 which made it treason to speak or think in opposition to the views of the monarch, supposedly to quell opposition to the religious changes and his new marriage to Anne Boleyn. Another Treason Act was introduced under Edward VI in 1547 and then again under Mary I in 1554. The 1554 Treason Act undid all forms of treason created since 1351 except the 1351 Treason Act itself. It remained in effect until it was repealed in two parts in 1863 and 1967. Researching this book and the history of treason it was interesting to see just how much definitions had changed and how far the nobles discussed in this book were executed under different treason laws and slightly varied definitions. Had a different treason law been in place, would they still have been guilty? It is difficult to say.

What is certain is the nobility were severely depleted under the Tudors, as fewer nobles were created, and many were executed. It highlights just how insecure the dynasty felt on the throne and how, even after a century of the Tudors in power, Elizabeth I still executed an anointed queen who threatened her position. Though this was after much pushing from her parliament and changing her mind several times. But it did pave the way for the execution of Charles I in 1649 during the English Civil War. The execution of Mary Queen of Scots could be seen as the first execution of a regnant queen in England, following on the heels of the executions of queen consorts Anne Boleyn and Katherine Howard. It depends on whether you accept Jane Grey as queen of England, otherwise Jane would be the first former regnant queen to be executed. The reigns of both Lady Jane Grey and Mary Queen of Scots were controversial in very different ways. It eroded the idea of a divine right to rule, which was the foundation of many monarchies across Europe. Divine right was not strictly Catholic or Protestant, but something that underpinned monarchy more generally in the Medieval and Early Modern periods. Mary Queen of Scots' execution stemmed from the belief the Tudors had that they could execute anyone, no matter how high or low, in order to maintain their power and hold on the English throne.

So many changes happened under the Tudors that it can be hard to keep them straight, particularly when nobles were executed for such varying reasons. Some were unquestionably guilty under the law at the time but morally questionable, some largely today considered to have been innocent of the crimes of which they were accused, and some seemingly forced into or unwittingly inveigled into committing treason. It was bloody, the result of paranoia and a seizure of the throne on a battlefield in 1485. It is certainly a defining period in the history of treason and noble executions.

References

Introduction
1. Wiesner-Hanks, Merry E., *Women and Gender in Early Modern Europe* (2008) p.278.
2. 'Treason, n.'. OED Online. Oxford University Press (June 2022). https://www.oed.com/view/Entry/205355.
3. *Treason Act 1351*. The National Archives.
4. *Treason Act 1534*, as quoted in Henry Gee & William John Hardy, *Documents Illustrative of English Church History* (1914) pp.247–251.
5. The National Archives, *A History of Treason: The Bloody History of Britain Through the Stories of its Most Notorious Traitors* (2022) p.93.
6. Harington, John, Of Treason. Poetry Nook. https://www.poetrynook.com/poem/treason-0.
7. Norton, Elizabeth, *Anne Boleyn: In her Own Words and the Words of Those Who Knew Her* (2011) p.237.
8. Kendall, Paul, *Queen Elizabeth I: Life and Legacy of the Virgin Queen* (2022) p.261.
9. Ibid, p.262.
10. The National Archives, *A History of Treason: The Bloody History of Britain Through the Stories of its Most Notorious Traitors* (2022) p.2.

Chapter 1: Edward Plantagenet, 17th Earl of Warwick – 1499
1. Fabyan, R., *The New Chronicles of England and France* (1811) p.666.
2. Amin, Nathen, *Henry VII and the Tudor Pretenders: Simnel, Warbeck and Warwick* (2020) p.64.
3. Carpenter, Christine, *Edward, styled earl of Warwick*. Oxford Dictionary of National Biography. https://doi.org/10.1093/ref:odnb/8525.
4. Amin, Nathen, *Henry VII and the Tudor Pretenders: Simnel, Warbeck and Warwick* (2020) p.67.
5. Ibid, p.68.
6. Carpenter, Christine, *Edward, styled earl of Warwick*. Oxford Dictionary of National Biography. https://doi.org/10.1093/ref:odnb/8525.
7. Amin, Nathen, *Henry VII and the Tudor Pretenders: Simnel, Warbeck and Warwick* (2020) p.70.
8. Loades, David, *The Tudors: History of a Dynasty* (2012) p.10.
9. Vergil, Polydore, *Anglica Historia* (2005) Book XXIV [XXVI] p.17.
10. *Rotuli Parliamentorum* (1767–77) pp.436–7.
11. Lisle, Leanda de, *Tudor: The Family Story* (2013) p.77.
12. Vergil, Polydore, *Anglica Historia* (2005) Book XXIV [XXVI] p.63.
13. Amin, Nathen, *Henry VII and the Tudor Pretenders: Simnel, Warbeck and Warwick* (2020) p.58.
14. Vergil, Polydore, *Anglica Historia* (2005) Book XXIV.
15. *The Great Chronicle of London* (1938) p.287.
16. Amin, Nathen, *Henry VII and the Tudor Pretenders: Simnel, Warbeck and Warwick* (2020) p.278.
17. Amin, Nathen, *Henry VII and the Tudor Pretenders: Simnel, Warbeck and Warwick* (2020) p.316.
18. 'Letter from Ferdinand and Isabella to De Puebla on 20 January 1500', *Calendar of State Papers: Spain*, Volume 1.
19. Gunn, S.J., *Wilford [Wulford] Ralph*, Oxford Dictionary of National Biography. https://doi.org/10.1093/ref:odnb/30094.
20. Weir, Alison, *Elizabeth of York: The First Tudor Queen* (2014) p.336.

21. Ibid, p.336.
22. Hall, Edward, *Hall's Chronicle* (1809) p.491.
23. Amin, Nathen, *Henry VII and the Tudor Pretenders: Simnel, Warbeck and Warwick* (2020) p.296.
24. Bacon, Francis, *History of the Reign of King Henry VII* (1902) p.176.
25. Amin, Nathen, *Henry VII and the Tudor Pretenders: Simnel, Warbeck and Warwick* (2020) p.297.
26. *Treason Act 1351.* The National Archives. https://www.legislation.gov.uk/aep/Edw3Stat5/25/2.
27. Weir, Alison, *Elizabeth of York: The First Tudor Queen* (2014) p.336.
28. Hall, Edward, *Hall's Chronicle* (1809) p.491.
29. Bacon, Francis, *History of the Reign of King Henry VII* (1902) p.177.
30. *Select Cases in the Council of Henry VII* (ed. C.G. Bayne & W.H. Dunham, London, 1958) quoted in Nathan Amin, *Henry VII and the Tudor Pretenders: Simnel, Warbeck and Warwick* (2020) p.300.
31. Bacon, Francis, *History of the Reign of King Henry VII* (1902) p.177.
32. Hall, Edward, *Hall's Chronicle* (1809) p.491.
33. Gairdner, James, 'A Supposed Conspiracy against Henry VII', *Transactions of the Royal Historical Society* (1904) p.187.
34. Weir, Alison, *Elizabeth of York: The First Tudor Queen* (2014) p.336.
35. 'Letter from Rodrigo Gonzalez de Puebla to Ferdinand and Isabella of Spain on 11 January 1500', *Calendar of State Papers: Spain*, Volume 1.
36. Bacon, Francis, *History of the Reign of King Henry VII* (1902) p.179.

Chapter 2: Edward Stafford, 3rd Duke of Buckingham – 1521

1. Davies, C.S.L., Stafford, *Edward, third duke of Buckingham.* Oxford Dictionary of National Biography. https://www.oxforddnb.com/view/10.1093/ref:odnb/9780198614128.001.0001/odnb-9780198614128-e-26202.
2. Jones, Philippa, *The Other Tudors: Henry VIII's Mistresses and Bastards* (2010) p.59.
3. Ibid, p.61.
4. Ibid.
5. 'Letter from Luis Caroz to Duke of Almazan on 28 May 1510', *Letters and Papers of the Reign of Henry VIII*, Volume 1.
6. Claiden-Yardley, Kirsten, *The Man Behind the Tudors: Thomas Howard, 2nd Duke of Norfolk* (2020) p.118.
7. Lisle, Leanda de, *Tudor: The Family Story* (2013) p.156.
8. Gairdner, James, 'A Supposed Conspiracy against Henry VII', *Transactions of the Royal Historical Society* (1904) p.187.
9. 'Trial documents for Edward Stafford, 3rd Duke of Buckingham, on 13 May 1521', *Letters and Papers of the Reign of Henry VIII*, Volume 3.
10. Loades, David, *The Tudors: History of a Dynasty* (2012) p.80.
11. Loades, David, *Henry VIII* (2011) p.119.
12. 'Letter from William Fitzwilliam to Cardinal Thomas Wolsey on 22 April 1521', *Letters and Papers of the Reign of Henry VIII*, Volume 3.
13. Seward, Desmond, *The Last White Rose: The Secret Wars of the Tudors* (2011) p.206.
14. Claiden-Yardley, Kirsten, *The Man Behind the Tudors: Thomas Howard, 2nd Duke of Norfolk* (2020) p.119.
15. Shakespeare, William, *King Henry the Eighth*, in W.J. Craig (ed.) *The Complete Works of William Shakespeare* (1998) p.687.
16. Ibid, p.691.
17. Seward, Desmond, *The Last White Rose: The Secret Wars of the Tudors* (2011) p.205.
18. Lisle, Leanda de, *Tudor: The Family Story* (2013) p.157.
19. Matusiak, John, *Henry VIII: The Life and Rule of England's Nero* (2014) p.112.

20 'Letter from Edward Stafford to Robert Gilbert on 26 November 1520', *Letters and Papers of the Reign of Henry VIII*, Volume 3.

21. Ackroyd, Peter, *The History of England Vol.2: Tudors* (2012) p.36.

22. Claiden-Yardley, Kirsten, *The Man Behind the Tudors: Thomas Howard, 2nd Duke of Norfolk* (2020) p.118.

23. Seward, Desmond, *The Last White Rose: The Secret Wars of the Tudors* (2011) p.206.

24. 'Trial documents for Edward Stafford, 3rd Duke of Buckingham, on 13 May 1521', *Letters and Papers of the Reign of Henry VIII*, Volume 3.

25. Loades, David, *The Tudors: History of a Dynasty* (2012) p.79.

26. Claiden-Yardley, Kirsten, *The Man Behind the Tudors: Thomas Howard, 2nd Duke of Norfolk* (2020) p.118.

27. Seward, Desmond, *The Last White Rose: The Secret Wars of the Tudors* (2011) p.210.

28. Guy, John, *The Children of Henry VIII* (2013) p.28.

29. 'Trial documents for Edward Stafford, 3rd Duke of Buckingham, on 13 May 1521', *Letters and Papers of the Reign of Henry VIII*, Volume 3.

30. Ibid.

31. Ibid.

32. Hall, Edward, *Hall's Chronicle* (1809) p.623.

33. Ibid.

34. Hutchinson, Robert, *House of Treason: The Rise and Fall of a Tudor Dynasty* (2009) p.48.

35. Ibid, p.49.

Chapter 3: Queen Anne Boleyn & George Boleyn, Viscount Rochford – 1536

1. Licence, Amy, *Tudor Roses: From Margaret Beaufort to Elizabeth I* (2022) p.218.

2. Ives, Eric, *The Life and Death of Anne Boleyn* (2005) p.6.

3. Emmerson, Owen & McCaffrey, Kate, *Becoming Anne: Connections, Culture, Court* (2022) pp.21–23.

4. Ives, Eric, *The Life and Death of Anne Boleyn* (2005) p.14–15.

5. Norton, Elizabeth, *Anne Boleyn: In her Own Words and the Words of Those Who Knew Her* (2011) p.25.

6. Morris, Sarah & Grueninger, Natalie, *In the Footsteps of the Six Wives of Henry VIII* (2016) p.114.

7. Norton, Elizabeth, *Anne Boleyn: In her Own Words and the Words of Those Who Knew Her* (2011) p.25.

8. Telford, Lynda, *Tudor Victims of the Reformation* (2016) p.32.

9. Norton, Elizabeth, *Anne Boleyn: In her Own Words and the Words of Those Who Knew Her* (2011) p.32.

10. Ives, Eric, *The Life and Death of Anne Boleyn* (2005) p.83.

11. Henry VIII, *Love Letters of Henry VIII to Anne Boleyn* (2009) p.40

12. Ibid, p.10.

13. 'Letter from Chapuys to Charles V on 10 February 1536', *Letters and Papers of the Reign of Henry VIII*, Volume 10.

14. 'Letter from Chapuys to Charles V on 29 January 1536', *Letters and Papers of the Reign of Henry VIII*, Volume 10.

15. Sander, Nicholas, *Rise and Growth of the Anglican Schism* (1877) p.25.

16. 'Letter from Chapuys to Charles V on 19 May 1536', *Letters and Papers of the Reign of Henry VIII*, Volume 10.

17. Whitley, Catrina Banks & Kramer Kyra, 'A New Explanation for the Reproductive Woes and Midlife Decline of Henry VIII', *The Historical Journal* (2010) pp.833–834.

18. Strype, John, *Ecclesiastical Memorials* (1721) p.113.

19. 'Letter from Chapuys to Charles V on 2 May 1536', *Letters and Papers of the Reign of Henry VIII*, Volume 10.

20. Ibid.
21. 'Letter from Chapuys to Charles V on 10 February 1536', *Letters and Papers of the Reign of Henry VIII*, Volume 10.
22. 'Letter from Chapuys to Charles V on 2 May 1536', *Letters and Papers of the Reign of Henry VIII*, Volume 10.
23. Ibid.
24. 'Letter from William Kingston to Thomas Cromwell on 3 May 1536', *Letters and Papers of the Reign of Henry VIII*, Volume 10.
25. Ibid.
26. 'Letter from Chapuys to Charles V on 19 May 1536', *Letters and Papers of the Reign of Henry VIII*, Volume 10.
27. Ibid.
28. Baldwin Smith, Lacey, 'English Treason Trials and Confessions in the Sixteenth Century', *Journal of the History of Ideas* (1954) p.472.
29. 'Account of Executions of Anne and George Boleyn from Vienna Archives', *Letters and Papers of the Reign of Henry VIII*, Volume 10.
30. *The Chronicle of Calais in the Reigns of Henry VII and Henry VIII*, 1846, quoted in Alison Weir's *The Lady in the Tower: The Fall of Anne Boleyn* (2009) p.242–3.
31. Denny, Joanna, *Anne Boleyn: A New Life of England's Tragic Queen* (2008) p.308.
32. Ibid, p.309.
33. Ives, Eric, *The Life and Death of Anne Boleyn* (2005) p.423.
34. Foxe, John, *Acts and Monuments* (1838) p.135.
35. Ibid, p.135–6.
36. Ibid.
37. Bernard, G.W., *Anne Boleyn: Fatal Attractions* (2011) p.192.
38. McGrath, Carol, *Sex and Sexuality in Tudor England* (2022) p.90.
39. Castor, Helen, *Elizabeth I: A Study in Insecurity* (2019) p.3.

Chapter 4: Margaret Pole, Countess of Salisbury – 1541

1. Pollard, A.J., *Edward IV: The Summer King* (2019) p.77.
2. *Treason Act 1351*. The National Archives.
3. Jones, Dan, *The Hollow Crown: The Wars of the Roses and the Rise of the Tudors* (2015) pp.276–277.
4. 'Letter from Margaret Pole to Reginald Pole on 19 July 1536', *Letters and Papers of the Reign of Henry VIII*, Volume 11.
5. Ridley, Jasper, *A Brief History of the Tudor Age* (2002) p.82.
6. Pole, Reginald, *Pro ecclesiasticae unitatis Defensione* (1965) p.9.
7. Seward, Desmond, *The Last White Rose: The Secret Wars of the Tudors* (2011) p.326.
8. Beccadelli, Ludovico, *The Life of Cardinal Reginald Pole* (1776) p.10.
9. Seward, Desmond, *The Last White Rose: The Secret Wars of the Tudors* (2011) pp.324–325.
10. Weir, Alison, *Henry VIII: King and Court* (2002) p.416.
11. Ibid.
12. Coby, J. Patrick, *Thomas Cromwell: Henry VIII's Henchman* (2012) p.158.
13. 'Letter from Eustace Chapuys to Charles V on 27 September 1533', *Letters and Papers of the Reign of Henry VIII*, Volume 6.
14. Seward, Desmond, *The Last White Rose: The Secret Wars of the Tudors* (2011) pp.327.
15. Higginbotham, Susan, *Margaret Pole: The Countess in the Tower* (2017) p.128.
16. 'Letter from Margaret Pole to Reginald Pole on 19 July 1536', *Letters and Papers of the Reign of Henry VIII*, Volume 11.
17. Beccadelli, Ludovico, *The Life of Cardinal Reginald Pole* (1776) p.155.
18. Elton, G.R., *England Under the Tudors* (2006) p.155.
19. Loades, David, *The Tudors: History of a Dynasty* (2012) p.14.

20. Seward, Desmond, *The Last White Rose: The Secret Wars of the Tudors* (2011) pp.330.
21. 'Letter from Charles de Marillac to Francis I of France on 29 May 1541', *Letters and Papers of the Reign of Henry VIII*, Volume 16.
22. Ackroyd, Peter, *The History of England Vol.2: Tudors* (2012) p.135.
23. 'Letter from Eustace Chapuys to Anne of Bohemia, Queen of Hungary and Archduchess of Austria, on 10 June 1541', *Letters and Papers of the Reign of Henry VIII*, Volume 16.
24. Breverton, Terry, *Everything You Ever Wanted to Know About the Tudors but Were Afraid to Ask* (2014) p.145.
25. Matusiak, John, *A History of the Tudors in 100 Objects* (2019) p.296.
26. Herbert, Edward, *The Life and Reigne of King Henry the Eighth* (1649) p.468.
27. Higginbotham, Susan, *Margaret Pole: The Countess in the Tower* (2017) p.135.
28. 'Letter from Charles de Marillac to Francis I of France on 29 May 1541', *Letters and Papers of the Reign of Henry VIII*, Volume 16.
29. 'Letter from Eustace Chapuys to Anne of Bohemia, Queen of Hungary and Archduchess of Austria, on 10 June 1541', *Letters and Papers of the Reign of Henry VIII*, Volume 16.
30. Ibid.
31. Breverton, Terry, *Everything You Ever Wanted to Know About the Tudors but Were Afraid to Ask* (2014) p.262.
32. Higginbotham, Susan, *Margaret Pole: The Countess in the Tower* (2017) p.135.
33. Matusiak, John, *A History of the Tudors in 100 Objects* (2019) p.297.

Chapter 5: Queen Katherine Howard & Jane Boleyn, Viscountess Rochford – 1542
1. Wilkinson, Josephine, *Katherine Howard: The Tragic Story of Henry VIII's Fifth Queen* (2016) p.247.
2. 'Letter from Charles de Marillac to Francis I of France on 11 November 1541', *Letters and Papers of the Reign of Henry VIII*, Volume 16.
3. Byrne, Conor, *Katherine Howard: Henry VIII's Slandered Queen* (2019) p.70.
4. Wilkinson, Josephine, *Katherine Howard: The Tragic Story of Henry VIII's Fifth Queen* (2016) p.58.
5. Loades, David, *The Six Wives of Henry VIII* (2010) p.119.
6. Ibid.
7. Seward, Desmond, *The Last White Rose: The Secret Wars of the Tudors* (2011) p.327.
8. 'Letter from Ralph Sadler to Archbishop Thomas Cranmer and others on 12 November 1541', *Letters and Papers of the Reign of Henry VIII*, Volume 16.
9. Wilkinson, Josephine, *Katherine Howard: The Tragic Story of Henry VIII's Fifth Queen* (2016) p.148.
10. 'Letter from the Privy Council to William Paget, Ambassador to France, on 12 November 1541', *Letters and Papers of the Reign of Henry VIII*, Volume 16.
11. Byrne, Conor, *Katherine Howard: Henry VIII's Slandered Queen* (2019) p.160.
12. Ibid, p.161.
13. Burnet, Gilbert, *The History of the Reformation of the Church of England*, Volume 4 (1843) pp.504–505.
14. 'Letter from Charles de Marillac to Francis I of France on 11 November 1541', *Letters and Papers of the Reign of Henry VIII*, Volume 16.
15. 'Letter from Charles de Marillac to Francis I of France on 14 November 1541', *Letters and Papers of the Reign of Henry VIII*, Volume 16.
16. 'Letter from Ralph Sadler to Archbishop Thomas Cranmer and others on 12 November 1541', *Letters and Papers of the Reign of Henry VIII*, Volume 16.
17. 'Depositions against Katherine Howard on 13 November 1541', *Letters and Papers of the Reign of Henry VIII*, Volume 16.

18. Wilkinson, Josephine, *Katherine Howard: The Tragic Story of Henry VIII's Fifth Queen* (2016) p.65

19. 'Depositions against Katherine Howard on 13 November 1541', *Letters and Papers of the Reign of Henry VIII*, Volume 16.

20. Ibid.

21. Ibid.

22. 'Letter from Charles de Marillac to Francis I of France on 11 November 1541', *Letters and Papers of the Reign of Henry VIII*, Volume 16.

23. 'Letter from the Privy Council to William Paget, Ambassador to France, on 12 November 1541', *Letters and Papers of the Reign of Henry VIII*, Volume 16.

24. Fox, Julia, *Jane Boleyn: The Infamous Lady Rochford* (2007) p.308.

25. 'Letter from Eustace Chapuys to Charles V, Holy Roman Emperor, on 9 February 1542', *Calendar of State Papers, Spain*, Volume 6.

26. 'Letter from Eustace Chapuys to Charles V, Holy Roman Emperor, on 25 February 1542', *Calendar of State Papers: Spain*, Volume 6.

27. Byrne, Conor, *Katherine Howard: Henry VIII's Slandered Queen* (2019) p.173.

28. 'Letter from Charles de Marillac to Francis I of France on 13 February 1542', *Letters and Papers of the Reign of Henry VIII*, Volume 17.

29. 'Letter from Eustace Chapuys to Charles V, Holy Roman Emperor, on 25 February 1542', *Calendar of State Papers: Spain*, Volume 6.

30. 'Letter from Charles de Marillac to Francis I of France on 13 February 1542', *Letters and Papers of the Reign of Henry VIII*, Volume 17; & 'Letter from Eustace Chapuys to Charles V, Holy Roman Emperor, on 25 February 1542', *Calendar of State Papers: Spain*, Volume 6.

31. 'Letter from Charles de Marillac to Francis I of France on 13 February 1542', *Letters and Papers of the Reign of Henry VIII*, Volume 17.

32. Hume, Martin, *The Chronicle of King Henry VIII of England* (1889) p.86.

33. Ibid.

34. Hall, Edward, *Hall's Chronicle* (1809) p.843.

35. 'Letter from Eustace Chapuys to Charles V, Holy Roman Emperor, on 25 February 1542', *Calendar of State Papers: Spain*, Volume 6.

36. 'Letter from Charles de Marillac to Francis I of France on 13 February 1542', *Letters and Papers of the Reign of Henry VIII*, Volume 17.

37. Ibid.

38. Wilkinson, Josephine, *Katherine Howard: The Tragic Story of Henry VIII's Fifth Queen* (2016) p.247.

39. 'Letter from Eustace Chapuys to Charles V, Holy Roman Emperor, on 25 February 1542', *Calendar of State Papers: Spain*, Volume 6.

40. 'Letter from Charles de Marillac to Francis I of France on 13 February 1542', *Letters and Papers of the Reign of Henry VIII*, Volume 17.

41. 'Letter from Eustace Chapuys to Charles V, Holy Roman Emperor, on 25 February 1542', *Calendar of State Papers: Spain*, Volume 6.

42. Wilkinson, Josephine, *Katherine Howard: The Tragic Story of Henry VIII's Fifth Queen* (2016) p.247.

Chapter 6: Henry Howard, Earl of Surrey – 1547

1. Brigden, Susan, *Howard, Henry, earl of Surrey*. Oxford Dictionary of National Biography. https://doi.org/10.1093/ref:odnb/13905.

2. 'Letter from the Earl of Surrey to the Council on 13 December 1546', *Letters and Papers of the Reign of Henry VIII*, Volume 21.

3. Brigden, Susan, *Howard, Henry, earl of Surrey*. Oxford Dictionary of National Biography. https://doi.org/10.1093/ref:odnb/13905.

4. Howard, Henry, *Eache Beast can choose his fere*. Luminarium.
5. Ibid.
6. Loades, David, *The Tudors: History of a Dynasty* (2012) p.80.
7. 'Letter from François Van der Delft to Charles V on 14 December 1546', *Letters and Papers of the Reign of Henry VIII*, Volume 21.
8. 'Letter from François Van der Delft to Mary of Hungary on 14 December 1546', *Letters and Papers of the Reign of Henry VIII*, Volume 21.
9. Childs, Jessie, *Henry VIII's Last Victim: The Life and Times of Henry Howard, Earl of Surrey* (2008) p.4.
10. Ibid, p.150
11. 'Letter from Thomas Howard, 3rd Duke of Norfolk, to Henry VIII on 15 December 1541', *Letters and Papers of the Reign of Henry VIII*, Volume 16.
12. Hutchinson, Robert, *The Last Days of Henry VIII* (2006) p.49.
13. Heath, Richard, *Henry VIII and Charles V: Rival Monarchs, Uneasy Allies* (2023) p.154.
14. Brigden, Susan, *Howard, Henry, earl of Surrey*. Oxford Dictionary of National Biography. https://doi.org/10.1093/ref:odnb/13905.
15. Ibid.
16. Hutchinson, Robert, *House of Treason: The Rise and Fall of a Tudor Dynasty* (2009) p.188.
17. *Treason Act 1534*, in *Documents Illustrative of English Church History* (1914) p.247–251.
18. Childs, Jessie, *Henry VIII's Last Victim: The Life and Times of Henry Howard, Earl of Surrey* (2008) p.261.
19. Hart, Kelly, *The Mistresses of Henry VIII* (2011) p.195.
20. Hutchinson, Robert, *House of Treason: The Rise and Fall of a Tudor Dynasty* (2009) p.183.
21. 'Letter from François Van der Delft to Charles V on 14 December 1546', *Letters and Papers of the Reign of Henry VIII*, Volume 21.
22. Hutchinson, Robert, *House of Treason: The Rise and Fall of a Tudor Dynasty* (2009) p.174.
23. 'Letter from Odet de Selve to Claude d'Annebault on 12 December 1546', *Letters and Papers of the Reign of Henry VIII*, Volume 21.
24. 'Interrogatories for the Earl of Surrey', *Letters and Papers of the Reign of Henry VIII*, Volume 21.
25. Ibid.
26. 'Letter from the Duke of Norfolk to Henry VIII on 13 December 1546', *Letters and Papers of the Reign of Henry VIII*, Volume 21.
27. 'Letter from the Earl of Surrey to the Council on 13 December 1546', *Letters and Papers of the Reign of Henry VIII*, Volume 21.
28. 'Thomas Howard, 3rd Duke of Norfolk, to the Council, December 1546', *Letters and Papers of the Reign of Henry VIII*, Volume 21.
29. Ibid.
30. 'Letter from Sir John Gates, Sir Richard Southwell, and Wymond Carew to Henry VIII on 14 December 1546', *Letters and Papers of the Reign of Henry VIII*, Volume 21.
31. Ibid.
32. 'Thomas Howard, 3rd Duke of Norfolk, to the Council, December 1546', *Letters and Papers of the Reign of Henry VIII*, Volume 21.
33. Lisle, Leanda de, *Tudor: The Family Story* (2013) p.237.

Chapter 7: Thomas Seymour, 1st Baron Seymour of Sudeley –1549

1. Loades, David, *The Seymours of Wolf Hall: A Tudor Family Story* (2015) p.11.
2. 'Letter from Chapuys to Charles V on 10 February 1536', *Letters and Papers of the Reign of Henry VIII*, Volume 10.
3. Loades, David, *The Seymours of Wolf Hall: A Tudor Family Story* (2015) p.181.
4. Porter, Linda, *Katherine the Queen: The Remarkable Life of Katherine Parr, the Last Wife of Henry VIII* (2010) p.285.

5. Ibid, p.294.
6. Loades, David, *The Seymours of Wolf Hall: A Tudor Family Story* (2015) p.191.
7. Lisle, Leanda de, *Tudor: The Family Story* (2013) p.247.
8. Williams, Penry, *The Later Tudors: England 1547–1603* (1998) p.56.
9. Kramer, Kyra, *Interpreting the Death of Edward VI: The Brief Life and Mysterious Demise of the Last Tudor King* (2022) p.90.
10. Ibid, p.91.
11. Elizabeth I, *Collected Works* (2000) p.17.
12. Ibid, p.23.
13. Somerset, Anne, *Elizabeth I* (1997) p.31.
14. Elizabeth I, *Collected Works* (2000) p.24.
15. Castor, Helen, *Elizabeth I: A Study in Insecurity* (2019) p.14.
16. Kramer, Kyra, *Interpreting the Death of Edward VI: The Brief Life and Mysterious Demise of the Last Tudor King* (2022) p.97.
17. Chapman, Hester, *The Last Tudor King: A Study of Edward VI* (1958) p.126.
18. Ackroyd, Peter, *History of England Vol.2: Tudors* (2012) p.203.
19. Kramer, Kyra, *Interpreting the Death of Edward VI: The Brief Life and Mysterious Demise of the Last Tudor King* (2022) p.97.
20. Elizabeth I, *Collected Works* (2000) p.31.
21. Ibid, p.25–26.
22. Ibid, p.33–35.
23. Ibid.
24. Skidmore, Chris, *Edward VI: The Lost King of England* (2008) p.102.
25. Porter, Linda, *Katherine the Queen: The Remarkable Life of Katherine Parr, the Last Wife of Henry VIII* (2010) p.329.
26. Ibid, p.333.
27. Loades, David, *The Seymours of Wolf Hall: A Tudor Family Story* (2015) p.191.
28. 'Deposition of John Fowler', *The National Archives* SP 10/6/10, quoted in David Loades, *The Seymours of Wolf Hall: A Tudor Family Story* (2015) p.194.
29. Chapman, Hester, *The Last Tudor King: A Study of Edward VI* (1958) p.131.
30. Norton, Elizabeth, *The Temptation of Elizabeth Tudor* (2015) p.273.
31. Chapman, Hester, *The Last Tudor King: A Study of Edward VI* (1958) p.132.
32. Norton, Elizabeth, *The Temptation of Elizabeth Tudor* (2015) p.279.
33. Kramer, Kyra, *Interpreting the Death of Edward VI: The Brief Life and Mysterious Demise of the Last Tudor King* (2022) p.97.
34. Porter, Linda, *Katherine the Queen: The Remarkable Life of Katherine Parr, the Last Wife of Henry VIII* (2010) p.338.
35. Latimer, Hugh, *Sermons* (1844) p.161–162.
36. Seymour, Thomas, *Forgetting God*, Poetry Nook. https://www.poetrynook.com/poem/forgetting-god.
37. Skidmore, Chris, *Edward VI: The Lost King of England* (2008) p.108.
38. Ackroyd, Peter, *The History of England Vol.2: Tudors* (2012) p.205.

Chapter 8: Edward Seymour, 1st Duke of Somerset – 1552
1. Loades, David, *The Seymours of Wolf Hall: A Tudor Family Story* (2015) p.11.
2. Ibid, p.98.
3. Foxe, John, *Acts and Monuments* (1838) p.703.
4. Sander, Nicholas, *Rise and Growth of the Anglican Schism* (1877) p.171.
5. Loades, David, *Intrigue and Treason: The Tudor Court 1547–1558* (2004) p.30.
6. Lisle, Leanda de, *Tudor: The Family Story* (2013) p.248.

7. Kramer, Kyra, *Interpreting the Death of Edward VI: The Brief Life and Mysterious Demise of the Last Tudor King* (2022) p.89.

8. BL Add. MS 48126, fols.1–4 quoted in David Loades, *Intrigue and Treason: The Tudor Court 1547–1558* (2004) p.29.

9. Kramer, Kyra, *Interpreting the Death of Edward VI: The Brief Life and Mysterious Demise of the Last Tudor King* (2022) p.89.

10. Heath, Richard, *Henry VIII and Charles V: Rival Monarchs, Uneasy Allies* (2023) p.168.

11. Ridley, Jasper, *A Brief History of the Tudor Age* (2002) p.18.

12. Heath, Richard, *Henry VIII and Charles V: Rival Monarchs, Uneasy Allies* (2023) p.169.

13. 'Circular Letter sent 1 July 1549', *Calendar of State Papers Domestic: Edward VI, Mary and Elizabeth, 1547–80*, Edward VI – Volume 8.

14. Shagan, Ethan H., *Protector Somerset and the 1549 Rebellions: New Sources and New Perspectives* (1999) p.45.

15. Heath, Richard, *Henry VIII and Charles V: Rival Monarchs, Uneasy Allies* (2023) p.169.

16. Foxe, John, *Acts and Monuments* (1838) p.703.

17. Sander, Nicholas, *Rise and Growth of the Anglican Schism* (1877) p.190.

18. Kramer, Kyra, *Interpreting the Death of Edward VI: The Brief Life and Mysterious Demise of the Last Tudor King* (2022) p.104.

19. Loades, David, *Intrigue and Treason: The Tudor Court 1547–1558* (2004) p.46.

20. Halliwell, James Orchard, *Letters of the Kings of England, Volume 2* (1848) pp.36–7.

21. Kramer, Kyra, *Interpreting the Death of Edward VI: The Brief Life and Mysterious Demise of the Last Tudor King* (2022) p.105.

22. Heath, Richard, *Henry VIII and Charles V: Rival Monarchs, Uneasy Allies* (2023) p.170.

23. Hume, Martin, *The Chronicle of King Henry VIII of England* (1889) p.193.

24. Ibid, p.192

25. Lisle, Leanda de, *Tudor: The Family Story* (2013) p.254.

26. Alford, Stephen, *Edward VI: The Last Boy King* (2018) p.51.

27. Guy, John, *The Children of Henry VIII* (2013) p.135.

28. Chapman, Hester, *The Last Tudor King: A Study of Edward VI* (1958) p.235.

29. Ibid, p.236.

30. Ibid.

31. Edward VI, *England's Boy King: The Diary of Edward VI 1547–1553* (2005) p.132.

32. Foxe, John, *Acts and Monuments* (1838) p.400.

Chapter 9: John Dudley, 1st Duke of Northumberland – 1553; & Queen Jane Grey – 1554

1. Lisle, Leanda de, *The Sisters Who Would Be Queen: Mary, Katherine, and Lady Jane Grey* (2008) p.8.

2. Ascham, Roger, *The Schoolmaster* (1570) p.36.

3. Ibid.

4. Lisle, Leanda de, *The Sisters Who Would Be Queen: Mary, Katherine, and Lady Jane Grey* (2008) p.26.

5. 'Letter from Henry Grey to Thomas Seymour', quoted in Ida Ashworth Taylor, *Lady Jane Grey and Her Times* (1822) p.157.

6. 'Letter from Lady Jane Grey to Thomas Seymour', *The National Archives*, EXT 9/42/2.

7. Tallis, Nicola, *Crown of Blood: The Deadly Inheritance of Lady Jane Grey* (2016) p.71.

8. Paul, Joanne, *The House of Dudley: A New History of Tudor England* (2022) p.201.

9. Edward VI, *Devise for the Succession* (1553).

10. Ibid.

11. Loades, David, *The Tudors: History of a Dynasty* (2012) p.37.

12. Ridley, Jasper, *A Brief History of the Tudor Age* (2002) p.235.

13. Kramer, Kyra, *Interpreting the Death of Edward VI: The Brief Life and Mysterious Demise of the Last Tudor King* (2022) p.159.

14. Paul, Joanne, *The House of Dudley: A New History of Tudor England* (2022) p.216.

15. Lisle, Leanda de, *Tudor: The Family Story* (2013) p.277.

16. Paul, Joanne, *The House of Dudley: A New History of Tudor England* (2022) p.223.

17. Elton, G.R., *England Under the Tudors* (2006) p.216.

18. Tallis, Nicola, *Crown of Blood: The Deadly Inheritance of Lady Jane Grey* (2016) p.211.

19. Ibid, p.207.

20. Lisle, Leanda de, *The Sisters Who Would Be Queen: Mary, Katherine, and Lady Jane Grey* (2008) p.124.

21. Lady Jane Grey, *An epistle of the Ladye Iane, a righte vertuous woman, to a learned man of late falne from the truth of Gods most holy word* (1554).

22. Jones, Nigel, *Tower: An Epic History of the Tower of London* (2012) p.242.

23. Lady Jane Grey, *An epistle of the Ladye Iane, a righte vertuous woman, to a learned man of late falne from the truth of Gods most holy word* (1554).

24. *Lady Jane Grey's Prayer Book*. British Library, Harley MS 2342.

25. Nichols, J.G., *The Chronicle of Queen Jane* (1850) p.55.

26. Ibid, pp.56–57.

27. Plowden, Alison, *Lady Jane Grey: Nine Days Queen* (2006) p.164.

28. Ibid.

29. *Lady Jane Grey's Prayer Book*. British Library, Harley MS 2342.

30. Plowden, Alison, *Lady Jane Grey: Nine Days Queen* (2006) p.165.

Chapter 10: Thomas Howard, 4th Duke of Norfolk – 1572

1. Graves, Michael A.R., *Howard, Thomas, fourth duke of Norfolk*. Oxford Dictionary of National Biography. https://www.oxforddnb.com/display/10.1093/ref:odnb/9780198614128.001.0001/odnb-9780198614128-e-13941.

2. Ibid.

3. Ibid.

4. Ibid.

5. Doran, Susan, *Elizabeth I and Her Circle* (2015) p.79.

6. The National Archives, *A History of Treason: The Bloody History of Britain through the Stories of its Most Notorious Traitors* (2022) p.132.

7. Ibid.

8. Kendall, Paul, *Queen Elizabeth I: Life and Legacy of the Virgin Queen* (2022) p.147.

9. 'Letter from Francis Walsingham to William Cecil on 8 October 1571', *Calendar of State Papers, Foreign: Elizabeth 1569–1571*, Volume 9.

10. Brennan, Laura, *Elizabeth I: The Making of a Queen* (2020) p.120.

11. The National Archives, *A History of Treason: The Bloody History of Britain through the Stories of its Most Notorious Traitors* (2022) p.131.

12. Plowden, Alison, *Danger to Elizabeth: The Catholics Under Elizabeth I* (1973) p.101.

13. Brennan, Laura, *Elizabeth I: The Making of a Queen* (2020) p.120.

14. Plowden, Alison, *Danger to Elizabeth: The Catholics Under Elizabeth I* (1973) p.103.

15. The National Archives, *A History of Treason: The Bloody History of Britain through the Stories of its Most Notorious Traitors* (2022) p.133.

16. 'Letter from Dr Thomas Wilson to William Cecil, Lord Burghley, on 1 October 1571', *Calendar of the Cecil Papers in Hatfield House*, Volume 1.

17. Kendall, Paul, *Queen Elizabeth I: Life and Legacy of the Virgin Queen* (2022) p.147.

18. 'Message from the Duke of Norfolk to the Earl of Bedford, the Lord Admiral, the Lord Chamberlain, and Lord Burghley, on 11 October 1571', *Calendar of the Cecil Papers in Hatfield House*, Volume 1.

19. Brennan, Laura, *Elizabeth I: The Making of a Queen* (2020) p.122.
20. *National Archives*, KB 8/42, roll and file of court of Lord High Steward, quoted in Robert Hutchinson, *House of Treason: The Rise and Fall of a Tudor Dynasty* (2009) pp.234–235.
21. *Treason Act 1351*. The National Archives.
22. Hutchinson, Robert, *House of Treason: The Rise and Fall of a Tudor Dynasty* (2009) p.235.
23. Ibid, p.236.
24. Weir, Alison, *Elizabeth the Queen* (2009) p.280.
25. Hutchinson, Robert, *House of Treason: The Rise and Fall of a Tudor Dynasty* (2009) p.240.
26. Kendall, Paul, *Queen Elizabeth I: Life and Legacy of the Virgin Queen* (2022) p.148.
27. Camden, William, *The history of the most renowned and Virtuous Princess Elizabeth* (1675) p.177–178.
28. Ibid, p.178.
29. Ibid, p.180.
30. Hutchinson, Robert, *House of Treason: The Rise and Fall of a Tudor Dynasty* (2009) p.236.

Chapter 11: Robert Devereux, 2nd Earl of Essex – 1601

1. Baldwin Smith, Lacey, 'English Treason Trials and Confessions', *Journal of the History of Ideas* (1984) p.494.
2. Routh, C.R.N., *Who's Who in British History: Tudor England 1485–1603* (2001) p.208.
3. Stedall, Robert, *Elizabeth I's Final Years: Her Favourites and Her Fighting Men* (2022) p.xi.
4. Hammer, Paul E.J., *Devereux, Robert, second earl of Essex (1565–1601), soldier and politician.* Oxford Dictionary of National Biography. https://www.oxforddnb.com/view/10.1093/ref:odnb/9780198614128.001.0001/odnb-9780198614128-e-7565.
5. Ibid.
6. Guy, John, *Elizabeth: The Forgotten Years* (2016) p.128.
7. Kendall, Paul, *Queen Elizabeth I: Life and Legacy of the Virgin Queen* (2022) p.258.
8. The National Archives, *A History of Treason: The Bloody History of Britain Through the Stories of its Most Notorious Traitors* (2022) p.143.
9. Kendall, Paul, *Queen Elizabeth I: Life and Legacy of the Virgin Queen* (2022) p.259.
10. Brennan, Laura, *Elizabeth I: The Making of a Queen* (2020) p.155.
11. Stedall, Robert, *Elizabeth I's Final Years: Her Favourites and Her Fighting Men* (2022) p.xxviii.
12. Guy, John, *Elizabeth: The Forgotten Years* (2016) p.128.
13. Veerapen, Steven, *Elizabeth and Essex: Power, Passion, and Politics* (2019) p.231.
14. Stedall, Robert, *Elizabeth I's Final Years: Her Favourites and Her Fighting Men* (2022) p.181.
15. Bacon, Francis, *A Declaration of the Practises and Treasons attempted and committed by Robert late Earle of Essex* (1601).
16. Elizabeth I, *Collected Works* (2000) p.394.
17. Ibid, p.395.
18. Harrison, Helene, *Elizabethan Rebellions: Conspiracy, Intrigue and Treason* (2023) p.154.
19. The National Archives, *A History of Treason: The Bloody History of Britain Through the Stories of its Most Notorious Traitors* (2022) p.143.
20. Bacon, Francis, *A Declaration of the Practises and Treasons attempted and committed by Robert late Earle of Essex* (1601).
21. Shakespeare, William, 'The Tragedy of Richard II', in *The Complete Works of William Shakespeare* (1998) p.440.
22. Loades, David, *Tudors: History of a Dynasty* (2012) p.89; and Doran, Susan, *Elizabeth I and Her Circle* (2015) p.189.
23. Rex, Richard, *The Tudors* (2015) p.264; and Hilton, Lisa, *Elizabeth: Renaissance Prince* (2015) p.312; and Plowden, Alison, *Elizabethan England: Life in an Age of Adventure* (1982) p.275; and John, Judith, *Dark History of the Tudors* (2017) p.209.

24. Williams, Penry, *The Later Tudors: England 1547–1603* (1998) p.374.
25. Stedall, Robert, *Elizabeth I's Final Years: Her Favourites and Her Fighting Men* (2022) p.180.
26. Bacon, Francis, *A Declaration of the Practises and Treasons attempted and committed by Robert late Earle of Essex* (1601).
27. Somerset, Anne, *Elizabeth I* (1997) p.689.
28. Hilton, Lisa, *Elizabeth: Renaissance Prince* (2015) p.313.
29. 'Letter from the Earl of Southampton to Lady Southampton on 8 Feb 1601', *Cecil Papers in Hatfield House*, Volume 11 (1601).
30. Kendall, Paul, *Queen Elizabeth I: Life and Legacy of the Virgin Queen* (2022) p.258.
31. Ibid, p.260.
32. Hume, David, *A History of England*, Volume 5 (1807) pp.445–446.
33. Veerapen, Steven, *Elizabeth and Essex: Power, Passion, and Politics* (2019) p.239.
34. Stedall, Robert, *Elizabeth I's Final Years: Her Favourites and Her Fighting Men* (2022) p.186.
35. Baldwin Smith, Lacey, *Treason in Tudor England: Politics and Paranoia* (2006) p.239.
36. *Lamentable new Ballad upon the Earle of Essex his death* (1635).

Epilogue
1. The National Archives, *A History of Treason: The Bloody History of Britain Through the Stories of its Most Notorious Traitors* (2022) p.2.

Bibliography

Primary Sources

State Papers

Calendar of the Cecil Papers in Hatfield House. Edited by R A Roberts. London: His Majesty's Stationery Office, 1906. British History Online. http://www.british-history.ac.uk/cal-cecil-papers/

Calendar of State Papers, Domestic: Edward VI, Mary and Elizabeth 1547–80. Edited by Robert Lemon. London: Her Majesty's Stationery Office, 1856. British History Online. https://www.british-history.ac.uk/cal-state-papers/domestic/edw-eliz/1547-80

Calendar of State Papers Foreign: Elizabeth. Edited by Allan James Crosby. London: Her Majesty's Stationery Office, 1874. British History Online. http://www.british-history.ac.uk/cal-state-papers/foreign/

Calendar of State Papers: Spain. Edited by Pascual de Gayangos. London: Her Majesty's Stationery Office, 1890. British History Online. https://www.british-history.ac.uk/search/series/cal-state-papers--spain

Letters and Papers, Foreign and Domestic, Henry VIII. Edited by James Gairdner. London: Her Majesty's Stationery Office, 1888. British History Online. http://www.british-history.ac.uk/letters-papers-hen8/

Online Sources

Bacon, Francis, *A Declaration of the Practises & Treasons attempted and committed by Robert late Earle of Essex and his Complices, against her Maiestie and her Kingdoms, and of the proceedings as well at the Arraignments & Conuictions of the said late Earle, and his adherents.* 1601. Oxford University Press Text Creation Partnership. https://ota.bodleian.ox.ac.uk/repository/xmlui/bitstream/handle/20.500.12024/A01216/A01216.html

Edward VI, *Devise for the Succession,* 1553. Luminarium Encyclopedia Project. https://luminarium.org/encyclopedia/edward6devise.htm

Grey, Lady Jane, *An epistle of the Ladye Iane, a righte vertuous woman, To a learned man of late falne from the truth of Gods most holy word, for fear of the worlde. Read it, to thy consolacion. VVhereunto is added the communication that she had with Master Feckenham vpon her faith, and belefe of the Sacraments. Also another epistle whiche she wrote to her sister, with the words she spake vpon the Scaffold befor she suffered, anno. M.D.Liiii.* 1554. Oxford University Press Text Creation Partnership. https://ota.bodleian.ox.ac.uk/repository/xmlui/bitstream/handle/20.500.12024/A20904/A20904.html

Lady Jane Grey's Prayer Book, created c.1539–1544. British Library, Harley MS 2342. https://www.bl.uk/collection-items/lady-jane-greys-prayer-book

A Lamentable new Ballad upon the Earle of Essex his death. To the tune of, Essex last goodnight, 1635. Oxford University Press Text Creation Partnership. https://ota.bodleian.ox.ac.uk/repository/xmlui/bitstream/handle/20.500.12024/A20381/A20381.html

The National Archives. https://discovery.nationalarchives.gov.uk/

Treason Act 1351. The National Archives. https://www.legislation.gov.uk/aep/Edw3Stat5/25/2

1

Vergil, Polydore, *The Anglica Historia of Polydore Vergil A.D. 1485–1537*, ed. Dana J. Sutton. Library of Humanistic Texts at the Philological Museum of University of Birmingham's Shakespeare Institute, 2005. http://www.philological.bham.ac.uk/polverg/

Printed Sources
Ascham, Roger, *The Schoolmaster* (London: John Day, 1570).
Bacon, Francis, *History of the Reign of King Henry VII* (London: C.J. Clay & Sons, 1902).
Beccadelli, Ludovico, *The Life of Cardinal Reginald Pole by Ludovico Beccatelli, Archbishop of Ragusa*. Translated by Benjamin Pye (London: C. Bathurst, 1766).
Burnet, Gilbert, *The History of the Reformation of the Church of England* (New York: D. Appleton & Company, 1843).
Camden, William, *The history of the most renowned and victorious Princess Elizabeth, the late queen of England* (London: E. Flesher, 1675).
Edward VI, *England's Boy King: The Diary of Edward VI 1547–1553*. Edited by Jonathan North (Welwyn Garden City: Ravenhall Books, 2005).
Elizabeth I, *Collected Works*, 2nd Edition. Edited by L.S. Marcus, J. Mueller & M.B. Rose (London & Chicago: University of Chicago Press, 2000).
Fabyan, R., *The New Chronicles of England and France* (London: H. Ellis, 1811).
Foxe, John, *Acts and Monuments*, Edited by George Townsend (London: Seeley, Burnside and Seeley, 1838).
Gairdner, James (ed.), *Letters and Papers Illustrative of the Reigns of Richard III and Henry VII* (London: Longman, Green, Longman, Roberts and Green, 1863).
Gee, Henry & Hardy, William John (eds.), *Documents Illustrative of English Church History* (London: Macmillan, 1914).
The Great Chronicle of London. Edited by A.H. Thomas & I.D. (Thornley, London, 1938).
Hall, Edward, *Hall's Chronicle; Containing the History of England During the Reign of Henry the Fourth and the Succeeding Monarchs to the End of the Reign of Henry VIII, in Which are Particularly Described the manners and Customs of Those Periods*. Edited by Ellis, Henry (London: J. Johnson, 1809).
Halliwell, James Orchard (ed.), *Letters of the Kings of England* (London: Henry Colburn Publishers, 1848).
Henry VIII, *Love Letters of Henry VIII to Anne Boleyn*. Edited by Phillips, J.O. (Gearhart, OR: Merchant Books, 2009).
Herbert, Edward, *The Life and Reigne of King Henry the Eighth* (London: Thomas Whitaker, 1649).
Hume, David, *The History of England from the Invasion of Julius Caesar to the Revolution in 1688, in Eight Volumes* (London: J. McCreery, 1807).
Hume, Martin, *The Chronicle of King Henry VIII of England, Being a Contemporary Record of Some of the Principal Events of the Reigns of Henry VIII and Edward VI* (London: George Bell & Sons, 1889).
Latimer, Hugh, *Sermons* (Cambridge: Cambridge University Press, 1844).
Nichols, J.G., *The Chronicle of Queen Jane, and of two years of Queen Mary, and especially of the rebellion of Sir Thomas Wyatt* (London: J.B. Nichols, 1850).
Norton, Elizabeth, *Anne Boleyn: In her Own Words and the Words of Those Who Knew Her* (Stroud: Amberley Publishing, 2011).
Pole, Reginald, *Pro ecclesiasticae unitatis Defensione*. Edited by Dwyer, Joseph G. (London: Newman Press, 1965).
Rotuli Parliamentorum (also known as the Parliamentary Rolls of Medieval England), Volumes 1 to 6 (London: 1767–77).
Sander, Nicholas, *Rise and Growth of the Anglican Schism*. Edited by Lewis, David (London: Burns and Oates, 1877).

Shakespeare, William, *The Complete Works of William Shakespeare*. Edited by W.J. Craig (Cockfosters: Henry Pordes, 1998).

Strype, John, *Ecclesiastical Memorials: relating chiefly to religion and the reformation of it, and the emergencies of the Church of England, under King Henry VIII, King Edward VI and Queen Mary the First* (London: John Wyat, 1721).

Taylor, Ida Ashworth, *Lady Jane Grey and Her Times* (London: Sherwood, Neely, and Jones, 1822).

Turpin, Richard, *The Chronicle of Calais in the Reigns of Henry VII and Henry VIII, to the year 1540* (London: The Camden Society, 1846).

Secondary Sources

Books

Ackroyd, Peter, *The History of England Vol.2: Tudors* (London: Macmillan, 2012).

Alford, Stephen, *Edward VI: The Last Boy King* (London: Penguin Books, 2018).

Amin, Nathen, *Henry VII and the Tudor Pretenders: Simnel, Warbeck and Warwick* (Stroud: Amberley Publishing, 2020).

Bernard, G.W., *Anne Boleyn: Fatal Attractions* (London: Yale University Press, 2011).

Brennan, Laura, *Elizabeth I: The Making of a Queen* (Barnsley: Pen and Sword Books, 2020).

Breverton, Terry, *Everything You Ever Wanted to Know About the Tudors but Were Afraid to Ask* (Stroud: Amberley Publishing, 2014).

Byrne, Conor, *Katherine Howard: Henry VIII's Slandered Queen* (Stroud: The History Press, 2019).

Castor, Helen, *Elizabeth I: A Study in Insecurity* (London: Penguin Books, 2019).

Chapman, Hester, *The Last Tudor King: A Study of Edward VI* (London: Jonathan Cape, 1958).

Childs, Jessie, *Henry VIII's Last Victim: The Life and Times of Henry Howard, Earl of Surrey* (London: Vintage, 2008).

Claiden-Yardley, Kirsten, *The Man Behind the Tudors: Thomas Howard, 2nd Duke of Norfolk* (Barnsley: Pen and Sword Books, 2020).

Denny, Joanna, *Anne Boleyn: A New Life of England's Tragic Queen* (London: Piatkus Books, 2008).

Doran, Susan, *Elizabeth I and Her Circle* (Oxford: Oxford University Press, 2015).

Doran, Susan, *The Tudor Chronicles 1485–1603* (London: Quercus Publishing, 2008).

Elton, G.R., *England Under the Tudors* (Abingdon: Routledge, 2006).

Emmerson, Owen & McCaffrey, Kate, *Becoming Anne: Connections, Culture, Court* (Norwich: Jigsaw Publishing, 2022).

Fox, Julia, *Jane Boleyn: The Infamous Lady Rochford* (London: Weidenfeld & Nicholson, 2007).

Friedman, P, *Anne Boleyn* (Stroud: Amberley Publishing, 2010).

Guy, John, *The Children of Henry VIII* (Oxford: Oxford University Press, 2013).

Guy, John, *Elizabeth: The Forgotten Years* (London: Viking Books, 2016).

Harrison, Helene, *Elizabethan Rebellions: Conspiracy, Intrigue and Treason* (Barnsley: Pen and Sword Books, 2023).

Hart, Kelly, *The Mistresses of Henry VIII* (Stroud: The History Press, 2011).

Heath, Richard, *Henry VIII and Charles V: Rival Monarchs, Uneasy Allies* (Barnsley: Pen and Sword Books, 2023).

Higginbotham, Susan, *Margaret Pole: The Countess in the Tower* (Stroud: Amberley Publishing, 2017).

Hilton, Lisa, *Elizabeth: Renaissance Prince* (London: Weidenfeld & Nicolson, 2015).

Hutchinson, Robert, *House of Treason: The Rise and Fall of a Tudor Dynasty* (London: Phoenix, 2009).

Hutchinson, Robert, *The Last Days of Henry VIII* (London: Phoenix, 2006).

Ives, Eric, *The Life and Death of Anne Boleyn* (Oxford: Blackwell Publishing, 2005).

John, Judith, *Dark History of The Tudors* (London: Amber Books, 2017).

Jones, Dan, *The Hollow Crown: The Wars of the Roses and the Rise of the Tudors* (London: Faber and Faber, 2015).

Jones, Nigel, *Tower: An Epic History of The Tower Of London* (London: Windmill Books, 2012).

Jones, Philippa, *The Other Tudors: Henry VIII's Mistresses and Bastards* (London: New Holland Publishers, 2010).

Kendall, Paul, *Queen Elizabeth I: Life and Legacy of the Virgin Queen* (Barnsley: Frontline Books, 2022).

Kramer, Kyra, *Interpreting the Death Of Edward VI: The Brief Life and Mysterious Demise of the Last Tudor King* (Barnsley: Pen and Sword Books, 2022).

Licence, Amy, *Anne Boleyn: Adultery, Heresy, Desire* (Stroud: Amberley Publishing, 2017).

Licence, Amy, *Tudor Roses: From Margaret Beaufort to Elizabeth I* (Stroud: Amberley Publishing, 2022).

Lisle, Leanda De, *The Sisters Who Would Be Queen: Mary, Katherine, and Lady Jane Grey* (New York: Ballantine Books, 2008).

Lisle, Leanda De, *Tudor: The Family Story* (London: Chatto and Windus, 2013).

Loades, David, *Catherine Howard: The Adulterous Wife of Henry VIII* (Stroud: Amberley Publishing, 2012).

Loades, David, *Henry VIII* (Stroud: Amberley Publishing, 2011).

Loades, David, *Intrigue and Treason: The Tudor Court 1547–1558* (Harlow: Pearson Education Limited, 2004).

Loades, David, *The Seymours of Wolf Hall: A Tudor Family Story* (Stroud: Amberley Publishing, 2015).

Loades, David, *The Six Wives of Henry VIII* (Stroud: Amberley Publishing, 2010).

Loades, David, *The Tudors: History of A Dynasty* (London: Continuum International Publishing Group, 2012).

Mackay, Lauren, *Inside the Tudor Court: Henry VIII and his Six Wives Through the Eyes of the Spanish Ambassador* (Stroud: Amberley Publishing, 2015).

Matusiak, John, *Henry VIII: The Life and Rule of England's Nero* (Stroud: The History Press, 2014).

Matusiak, John, *A History of the Tudors In 100 Objects* (Stroud: The History Press, 2019).

McGrath, Carol, *Sex and Sexuality in Tudor England* (Barnsley: Pen and Sword Books, 2022).

Morris, Sarah, and Grueninger, Natalie, *In the Footsteps of the Six Wives of Henry VIII* (Stroud: Amberley Publishing, 2016).

Norton, Elizabeth, *The Temptation of Elizabeth Tudor* (London: Head of Zeus, 2015).

Paul, Joanne, *The House of Dudley: A New History of Tudor England* (London: Michael Joseph, 2022).

Penn, Thomas, *Winter King: The Dawn of Tudor England* (London: Penguin Books, 2012).

Plowden, Alison, *Danger to Elizabeth: The Catholics Under Elizabeth I* (Bungay: The Chaucer Press, 1973).

Plowden, Alison, *Elizabethan England: Life in an Age Of Adventure* (London: Reader's Digest, 1982).

Plowden, Alison, *Lady Jane Grey: Nine Days Queen* (Stroud: Sutton Publishing, 2004).

Pollard, A.J. *Edward IV: The Summer King* (London: Penguin Books, 2019).

Porter, Linda, *Katherine the Queen: The Remarkable Life of Katherine Parr, The Last Wife of Henry VIII* (New York: St Martin's Press, 2010).

Rex, Richard, *The Tudors* (Stroud: Tempus Publishing, 2015).

Ridley, Jasper, *A Brief History of the Tudor Age* (London: Constable and Robinson, 2002).

Routh, C.R.N., *Who's Who in British History: Tudor England 1485–1603* (Mechanicsburg PA: Stackpole Books, 2001).

Seward, Desmond, *The Last White Rose: The Secret Wars of the Tudors* (London: Constable And Robinson, 2011).

Skidmore, Chris, *Edward VI: The Lost King of England* (London: Phoenix, 2008).

Smith, Lacey Baldwin, *Anne Boleyn: Queen of Controversy* (Stroud: Amberley Publishing, 2013).

Smith, Lacey Baldwin, *Treason in Tudor England: Politics and Paranoia* (London: Pimlico, 2006).

Somerset, Anne, *Elizabeth I* (London: Phoenix, 1997).

Starkey, David, *Six Wives: The Queens of Henry VIII* (London: Vintage, 2004).

Stedall, Robert, *Elizabeth I's Final Years: Her Favourites and her Fighting Men* (Barnsley: Pen and Sword Books, 2022).

Tallis, Nicola, *Crown of Blood: The Deadly Inheritance of Lady Jane Grey* (London: Michael O'Mara Books, 2016).

Telford, Lynda, *Tudor Victims of the Reformation* (Barnsley: Pen and Sword Books, 2016).

The National Archives, *A History of Treason: The Bloody History of Britain Through the Stories of its Most Notorious Traitors* (London: John Blake Publishing, 2022).

Veerapen, Steven, *Elizabeth and Essex, Power, Passion, and Politics* (London: Sharpe Books, 2019).

Warnicke, Retha, *The Rise and Fall of Anne Boleyn* (Cambridge: Cambridge University Press, 2010).

Weir, Alison, *Britain's Royal Families: The Complete Genealogy* (London: Vintage, 2008).

Weir, Alison, *Elizabeth of York: The First Tudor Queen* (London: Vintage, 2014).

Weir, Alison, *Elizabeth the Queen* (London: Vintage, 2009).

Weir, Alison, *Henry VIII: King and Court* (London: Vintage, 2002).

Weir, Alison, *The Lady in the Tower: The Fall of Anne Boleyn* (London: Jonathan Cape, 2009).

Whitelock, Anna, *Mary Tudor: Princess, Bastard, Queen* (London: Random House, 2009).

Wiesner-Hanks, Merry E., *Women and Gender in Early Modern Europe* (Cambridge: Cambridge University Press, 2008).

Wilkinson, Josephine, *Katherine Howard: The Tragic Story of Henry VIII's Fifth Queen* (London: John Murray, 2016).

Williams, Penry, *The Later Tudors: England 1547–1603* (Oxford: Oxford University Press, 1998).

Articles

Banks-Whitley, Catrina, and Kramer, Kyra, 'A New Explanation for the Reproductive Woes and Midlife Decline of Henry VIII', *The Historical Journal*, Vol.53, No.4 (December 2010) pp.827–848.

Bernard, G.W., 'The Fall of Anne Boleyn', *The English Historical Review*, Vol.106, No.420 (July 1991) pp.584–610.

Gairdner, James, 'A Supposed Conspiracy Against Henry VII', *Transactions of the Royal Historical Society*, New Series, Vol.18 (1904) pp.157–194.

Ives, Eric, 'The Fall of Anne Boleyn Reconsidered', *The English Historical Review*, Vol.107, No.424 (July 1992) pp.651–664.

Shagan, Ethan H., 'Protector Somerset and the 1549 Rebellions: New Sources and New Perspectives', *The English Historical Review*, Vol.114, No.455 (Feb 1999) pp.34–63.

Smith, Lacey Baldwin, 'English Treason Trials and Confessions', *Journal of the History of Ideas*, Vol.15, No.4 (October 1954) pp.471–498.

Walker, Greg, 'Rethinking the Fall of Anne Boleyn', *The Historical Journal*, Vol.45, No.1 (2002) pp.1–29.

Warnicke, Retha, 'Sexual Heresy at the Court of Henry VIII', *The Historical Journal*, Vol.30, No.2 (1987) pp.247–268.

Whitelock, Anna, 'Princess Mary's Household and the Succession Crisis, July 1553', *The Historical Journal*, Vol.50, No.2 (2007) pp.265–287.

Other Resources

Becoming Elizabeth, one season (2022). [Amazon Prime] Created by Anya Reiss. United Kingdom: Starz.

Luminarium: Anthology of English Literature. https://www.luminarium.org/

National Archives Currency Converter 1270–2017. The National Archives. https://www.nationalarchives.gov.uk/currency-converter/#

Oxford Dictionary of National Biography. Oxford University Press. https://www.oxforddnb.com/

Oxford English Dictionary Online. Oxford University Press. https://www.oed.com/

Poetry Nook. https://www.poetrynook.com/

The Tudors, four seasons (2007–2011). [DVD] Created by Michael Hirst. United Kingdom: Showtime.

Index

Peers are ordered by surname and then title i.e., Howard, Thomas, 2nd Duke of Norfolk / Howard, Thomas, 3rd Duke of Norfolk